Psychological Management of Physical Disabilities

The successful integration of psychological factors into the management of physical disabilities is critical to successful healthcare delivery. This book provides a comprehensive and accessible guide to the best practice and approaches in this field.

Paul Kennedy brings together contributions from a range of experienced researchers and practitioners, who explore the emotional, motivational and psychological factors associated with the rehabilitation and treatment of people with a range of physical disabilities, including spinal cord injury, stroke and chronic pain. The book is divided into three parts, covering:

- The scope of psychological processes in physical rehabilitation.
- Psychological applications and practitioner perspectives.
- General organisational challenges and developments.

Psychological Management of Physical Disabilities will be of great interest to all clinical psychologists, health psychologists, occupational therapists, counsellors, physiotherapists, physicians and rehabilitation nurses. Service providers know how important psychological factors are. This book explains why and how psychological models and research can support rehabilitation and improve individual well-being.

Paul Kennedy is Professor of Clinical Psychology and Academic Director of the Oxford Doctoral Course in Clinical Psychology at the University of Oxford.

Psychological Management of Physical Disabilities

A practitioner's guide

Edited by Paul Kennedy

Routledge
Taylor & Francis Group

LONDON AND NEW YORK

First published 2007
by Routledge
27 Church Road, Hove, East Sussex BN3 2FA

Simultaneously published in the USA and Canada
by Routledge
270 Madison Avenue, New York, NY 10016

Routledge is an imprint of the Taylor & Francis Group, an informa business

Typeset in Times by Garfield Morgan, Swansea, West Glamorgan
Printed and bound in Great Britain by TJ International Ltd, Padstow,
Cornwall
Paperback cover design by Design Deluxe

British Library Cataloguing-in-Publication Data
A catalogue record for this book is available from the British Library

Library of Congress Cataloging in Publication Data
Psychological management of physical disabilities : a practitioner's
    guide / edited by Paul Kennedy.
        p. cm.
    Includes bibliographical references and index.
    ISBN-13: 978-1-58391-712-1 (hbk)
    ISBN-10: 1-58391-712-8 (hbk)
    ISBN-13: 978-1-58391-713-8 (pbk)
    ISBN-10: 1-58391-713-6 (pbk)
    1. People with disabilities—Mental health. 2. People with disabilities
—Rehabilitation—Psychological aspects. 3. Disabilities—Psychological
aspects. 4. Wounds and injuries—Psychological aspects. 5. Rehabilitation—Psychological aspects. I. Kennedy, Paul, 1959–   .
    [DNLM: 1. Disabled Persons—psychology. 2. Disabled Persons—
rehabilitation. WB 320 P974 2007]
    RC451.4.H35P729 2007
    362.4–dc22

                                                        2006021371

ISBN: 978-1-58391-712-1 (hbk)
ISBN: 978-1-58391-713-8 (pbk)

This book is dedicated to all those whose shared knowledge (through personal experience, service provision or research endeavours) has contributed to our understanding and management of disability.

Contents

Contributors

Jane Barton is a Consultant Clinical Psychologist working in Sheffield, UK, with a special interest in stroke rehabilitation and older people. She graduated from Sheffield University with a BA (Hons) in Psychology, completed her doctoral training in Clinical Psychology at the University of Leeds, and has an MSc in Occupational Psychology from Sheffield University. Her special interests are in post-traumatic stress following stroke, and in driving after stroke.

Paul Bennett is Research Professor in the School of Nursing and Midwifery at Cardiff University, UK. His career has combined work as a Clinical Psychologist and academic in Cardiff, Bristol, and the University of Wales, Swansea. He has published over 100 journal articles and chapters, as well as authored five books on clinical and health psychology. His main areas of research interest include the emotional impact of disease or risk of disease, and how people cope with the challenges this presents.

Donna Caruthers is a post-doctoral Research Associate at the University of Pittsburgh School of Nursing, Pittsburgh, USA. She currently serves as a co-investigator and the Project Director on Dr Erlen's NIH/NINR-funded study examining medication adherence interventions with persons infected with HIV who are prescribed antiretroviral therapy. Dr Caruthers' research and clinical focus pertains to treatment adherence in chronic disorders, specifically patients with multiple co-morbid disorders. She has served as a Research Assistant on studies centring on adherence interventions in patients with rheumatoid arthritis and diabetes management. Her dissertation was entitled 'Enhancing tobacco abstinence following hospitalization'.

Zoë Clyde obtained a doctorate in Clinical Psychology from the University of Leeds, UK, in 2000. After qualifying, she worked for three years at Input residential pain management programme, St Thomas Hospital, London. During this time she gained a Diploma in Cognitive Therapy from the Oxford Cognitive Therapy Centre. In 2004 she began working as a Clinical Psychologist at the National Spinal Injuries Centre, Stoke Mandeville Hospital.

Jane Duff is a Principal Clinical Psychologist who has worked in spinal cord injury at the National Spinal Injuries Centre, Stoke Mandeville Hospital, UK, for nearly 10 nine years. She obtained her BSc Honours degree in Psychology at the University of Plymouth in 1991 and her Doctorate in Clinical Psychology from the University of Southampton in 1997, completing her thesis on the psychological sequelae of trauma following spinal cord injury. She is an experienced clinician and researcher and her main areas of interest include coping, adjustment and quality of life in chronic health conditions, rehabilitation and goal planning, and post-traumatic stress disorder. She has also been active in a number of professional issues, including coordinating continuing professional development for the Oxford Branch of the Division of Clinical Psychology. She was a founder member of the former Special Interest Group in Physical Health and Disability, now the Faculty of Clinical Health Psychology, of the British Psychological Society.

Magnus L. Elfström is currently a Research Assistant at the Health Care Research Unit, Institute of Medicine, Sahlgrenska Academy at Göteborg University, Sweden. He is also a guest lecturer at various undergraduate courses in the Department of Psychology and the Institute of Odontology at Göteborg University.

Dr Elfström became a licensed Clinical Psychologist in 1999 and then worked with people with chronic pain and fatigue at the National Hospital of Insurance in Tranås and the Public Dental Service in Göteborg. The work at the Public Dental Service also included people with severe dental fear. Dr Elfström has had consulting assignments as Clinical Supervisor in Psychology at the diabetes clinic at the Sahlgrenska University Hospital and evaluator of a public primary care treatment of chronic pain and fatigue. In 2003 he was awarded a PhD at Göteborg University. His thesis dealt with coping strategies and health-related quality of life in persons with traumatic spinal cord lesion. Dr Elfström is currently involved in health psychological research on dental fear, orofacial pain, lung cancer and spinal cord lesion.

Timothy R. Elliott is a Professor in the Department of Educational Psychology at Texas A & M University in College Station, TX, USA. He obtained his PhD in Counselling Psychology from the University of Missouri-Columbia and he holds the diplomate in rehabilitation psychology from the American Board of Professional Psychology. He is a Fellow of the American Psychological Association (including the divisions of Rehabilitation, Health and Counselling Psychology).

Dr Elliott's research has been supported by the Centers of Disease Control, the National Institute of Disability Rehabilitation and Research, and the National Institute of Child and Human Development. The American Association of Spinal Cord Injury Psychologists and Social Workers presented him with the Essie Morgan Excellence Award for his research achievements in the area of spinal cord injury in 2002, and the Society for Counselling Psychology honoured him with the Dorothy Booz Black Award in 2004 for his contributions in counselling health psychology.

Judith A. Erlen is a Professor and the Doctoral Program Coordinator at the School of Nursing, and the Center for Bioethics & Health Law, University of Pittsburgh, Pittsburgh, USA. She is also the Associate Director and Director of the Research Development Core of the Center for Research in Chronic Disorders at the School of Nursing. Her programme of research focuses on medication adherence with patients with chronic disorders, specifically patients with HIV infection, Alzheimer's disease, and type 2 diabetes. She is currently funded by the National Institutes of Health/National Institute of Nursing Research (NIH/NINR). In addition to her peer-reviewed publications, she writes a column on ethical issues in nursing practice for *Orthopaedic Nursing*.

Maarten Fischer studied Social Psychology at the University of Groningen, the Netherlands. After graduating in 2000, he worked as a junior researcher at the Helen Dowling Institute for psycho-oncology on a quality of life study among Dutch prostate cancer patients. Since 2004 he has been undertaking a PhD at the Unit of Medical Psychology, Leiden University Medical Centre. His research focuses on the role of illness and treatment representations in the prediction of attendance and drop-out during respiratory rehabilitation for patients with chronic obstructive pulmonary disease.

Robert G. Frank is Dean of the College of Public Health and Health Professions at the University of Florida, USA, where he is also a Professor in the Department of Clinical and Health Psychology. His first appointment was at the University of Missouri-Columbia School of Medicine, Department of Physical Medicine and Rehabilitation, where he established the Division of Clinical Health Psychology and Neuropsychology. He was a Robert Wood Johnson Health Policy Fellow, sponsored by the Institute of Medicine, in 1991–1992 and worked in the United States Senate.

Dr Frank has a Doctorate in Clinical Psychology from the University of New Mexico. He is a Diplomate in Clinical Psychology from the American Board of Professional Psychology. He is past President of the Division of Rehabilitation Psychology of the American Psychological

Association and a Fellow in the Divisions of Rehabilitation Psychology and Health Psychology.

Philip Clarke Henshaw is Lead Clinical Psychologist in HIV and Sexual Health at The Ambrose King Centre, Royal London Hospital, Whitechapel, London. He graduated in Psychology from the University of Newcastle upon Tyne in 1987 and initially worked in Learning Disabilities. He graduated from the Oxford Clinical Psychology course in 1992 and worked at St Mary's Hospital, London with people with HIV. Sex and sexuality were central to this work and he has increasingly developed his academic and clinical interests in sexual health. Philip runs a busy male sexual dysfunction service with a medical colleague and manages an outreach service that provides sex and relationship therapies to people with HIV. He works with ethnically diverse populations of East London and spends much time practising via interpreters. He lectures on grief and loss, sexuality, psychological aspects of HIV, sex and relationship therapies, sexuality and intimate medical examinations. He is currently studying for a clinical doctorate and recent research interests include men's experience of genital examinations and the significance of language changes used for condomless sex in gay men.

Ad Kaptein is Professor of Medical Psychology at Leiden University Medical Center, Leiden, the Netherlands. His research focuses on illness perceptions in patients with chronic somatic disorders, in particular patients with respiratory disorders. He is co-editor of *Psychology & Health* and former editor-in-chief of this journal. He has edited 10 books on psychology as applied to medicine; the most recent one is *Health psychology* (Kaptein & Weinman, eds, 2004). He is a former President of the European Health Psychology Society (EHPS).

Paul Kennedy is Professor of Clinical Psychology at the University of Oxford, UK, Academic Director on the Oxford Doctoral Course in Clinical Psychology, and Trust Head of Clinical Psychology based at the National Spinal Injuries Centre, Stoke Mandeville Hospital. He studied at the University of Ulster and Queens University, Belfast and has worked in clinical health psychology since graduating from his clinical training in 1984. He has established clinical health psychology services in a number of areas.

Dr Kennedy is an active researcher with a broad portfolio of research on adjustment, coping and rehabilitation. He has published over 70 scientific papers for peer-reviewed journals, been a contributor to a number of book chapters and co-edited a book on clinical health psychology. He serves on the editorial board of the *Journal of Clinical Psychology in Medical Settings, Rehabilitation Psychology* and *Neurorehabilitation*. He was elected a Fellow of the British Psychological

Society in 1999, served on the Committee of the Division of Health Psychology, was made a Supernumerary Fellow of Harris Manchester College, University of Oxford in 2001 and was conferred Professor of Clinical Psychology in 2006. He is founding Chair of the Multi-disciplinary Association of Spinal Cord Injury Professionals. In 2002 he was awarded the Distinguished Service Award by the American Association of Spinal Cord Injury Psychologists and Social Workers and in 2005 he was awarded a visiting Fellowship to Australia by the New South Wales Government, Ministry of Science and Medical Research.

Andrea M. Lee completed her Bachelor of Arts (first class honors) degree in Psychology at Simon Fraser University in Burnaby, British Columbia, Canada, and her Master of Science degree in Clinical Psychology at the University of Florida. She is currently a PhD candidate at the University of Florida in the Department of Clinical and Health Psychology. She is a Graduate Research Assistant at the Florida Center for Medicaid and the Uninsured at the University of Florida.

Margreet Scharloo took her Masters degree in Social Psychology at Leiden University, the Netherlands. In 1992 she started working on a PhD project at the Unit of Medical Psychology, Department of Psychiatry at Leiden University. Her longitudinal study focused on which illness perceptions and coping strategies were predictive of outcome in patients with rheumatoid arthritis, chronic obstructive pulmonary disease and psoriasis. She was awarded her PhD by the Department of Clinical and Health Psychology at Leiden University in April 2002.

From 1999 to 2002 she worked as a researcher at Leiden University Medical Center on a Dutch Asthma Foundation-funded study of illness perceptions, coping and social support in patients with chronic obstructive pulmonary disease. Since November 2000 she has been employed as an Assistant Professor in Medical Psychology, Leiden University Medical Center.

Her research interests are in the factors that promote physical and psychological adjustment in chronic illness, especially coping and illness perceptions. Other research and academic interests are in behavioural medicine, chronic obstructive pulmonary disorder, cancer, illness beha-viour, and teaching behavioural medicine and communication skills to medical students and doctors.

Mary D. Slavin is a Physical Therapist with a doctoral degree in Experi-mental Psychology. She has been involved in rehabilitation for more than 30 years as a clinician and educator. She is actively involved in advancing evidence-based practice in rehabilitation. In her current position as the Director of Education and Dissemination at Boston

University's Health and Disability Research Institute, Boston, USA, Dr Slavin works to improve functional outcome measures used in rehabilitation. She also provides training for clinicians and educators in the use of outcome data to improve processes of care in rehabilitation.

Ann Marie Warren is Rehabilitation Psychologist in the Department of Physical Medicine and Rehabilitation at the Baylor Institute for Rehabilitation (BIR), Dallas, Texas, USA and the primary Psychologist with the Spinal Cord Injury Service. She obtained a BSc in Psychology at Texas Christian University and a PhD at the University of North Texas in Clinical Health Psychology and Behavioral Medicine. She completed her pre-doctoral internship at Eastern Virginia Medical School in Norfolk, Virginia and her post-doctoral requirements at the BIR. She is a member of the American Psychological Association, Division 22.

Dr Warren has worked in both clinical and research capacities at the BIR and BUMC. She has been the lead Rehabilitation Psychologist for the Spinal Cord Injury Team at BIR. In her research capacity, she is actively engaged in a variety of research projects, including a study of video education in the acute care setting for spinal cord injury patients. She has had a lead role in the development of the three projects on which her chapter with Timothy R. Elliott is based, and has presented research findings at recent conferences. She is a regular lecturer for the Department of Physical Medicine and Rehabilitation residents and clinical staff at BIR, as well as a guest lecturer at local universities. Her role at BIR also extends to the Administrative Coordinator of Rehabilitation Research. In this role she is engaged in funding activities, coordination of research professionals to conduct rehabilitation research, and working with administration on research-related activity.

Guinevere Webster is a Chartered Clinical Psychologist at the National Spinal Injuries Centre, Stoke Mandeville Hospital, UK. Since 2002 she has been involved in clinical practice and research with people with spinal cord injury, focusing on coping and adjustment, and is currently developing specialist research and practice in paediatric spinal cord injury. She has a particular interest in the family impact of acquired disability and has several publications in this area.

John Weinman is Professor of Psychology as applied to Medicine at the Institute of Psychiatry, University of London. He is a Fellow of the British Psychological Society and has played a major role in the development of academic and professional health psychology in the UK. His main research areas are cognition and health, communication and decision-making in health care, stress, wound healing and recovery from surgery, and self-regulation and self-management in chronic illness. He was the founding editor of *Psychology and Health: An International*

Journal and has edited and written a large number of books, chapters and research papers in the field of health psychology.

Amanda C. de C. Williams is a Reader in Clinical Health Psychology at University College London, and Consultant Clinical Psychologist in the pain service of the university hospital. She has been active in research and cognitive behavioural treatment of chronic pain for nearly 20 years, and has held an academic post since obtaining her PhD in 1996. Her particular research interests are in evaluation and evidence, depression in pain, expression of pain and how it is understood by clinicians, and pain from torture. She has written over 60 papers and chapters on aspects of pain and psychology and is on the editorial boards of several major pain journals.

Acknowledgements

I am grateful to all the contributors of this book who have made this project possible through the quality of their submissions, responsiveness to feedback and keeping to the timescale. This venture began following initial discussions with Michael Coombs, Freelance Publishing Adviser, and further communication with Joanna Forshaw, Senior Editor, at Routledge. I would like to thank them for their encouragement.

I have been well supported by a number of people, both directly and indirectly, in this project. I would particularly like to thank Mrs Linda Hall for her excellent support, communication and organisational skills.

Part 1

The scope of psychological processes in physical rehabilitation

Chapter 1

Introduction, context and overview

Paul Kennedy

> The assets of the person must receive considerable attention in the rehabilitation effort. A person's healthy physical and mental attributes can become a basis for alleviating as well as providing a source of gratification and enhancement of life.
>
> The active participation of the client in the planning and execution of the rehabilitation program is to be sought as fully as possible.
>
> (Beatrice Wright, 2005)

The fundamental integration of psychological factors into the management of physical disabilities is critical to successful healthcare delivery. This book explores the emotional, motivational and psychological factors associated with the rehabilitation and treatment of people with physical disabilities. In the past century there has been a major global shift in disease burden from the viral and bacterial killers of the early twentieth century, to chronic conditions of the twenty-first, namely coronary heart disease, stroke, cancer and diabetes. All these disease processes are greatly influenced by psycho-social factors that include behaviours, beliefs and relationships. Additionally, many of these conditions have age-related increases in their prevalence and will continue to grow as people are now living longer than ever before. The impact and consequences of these conditions stretch across all aspects of society, from the individual to their families, carers and communities. Demographic shifts have highlighted that fewer and fewer people will be available as service providers and carers (Kennedy and Llewelyn, 2006).

To help set the context for this book, it would be worth highlighting the results of the Pew Health Professions Commission (O'Neil, 1993). When considering healthcare outcomes for the twenty-first century, the Commission predicted that twenty-first century healthcare models would have a greater orientation towards health, with more emphasis on health promotion, and pay greater attention to environmental and occupational health outcomes. The Commission also predicted that there would be a greater focus on the consumer, with increased emphasis on patient involvement in decision making and increased coordination of services across settings, providers and units. They also proposed that more focus would be placed on treatment outcomes, cost effectiveness and the dissemination of evidence-based outcome research. There are a variety of stakeholders involved in healthcare and there is a growing need for greater integration and communication between them. Stakeholders include the patient and the family, as well as service providers, commissioners, the media and the academic and scientific community.

Psychological research and interventions have grown in significance, status and sophistication since the early 1970s. Abraham and Michie (2005) argue that health psychology research locates the determinants of health behaviour within the multi-layered biopsychosocial model which includes biological processes (e.g. the biochemistry of nicotine), cognition (e.g. understanding health risks), emotion (e.g. denial and avoidant coping), interpersonal processes (e.g. interactions between healthcare professionals and their patients), organisational and cultural effects (e.g. normative pressures experienced by healthcare professionals in everyday practice), and national and supranational policy frameworks (e.g. taxation and legislation). Smith *et al.* (2004) conclude that health psychology has maintained a major research and applied focus on the role of health behaviour in the development and prevention of serious illness and premature mortality, with the determinants of these behaviours and interventions designed to improve health behaviours being the central focus of theory, research and practice. They report on several notable accomplishments that include the identification of behavioural risk factors of the major healthcare problems of industrialised nations. Behaviour change intervention research has produced considerable evidence that risky health behaviours can be changed and health outcomes improved (Orleans, 2000). They indicate that the identification and modification of influences on the varying degrees of disability and distress that accompany a given condition can facilitate the compression of morbidity and maximise components of the individual's quality of life.

Rehabilitation psychology is the application of psychological knowledge and understanding on behalf of individuals with disabilities and society through such activities as research, clinical practice, teaching, public education, development of social policy and advocacy (Scherer *et al.*, 2000). Rehabilitation psychologists provide a broad range of services across diverse settings to a variety of health consumers. They have worked shoulder to shoulder with colleagues in medicine, nursing and education to address the varied health and social concerns of people with disabilities (Frank and Elliott, 2000). This book highlights how rehabilitation psychologists contribute to primary care, areas of specialist medicine and in broader research and health education capacities to increase function, minimise disability, and increase opportunities for engagement and greater social participation of people with disabilities and their families.

Table 1.1 Major conditions causing physical disability

Condition	UK prevalence	Causes
Neurological	1.5 million people	Stroke, epilepsy, Parkinson's disease, multiple sclerosis, motor neurone disease, muscular dystrophy, cerebral palsy, spinal cord injury.
Musculo-skeletal	3 million people	Osteoarthritis, rheumatoid arthritis, systemic lupus erythematosus, juvenile arthritis, osteoporosis, fractures and injuries.
Sensory	1 million have significant sight loss	Congenital, glaucoma, diabetes, retinopathy, otitis media, presbycusis, meningitis.
Chronic respiratory	3 million people	Cystic fibrosis, asthma, emphysema, chronic bronchitis.

Source: Kennedy and Llewelyn (2006).

It is estimated that there are 33 million persons with disabilities in the United States (US Census Bureau, 1997), many of whom require assistance in relation to bathing, dressing and toileting. According to the *Health Survey for England* (Joint Health Surveys Unit, 2002), 18 per cent of men and women aged 16 and over reported having one or more of five types of disability (locomotor, personal care, sight, hearing and communication) and 5 per cent of adults were found to have a serious disability. There are wide variations in the types and causes of disability and each of these has a different impact on the lifecycle. For example, spina bifida is a congenital condition which affects individuals throughout their lifespan, whereas the age of onset of asthma tends to be by the age of 8 or 12, and with other conditions such as rheumatoid arthritis, diabetes and coronary heart disease, increase in age is positively associated with greater physical disability. Disability may also result from accidents such as with spinal cord injury and traumatic amputations, or degenerative neurological diseases and cerebral vascular accidents. In the UK, the prevalence of severe disability remains stable until the age of 60, and from then on in, there is an increase in the prevalence, severity and range. In general, there are four broad conditions that account for most of the physical disabilities in the UK. These are illustrated in Table 1.1.

Yali and Revenson (2004) reported on the changing population and demographics in the United States and have highlighted that in addition to an increase in the number of people who are older, there will also be a significant increase in those who belong to a minority ethnic group, describe themselves as gay, or live in poverty, highlighting the need for psychologists to become aware of the overlap in context in which people live which will have an implication on research, clinical practice and training.

The biopsychosocial model promotes the idea that biological, psychological and social processes are integrally and interactively involved in physical health and illness. Suls and Rothman (2004) report that the initially provocative premise that people's psychological experiences and social behaviours are reciprocally related to biological processes has fuelled dramatic advances in this field since the early 1980s. This model has provided researchers, practitioners and policy makers with a critical framework that has promoted the integration of psychosocial factors into health and illness (Kennedy and Llewelyn, 2006; Suls and Rothman, 2004; Kaplan, 1990; Engel, 1977). The model developed because of the failure of the biomedical model to adequately explain health, illness and disability. That is not to say that the biomedical model is not appropriate in many aspects of healthcare, but there is a need to acknowledge its reductionist roots, explaining factors at the level of the cell and providing unidimensional explanations of outcome. It has also been helped by the maturity of behavioural science research since the early 1970s and the shift of focus from infectious disease to chronic conditions, with the associated recognition of bio-behavioural factors in the aetiology and maintenance of chronic disease. Suls and Rothman (2004) reviewed the evidence for the increased awareness of biopsychosocial factors in healthcare by reviewing the frequency of citations in Medline of the term 'biopsychosocial'. Between 1974 and 1977 it was mentioned in six articles, but between 1999 and 2001, it appeared in 350 publications. They also reported on the extent to which health psychologists examined multiple systems by assessing the work of researchers who had published papers in the American Psychiatric Association journal *Health Psychology* over a 12-month period between 2001 and 2002. They measured all four classes of variables associated with the biopsychosocial model, i.e. biological, psychological, social and macro (cultural socio-economic status and ethnicity). Not surprisingly, 94 per cent of the studies measured psychological variables, with just over half measuring social, biological and macro variables respectively. However, too often the findings and implications of basic research do not find their way into clinical practice, which remains a challenge for those involved in promoting the biopsychosocial perspective.

Nevertheless, it is acknowledged that the biomedical perspective remains dominant. The biomedical model is more often focused on single-causal pathways where the biopsychosocial perspective recognises the existence of multiple-causal pathways which reflect complex interactions of sub-systems. Treatment is not single-discipline dominant, but interdisciplinary, often involving a combination aimed at restoring the functioning of the whole person within their context. While the biomedical model is highly appropriate for straightforward disorders, it is poor in relation to chronic diseases and can often result in polarised views between doctors and patients.

The chronicity and extent of disabling conditions have also led to the growth of the biopsychosocial framework. Hoffman *et al.* (1996) report that

68 per cent of middle-aged adults and 88 per cent of older people have at least one medical condition that will be chronic. Nearly three-quarters of presenting symptoms in primary care are of an uncertain aetiology and are likely to have a psychosocial or behavioural dimension in origin (Kroenke and Mangelsdorff, 1989). Health expenditure on chronic conditions is considerable. Chronic illnesses account for as much as 76 per cent of total healthcare expenditure in the United States (Hoffman *et al.*, 1996).

Suls and Rothman (2004) conclude that basic applied research across a range of substantive areas has affirmed the value of the biopsychosocial perspective and demonstrated how biological, psychological and social processes operate together to affect physical health outcomes, reducing the stress and adverse consequences of medical procedures and facilitating the recovery and adaptations of persons with chronic illnesses. There are many challenges ahead for psychologists working in teams and with client groups. Suls and Rothman (2004) consider it essential to capture the complexity of processes that contribute to illness aetiology, prevention and treatment and develop a multi-system, multi-level, multi-varied orientation. It is fully recognised that there is a continuing challenge for practitioners to translate research findings into practice. The growing awareness of evidence-based approaches, however, will enhance this. One could reasonably predict that there will be a continuing growth of comprehensive intervention models as exemplified by pain management programmes (see Chapter 5). Pincus (2005) predicts that disease-specific psychological behavioural interventions will be routinely incorporated into chronic disease management systems within primary care. While we are a long way from this being implemented, Pruitt *et al.* (1998) propose a model to incorporate behavioural medicine expertise into existing primary care practice with the purpose of delivering integrated, comprehensive and efficient healthcare (see also Chapter 11).

The World Health Organization (WHO) has reformulated its model of disability (WHO, 1999) and proposes a model of disability that distinguishes between body functions and structure (impairment), activities (capacity to perform and limitations) and participation (capacity to engage and restrictions in wider social domains). It also recognises the interaction of the above with the contextual environment and personal factors. Environmental factors include physical, social and attitudinal constructions which may maximise or minimise the impact of disability. The experience of disability is not solely a condition of the individual and many of the negative experiences of disability are caused by architectural and social inaccessibilities which are physical and social creations in a society geared for and by non-disabled people. The creation of a more enabling physical and social environment can change the experience of disability.

Personal factors refer to the individual's background with respect to age, gender, ethnicity and experiences. This model of disability is often used as a framework to help understand the physical, psychological and social impact of disease-acquired injury and congenital disorders. Imrie (2004) proposed that the WHO model provides a coherent, albeit uneven, account of the competing conceptions of disability. It does, however, require further clarification with respect to biopsychosocial factors and disability definitions.

As mentioned, the impact of disability stretches from that on the individual to the systemic. It crosses many dimensions that include pain and suffering, beliefs and attitudes, losses and adjustment, coping and resilience. In this book, we have explored these issues in relation to a number of key themes and specific conditions.

The self-management approach is critical when integrating psychological aspects of disability. Devins and Binik (1996) outline three principles that are fundamental to the self-management of chronic disease. First, the emphasis is on self-management of disease, implying that the individual must accept responsibility for managing and enhancing his or her condition to the extent that is possible. They describe this as taking the form of actively monitoring physical and/or psychological well-being and taking appropriate actions as indicated. This also implies that patients must acquire considerable knowledge about their condition and treatment options. Second, self-management emphasises a partnership between service providers and recipients, meaning patient collaboration with healthcare professionals, rather than subservience to them. Activities particularly to be enhanced by active patient participation include communication with healthcare professionals, adhering to and implementing therapeutic regimens, reporting adverse reactions and modifying daily routines. Devin and Binik's third principle maintains that information acquired through patient education efforts must be implemented through effective coping skills and behaviour. Additionally, the potential benefits of increased illness-related knowledge must be actualised through effective self-management behaviour. Skills include scheduling of activity, exercising through behavioural contracting or other motivational strategies, applying a problem-solving approach, maintaining lifestyle balance and communication with the treatment team. Clark *et al.* (1991) outlined 12 self-management tasks commonly targeted in such interventions. These are illustrated in Table 1.2.

Dedicated self-care education training has been found to improve people's confidence and ability to take care of themselves and engage in collaborative shared decision making with health professionals (Bower, 2002; Kennedy *et al.*, 2003). The Chronic Disease Self-Management Programme (CDSMP) is one example of a programme for which there is clear evidence of effectiveness (Lorig *et al.*, 1999). This programme first began in working with people with arthritis and rheumatoid disease, and more recently has been generalised to apply across a variety of conditions. The programme combines a number of components with the objective of training, symptom management, collaboration with the healthcare team in controlling the disease and minimising illness-induced disruptions to preserve

Table 1.2 Twelve self-management tasks

1   Recognising and responding to symptoms
2   Using medications correctly
3   Managing emergencies
4   Maintaining nutrition and diet
5   Maintaining adequate exercise and activity
6   Giving up smoking
7   Using stress management techniques
8   Interacting with health service providers
9   Seeking information and using community resources
10   Adapting to work
11   Managing relationships with significant others
12   Managing psychological responses to disease.

Source: Clark et al. (1991).

quality of life. This programme is not simply about educating patients about their condition or giving information, nor is it solely about improving patients' compliance with instructions, but is aimed at developing confidence in patients to take effective control over their life and explore the ways in which their illness impacts upon their disability. The programme has demonstrated how patients can be more than the recipients of care, can be involved in becoming key decision makers and can take more responsibility for managing their condition. The programme specifically includes cognitive symptom management, exercise instructions, nutrition guidance, problem-solving skills and communication skills. They are facilitated by trained tutors who are often lay people with chronic illnesses themselves. The UK Department of Health has produced an anglicised version of the Stanford model that has been developed by Lorig and has called this the Expert Patient Programme (EPP) (Lorig et al., 1999).

Lorig et al. (2001) reported in a follow-up study that the benefits of chronic disease self-management courses remained two years at follow-up, despite the worsening disease. They found that participants with arthritis, heart disease, lung disease and stroke following a randomised control trial demonstrated significant improvements in their physical and psychological health status. Barlow et al. (2002) reviewed self-management approaches for people with chronic conditions. Most self-management approaches were found to be multi-component and half were based on randomised control trials. Their evidence suggests that self-management approaches are effective at increasing participants' knowledge, symptom management, use of self-management behaviours, self-efficacy and aspects of health status. The literature reviewed in this study suggests that self-management interventions have a beneficial effect on the well-being of participants in the short term. More research is required with particular populations such as children, and to ascertain whether benefits are sustained in the longer term. Barlow et al. (2005) conducted a qualitative investigation of chronic disease self-management courses. They found that sharing experiences, goal setting and upward social comparison were important themes. Anderson and Funnell (2005) insist that collaborative chronic disease management requires a new 'empowerment' paradigm and involves a fundamental redefinition of roles and relationships of healthcare professionals and patients. They suggest that greater reflective practice with healthcare professionals will lead to the adoption of a new paradigm focused on patient-centred collaborative management.

This book explores a number of themes. In the next chapter, Elliott and Warren review the major areas of psychological expertise in the rehabilitation process. They begin by providing an historical overview of rehabilitation psychology and clinical developments. They describe a working model for research and practice in disability and rehabilitation, and then review the key reasons why psychology is important in physical rehabilitation, such as the compelling evidence that psychological factors over physical aspects are more predictive of adjustment and how psychological expertise influences all levels of rehabilitation service development. In Chapter 3, Elfström reviews coping and cognitive behavioural models in physical and psychological rehabilitation. Elfström explains Lazurus and Folkman's theoretical framework of coping and discusses coping strategies and styles. He also highlights what coping is not, before going on to explain the cognitive behavioural framework as applied within the context of physical disability.

Part 2 of the book examines clinical interventions and the psychological contribution. In Chapter 4, Barton reviews the psychological aspects of stroke. She begins by describing the epidemiology and physical impact, before exploring the emotional, social and psychological consequences of stroke. Emotional and cognitive issues are identified, as well as the wider social impact of this condition. She highlights the problems of assessment and formulation following cerebral vascular accidents and provides an informative review of key psychological therapies and interventions. In Chapter 5, Williams and Clyde review the psychological management of chronic or persistent pain. This informed review highlights the psychological management of persistent pain in its physical and social context. The wide range of emotions associated with pain is identified and helpfully framed using a biopsychosocial formulation. This chapter concludes with a comprehensive review of the key components of psychological treatment.

In Chapter 6, Webster and Kennedy highlight the physical impact of spinal cord injury and then describe emotional responses, coping and adjustment. This chapter then reviews psychological care pathways and evidence-based interventions. Fischer, Scharloo, Weinman and Kaptein focus on rehabilitation programmes for people with chronic obstructive pulmonary disease (COPD) in Chapter 7. After describing the epidemiology and physical impact of COPD, they go on to review the key emotional, social and psychological consequences of this condition. They emphasise a comprehensive approach to rehabilitation and provide a helpful commentary on assessment, formulation and intervention.

In Chapter 8, Bennett provides an overview of cardiovascular rehabilitation. He examines the psychological impact of a number of outcomes of coronary heart disease and how psychological-based interventions benefit people with this condition. He considers a number of strategies facilitating behavioural change and emotional adjustment, which include motivational approaches, goal setting and cognitive behavioural therapy. In Chapter 9, Frank and Lee examine the intersections between primary care and physical rehabilitation and the opportunities for psychologists within these systems. They argue for a shift paradigm from patients to consumers and propose an alternative model of primary care which integrates psychological factors, recognises the collaboration that is required with consumers and emphasises the wide context of people's needs with chronic conditions. They caution against the cost-offset argument and argue that examination of the quality-of-life years created by effective psychological treatment will augment this field. Clarke Henshaw addresses sexual aspects of physical disabilities in Chapter 10. In this often ignored and neglected aspect of research and practice, he highlights how there have been considerable increases in our understanding of sex and sexuality over the last few decades. He describes the key conditions associated with sexual dysfunction and emphasises the critical role of accurate and comprehensive assessment. He then describes cognitive behavioural interventions for a variety of psychosexual issues.

In Part 3, this book explores organisational themes and advanced issues. In Chapter 11, Erlen and Caruthers review the ongoing issues associated with adherence to medical regimens. There has been little change since the early 1970s in the 50 per cent regimen adherence rates. They review the factors that influence treatment adherence, which include psychosocial, economic and system-related issues. They then review the treatment adherence research, highlighting a variety of methodologies and outcomes. Cultural and community challenges are highlighted, as well as the contribution of new technologies. Duff provides a comprehensive overview of rehabilitation planning in Chapter 12. This chapter reviews goal setting treatment theories and the key strategies of goal planning. Reference is also made to rehabilitation planning and practice, empowerment, as well as the expert patient model. Finally, in Chapter 13, Slavin reviews innovative applications of a range of technologies in the management, rehabilitation and assessment of a variety of conditions. She suggests a variety of transformations that could enhance service delivery and assessment.

Smith *et al.* (2004) discuss the new type of collaborations that will be required to manage new challenges in healthcare provision. They suggest that several new topics for research will emerge that will include: (a) the prevention of negative impacts of chronic disease; (b) the explication of the positive and negative impacts of medical screening procedures; (c) the implementation of empirically supported preventative interventions; and (d) a broadening of insufficiently studied aspects of health behaviour and prevention that will include phase of risk of disease development and lifecycle issues. Technologically, healthcare has become more complex in terms of treatments such as transplantation, but also in terms of prediction in relation to risk assessment and genetic markers. In parallel to these developments, new psychosocial technologies will also need to be developed, refined and formally tested (Pincus, 2003). We may need to review the current conception of psychotherapy as only occurring in a series of 45 to 50-minute face-to-face weekly sessions. Pincus suggests that some may be limited from 1 to 12 sessions, be of variable length (from 5 to 90 minutes), and administered face to face or through Broadband, video, the Internet or DVD in the primary care specialist's office. Much of these technologies will be packaged for specific target situations such as non-adherent adolescent diabetes and panic disorder.

These changing patterns in the delivery of healthcare also need to be mirrored in the training agenda of doctors, nurses and other health pro-fessionals. Teaching in aspects of multidisciplinary team care have been lacking in many medical training programmes. Crotty *et al.* (2000) reported that while 61 per cent of medical graduates recalled that they had been present at a replacement hip operation, less than half reported that they had ever attended a clinic where a physiotherapist or occupational therapist was present (43 per cent and 36 per cent respectively). Scullion (1999) reviewed the literature and suggested that nurses unwittingly promote 'disablism' and he recommended the promotion of a more socially orientated concept of disability within the nursing curriculum. Holman (2004) commented on the need for new clinical education and suggested that the inadequacy of clinical education is a consequence of the failure of healthcare and medical education to adapt to the two main transformations since the early 1950s that are central to good healthcare. In the first, chronic disease is replaced by acute disease as a dominant problem and is now the principal cause of disability and the use of healthcare expenditure, and the second is that chronic disease has dramatically transformed the role of the patient. The changed role of the patient and the physician bring complementary knowl-edge and reciprocal responsibility to the healthcare process, a partnership of patient and physician that embodies the central role of the patient, which is the crux of appropriate care for chronic disease.

When considering enhancing new healthcare paradigms for the manage-ment of chronic disease and disability, I think we need to be creative, collaborative and exploratory. We have access to tremendous health resources in the form of personnel, research, technology and organisations. The challenge will be for us to incorporate methods of ensuring effective collaborations across providers, users and planners. We also need to be more directed in our research agenda by broadening the base of our research participants to be more representative of the various societies within our communities. There is a continuing need to improve the scientific status and research evidence of the biopsychosocial models. Many models have matured, such as the coping model, the common-sense model and the theory of planned behaviour. For example, the theory of planned behaviour has been found to explain between 23 per cent and 34 per cent of the variance in measures of behaviour across reviews (Armitage and Connor, 2001). However, more convergence, clarity and parsimony are required along with the development of exploratory transdisciplinary research paradigms. Demographic shifts also mean that there will be fewer people to deliver healthcare in the future so more creative, cost-effective and time-limited interventions require research and development. However, Wardle and Steptoe (2005) highlight that it is not sufficient merely to demonstrate associations between psychological factors and health outcomes, or even to demonstrate the benefits of psychological interventions; it is also necessary to develop effective advocacy skills to ensure that research findings are implemented by health planners and policy makers at local and national levels. Little is known about the best strategies to facilitate active dissemination and rapid implementation of best evidence-based practice but Kerner *et al.* (2005) suggest that community health practice settings are perhaps the broadest and most diverse. This book with its focus on the psychological contribution and co-management of physical disability provides a clear agenda for these domains.

References

Abraham, C. and Michie, S. (2005). Towards a healthier nation. *The Psychologist*, 18(11), 670–671.

Anderson, R. N. and Funnell, M. (2005). Patient empowerment: Reflections on the challenge of fostering the adoption of a new paradigm. *Patient Education Evaluation*, 57, 153–157.

Armitage, C. J. and Connor, M. (2001). Efficacy of the theory of planned behaviour: A meta-analytic review. *British Journal of Social Psychology*, 40, 471–495.

Barlow, J., Bancroft, G. and Turner, A. (2005). Self management training for people with chronic disease – a shared learning experience. *Journal of Health Psychology*, 10, 863–872.

Barlow, J., Wright, C., Sheasby, J., Turner, A. and Hainsworth, J. (2002). Self management approaches for people with chronic conditions: A review. *Patient Education and Counselling*, 48, 177–187.

Bower, P. (2002). Primary care mental health workers: Models of working and evidence of effectiveness. *British Journal of General Practice*, 52, 926–933.

Clark, N., Becker, M., Janz, N., Lorig, K., Rakowski, W. and Anderson, L. (1991).

Self management of chronic disease by older adults. A review and questions for research. *Journal of Aging and Health*, 3, 3–27.

Crotty, M., Finucane, P. and Ahern, M. (2000). Teaching medical students about disability and rehabilitation: Methods and study feedback. *Medical Education*, 34, 659–664.

Devins, G. M. and Binik, Y. M. (1996). Facilitating coping in chronic physical illness. In M. Zeidner and N. S. Endler (eds) *The handbook of coping*, pp. 640–696. New York: Wiley.

Engels, G. (1977). The need for a new medical model: A challenge for biomedicine. *Science*, 196, 129–136.

Frank, R. and Elliott, T. (2000). *Handbook of rehabilitation psychology*. Washington, DC: American Psychological Association.

Hoffman, C., Rice, D. and Sung, H. (1996). Persons with chronic conditions: Their prevalence and cost. *Journal of the American Medical Association*, 276, 1473–1479.

Holman, H. (2004). Chronic disease – the need for a new clinical education. *Journal of the American Medical Association*, 292, 1057–1059.

Imrie, R. (2004). Demystifying disability: A review of the International Classification of Functioning, Disability and Health. *Sociology of Health and Illness*, 26, 287–305.

Joint Health Surveys Unit on behalf of the Department of Health (2002). *Health Survey for England 2001*. London: The Stationery Office.

Kaplan, R. (1990). Behaviour as the central outcome in healthcare. *American Psychologist*, 45, 1211–1220.

Kennedy, A., Nelson, E., Reeves, D., Richardson, G., Roberts, C., Robinson, A., Rogers, A., Sculpher, M. and Thompson, D. G. (2003). Randomised control trials to assess the impact of a package comprising a patient orientated, evidence-based self-help guidebook and patient centred consultations on disease management and satisfaction in irritable bowel disorder. *Health Technology Assessment*, 7, 1–126.

Kennedy, P. and Llewelyn, S. (2006). *Essential handbook of clinical health psychology*. Chichester: Wiley.

Kerner, J., Rimer, B. and Emmons, K. (2005). Dissemination research and research dissemination: How can we close the gap? *Health Psychology*, 24, 443–446.

Kroenke, K. and Mangelsdorff, A. D. (1989). Common symptoms in ambulatory care: Incidence, evaluation, therapy and outcome. *American Journal of Medicine*, 86, 262–266.

Lorig, K., Sobel, D., Ritter, P., Laurent, D. and Hobbs, M. (2001). Effective self management programme on patients with chronic disease. *Effective Clinical Practice*, 4, 256–262.

Lorig, K., Sobel, D., Stewart, A., Brown, B., Bandura, A., Ritter, P., Gonzalez, V., Laurent, D. and Holman, H. (1999). Evidence suggesting that a chronic disease self management programme can improve health status while reducing hospitalisation. *Medical Care*, 37, 5–14.

O'Neil, A. (1993). *Health professions' education for the future*. San Francisco: Pew Health Professions Commission.

Orleans, C. T. (2000). Promoting the maintenance of health behaviour change:

Recommendations for the next generation of research and practice. *Health Psychology*, 19 (supp. 1), 76–83.

Pincus, H. A. (2003). The future of behavioural health and primary care: Drowning in the mainstream or left on the bank? *Psychosomatics*, 44, 1–11.

Pruitt, S., Klapow, J., Epping-Jordan, J. and Dresselhaus, T. (1998). Moving behavioural medicine to the front line: a model for the integration of behavioural and medical sciences in primary care. *Professional Psychology: Research and Practice*, 29(3), 230–236.

Scherer, M., Blair, K., Banks, M., Brucker, B., Corrigan, J. and Wegener, S. (2000). Rehabilitation psychology. In E. Craighead and C. Nemeroff (eds) *The concise Corsini encyclopedia of psychology and behavioural science* (3rd edition), pp. 801–803. Chichester: Wiley.

Scullion, P. (1999). Conceptualising disability in nursing: Some evidence from students and their teachers. *Journal of Advanced Nursing*, 29, 648–657.

Smith, T. W., Orleans, C. and Jenkins, D. (2004). Prevention and health promotion: Decades of progress, new challenges and an emerging agenda. *Health Psychology*, 23, 126–131.

Suls, J. and Rothman, A. (2004). Evolution of the biopsychosocial model: Prospects and challengers for health psychology. *Health Psychology*, 23, 119–125.

US Census Bureau (1997). Current population reports: Americans with disabilities 1994–1995. Washington, DC: Census Bureau's Public Information Office.

Wardle, J. and Steptoe, A. (2005). Public health psychology. *The Psychologist*, 18(11), 672–675.

WHO (World Health Organization) (1999). *International Classification of Functioning, Disability and Health (ICFDH-2)*. Geneva, Switzerland: WHO.

Wright, B. A. (2005). Quotation. Personal correspondence.

Yali, A. and Revenson, T. (2004). How changes in population demographics will impact health psychology: Incorporating a broader notion of cultural confidence into the field. *Health Psychology*, 23, 147–155.

Chapter 2

Why psychology is important in rehabilitation

Timothy R. Elliott and Ann Marie Warren

Psychological expertise is an integral component of the continuum of rehabilitation processes from medical inpatient treatment for persons with acute-onset disabilities to the vocational training and placement for persons living with severe and chronic disabilities. Psychological perspectives were formally integrated into the vocational rehabilitation enterprise over a century ago; the ensuing decades and accompanying sophistication in research and practice intensified the role of psychologists at all levels of decision-making and service delivery across the rehabilitation service delivery spectrum.

In this chapter, we will review the major areas of psychological expertise in the rehabilitation process. This will entail an overview of important roles and supportive research. We will offer definitive examples of essential activities performed by psychologists and conclude with comments about future directions for practice and research.

Historical overview

Emotional issues and cognitive problems were recognized in the early days of modern medical rehabilitation as psychological concerns that complicated initial reactions to physical disability. However, the mortality rate of persons acquiring severe physical disability in the early twentieth century was quite dismal, and the clinical activities of psychologists of the day were rather circumscribed, so there was little psychological involvement of psychologists in the medical rehabilitation programs at that time. In contrast, persons who incurred disabling (but less life-threatening) physical or sensory disabilities in the evolving workplace that characterized the Industrial Revolution, and others who incurred disability in times of international conflict, experienced considerable difficulties as they returned to their communities. These persons eventually attracted attention and support from policymakers and charitable organizations. Psychologists participated in the vocational rehabilitation programs that emerged in the early to mid-twentieth century to help these individuals resume meaningful roles in their personal, social, and vocational roles (Elliott and Leung, 2005).

Psychologists' involvement in medical rehabilitation accelerated in the mid-twentieth century as medical interventions and technologies improved and many soldiers survived debilitating wounds incurred in wartime. Psychologists were hired in the medical systems established to provide rehabilitation services for veterans. Rehabilitation medicine was influenced tremendously by pioneers such as Sir Ludwig Guttmann who recognized the need for patients to actively participate in their therapies, resume leisure and recreational activities as part of their rehabilitation program, and pursue community reintegration. Academic psychology was informed by applications of field theory by protégés of Kurt Lewin who worked in clinics serving war veterans (Dunn and Elliott, 2005). Other psychologists entered medical rehabilitation settings to provide behavioral expertise in designing effective services for persons surviving industrial and pedestrian accidents with long-term concomitants that were not responsive to standard medical interventions (e.g. chronic pain; Fordyce, 1976).

New opportunities and formal recognition for professional psychology occurred in several pivotal events in the latter part of the twentieth century. In the United States, psychologists were involved in federal policy that created systems of care for persons who incurred spinal cord injuries (SCIs), and later for persons who sustained traumatic brain injuries (TBIs). SCI model systems were first initiated to create a shared database across medical centers that permitted the empirical study of medical and psychosocial issues and management techniques for this high-cost yet low-incidence disability. TBI model systems, in turn, were initiated later to address the complex needs of the increasing numbers of persons who sustained this injury. These systems (and other similar systems of care such as burn rehabilitation) provided influential and long-lasting roles for professional psychology in clinical, research, and administrative capacities.

Similarly, professional psychology was established as a required component of programs seeking accreditation from the Commission for the Accreditation of Rehabilitation Facilities (CARF). Other important landmarks include the emergence of related psychological specialties of health psychology, neuropsychology and geropsychology in medical settings, which directly enriched research and service throughout most medical specialties. These applied variants of professional psychology grew in direct association with the increasing numbers of persons with chronic diseases that culminate in disabling conditions (including several that reached epidemic proportions including HIV and diabetes mellitus), the increasing numbers of persons living into old age in the community, the increased life expectancy of persons with physical disabilities, and the increasing inability of traditional medical institutions and professions to meet the ongoing needs of persons living with these circumstances.

As a consequence of these various factors and events, an impressive literature base and repository of collective clinical and administrative experience now characterize the field of rehabilitation psychology. Furthermore, new conceptualizations of disability and rehabilitation have changed from the traditional medical model to others that acknowledge personal, social, and environmental factors that are well within the scientific and clinical purview of psychology.

Evolving models of disability and rehabilitation

Implied in the preceding discussion of the historical background and the contemporary context of rehabilitation was the evolving and shifting roles of medical professions and institutions in the rehabilitation enterprise. The medical model of disability is ultimately responsible for the rapid and effective delivery of medical interventions and coordinated ancillary therapies that met the acute physical needs of persons who sustain disabilities; many in these professions also were among the first to advocate improved social, psychological, community, and governmental services for those who survived acquired disabilities and needed specialized initiatives to improve their quality of life and expedite resumption of personal, social, and vocational activities (Elliott and Dreer, in press).

Ultimately, health care services based in a medical model assume a 'find it and fix it' approach to any presenting problem: A problem is diagnosed based on the best objective evaluation and an established and logical treatment is prescribed (Kaplan, 2002). This line of reasoning guided the development of acute care facilities and tertiary care programs designed to provide specialized services (as prescribed) to restore function in affective domains (or rehabilitate to the utmost capacity), and to evaluate the progress of the prescribed treatments. This approach relies heavily on the objective assessment and diagnosis of a condition and its concomitants, and as such, eventual success of the treatment does not depend on subjective reports and feedback from the patient receiving the service.

With improved emergency response interventions and medical rehabilitation services, more individuals survive acquired disabilities and the life expectancy for persons with physical disability has increased substantially (Crews, in press). The course of chronic disease and disability, including the prevention of disabling secondary complications and the attainment of optimal functioning and quality of life, is influenced primarily by behavioral and social mechanisms. Medically based models of service delivery and their associated institutions are best suited for acute care service delivery, and they are ill-suited for conceptualizing and directing services that address behavioral and social factors that can prevent complications and promote health and wellness. Traditional acute rehabilitation programs do not adequately meet the educational and therapeutic needs of persons with acquired disabilities who return to the community with considerable life expectancy (Frank *et al.*, 2004).

Moreover, the financial costs associated with the provision of health care services to persons with chronic disease and disability – including acute episodes of care for preventable complications – account for the majority of health care expenditures across most Western nations (Institute of Medicine, 2001; WHO, 2002). In attempts to manage these costs, most health care delivery systems have curtailed services and limited access to care for many persons with disability.

The limitations of the medical model of disability have been addressed in alternative models espoused by the Institute of Medicine (Institute of Medicine, 2001) and the World Health Organization (WHO, 2001), and a chapter devoted to health and well-being appeared in the most recent *Healthy people 2010* series (US Department of Health and Human Services, 2000). In the *International classification of functioning, disability, and health* (ICF), the WHO recommends separate ratings of impairment along dimensions of body structure impairment (and functioning) at the *organic* level, the degree of functional activity (or limitation) at the *person* level, and the degree of participation at the *societal* level. Environmental factors are recognized in this conceptualization as a major aspect of disablement. In the ICF, a specific medical condition (or physical disability) is an insufficient means of explaining, understanding, anticipating or rehabilitating any aspect of disability experienced by an individual. This highly influential model of disability places greater emphasis on behavioral and social factors in the optimal adjustment of persons who live with chronic disease and disability, and ratings are contingent upon objective evaluations and subjective reports from individuals with the condition.

Psychology and rehabilitation: a working model for research and practice

Psychologists have long understood that disability and rehabilitation is best expressed in the Lewinian equation

$$b = f(p \times e)$$

in which behavior is a function of the person and the environment (Wright, 1960). The degree to which psychologists place greater weight on the person or the environment side of the equation has varied, depending upon theoretical or clinical bias. Nevertheless, decades of research practice across literatures and clinical settings converge to provide a dynamic model for understanding adjustment following disability that can inform the current role of psychology at all levels of rehabilitation. As depicted in Figure 2.1, adjustment is a dynamic process that can be understood in the parallel

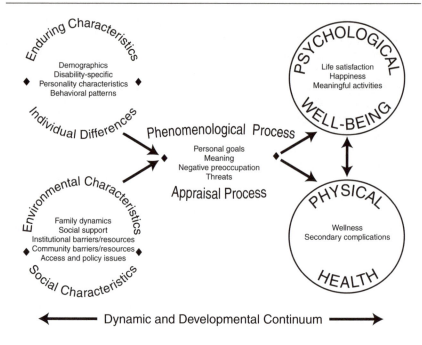

Figure 2.1 Dynamic model of adjustment of individuals living with chronic disease or disability

domains of physical health and personal well-being, and these domains are influenced by factors routinely studied in the broader fields of psychology including behavioral patterns, individual difference variables, social support, interpersonal and family relationships, and specific characteristics of the psychosocial environment that may affect adjustment including gender, culture, race and ethnic identity, and age-related and other developmental variables. Practically all of these reflect basic psychological processes that are studied among people in general, and the associated principles and properties of these psychological theories and constructs apply to persons with disabilities.

There are certain accommodations in this conceptualization to account for unique aspects of a specific disabling condition and environmental aspects that pertain to matters of policy and access. First, unique aspects and concomitants associated with a specific disability are subsumed under the domain labeled *Enduring Characteristics* and *Individual Differences*. This is at odds with medically based models that construe a diagnostic condition as a primary explanatory factor in the adjustment process. In contrast, the dynamic model explicitly recognizes the far-reaching implications of psychological characteristics and behavioral patterns for health and well-being.

Second, this model acknowledges the dynamic continuum in which behavior occurs, in terms of changes that follow in the wake of legislative and market trends, and in terms of changes that may be associated with age, family relationships, acquired abilities, and income. Third, the model concedes that individuals vary considerably in the environmental conditions in which they live that in turn may pose unique impediments to their adjustment (or unique supports that facilitate it), as contained in the component *Environmental Characteristics* and *Social Characteristics*.

However, the dynamic model recognizes that the relation of these factors to adjustment is mediated through phenomenological and appraisal processes unique to the individual; this component is an obvious concession to influential stress and coping models that have established the primacy of subjective appraisal activity in personal adjustment in times of stress (Lazarus and Folkman, 1984). The implications of this component are considerable and they derive from the known influence appraisals have on coping, motivation, and self-report measures of behavior, generally, and on various aspects of an individual's interpersonal and social world.

The dynamic model emphasizes elements of positive adjustment, and its focus is not confined to matters of pathology. Optimal adjustment among persons with physical disability is the fundamental outcome in the rehabilitation enterprise, and it is characterized by subjective well-being, meaningful activities, satisfying relationships, and good health. Too often rehabilitation programs – like most health care delivery systems, generally – are preoccupied with secondary complications, ill health, and psychopathology at the expense of adaptive behaviors, positive assets, and indicators of optimal adjustment (Elliott *et al.*, 2002a). This bias certainly reflects the problem-oriented (and problem-solving) mentality of rehabilitation programs, but it also demonstrates the ways in which people with disabilities are inadvertently defined by the existence and detection of problems and deficits, which relegates them to a second-class citizenship (Olkin, 1999; Wright, 1960). The dynamic model recognizes both positive and negatives aspects of adjustment over the lifespan, and stipulates that these outcomes are essentially predicted by similar psychosocial mechanisms.

Integrating the ICF and the dynamic model of adjustment

The ICF tacitly acknowledges the limited explanatory power of any given medical diagnosis in the prediction of any significant index of adjustment, and it recognizes the powerful influence of behavioral and social factors in subsequent adjustment. Unlike the medical model, which relies on professional and objective assessment of symptoms, signs, and outcomes, the ICF places considerable weight on the subjective experience of the individual, and upon the individual's report of personal, social, and environmental factors. The ICF also recognizes psychological well-being and social activity as essential elements of overall adjustment and it implies recognition of the intricate link between psychological adjustment and optimal physical health.

Yet the ICF is not a psychological model of adjustment; it does not provide explicit and testable hypotheses to advance our understanding of behavioral processes among people with chronic health conditions. However, the ICF acknowledges the importance of psychological well-being and personal independence in everyday routines, and thus it respects individual experience in ratings of adjustment and performance in various domains.

The ICF offers tremendous and unprecedented opportunities for psychologists to further illustrate the immense explanatory power and utility of psychological service, research, and consultation that stem from psychological theory expertise, which in turn will provide clear avenues for developing and implementing testable interventions and services for persons with chronic health conditions to facilitate their overall health and well-being (Johnstone, 1997). To a great extent, this scenario will permit psychologists to assume a lead role in promoting science-based, empirically driven service delivery systems for persons with chronic health conditions.

Reasons why psychology is important in rehabilitation

Within the context of the dynamic model of adjustment following disability, we can enumerate the basic tenets of rehabilitation that demonstrate the reasons why psychology is essential to the rehabilitation process, and we can delineate emerging roles in which psychology will realize more influential activity in administration, resource allocation, and policymaking. We can consider these essential functions in clinical and research activities across all components of the dynamic model.

First reason: psychological factors predict adjustment

Behavioral and social factors account for substantial variance in the prediction of important outcomes among persons with physical disability, above and beyond that attributable to immutable characteristics of any specific disabling condition (with some exceptions occurring in cases of severe brain-behavior deficits).

The WHO ICF model implicitly acknowledges that a specific disability diagnosis has insufficient explanatory power: There is considerable variation in the ways in which people adjust to their circumstances and pursue their routines, activities, and personal and social roles in everyday life. Evidence from the extant literature underlines this position: Both people in general and people with chronic health conditions vary in their ability to cope and adjust, and this is determined by an array of behavioral and social processes.

These factors are accommodated in the dynamic model of adjustment, but their importance is often obfuscated in clinical service programs and research designs that are constructed upon specific diagnostic entities: The diagnostic condition serves as the centerpiece for clinical and academic activity. Consonant with the medical model, this has considerable utility and convenience in acute care episodes in which necessary interventions are relatively circumscribed and focused on expert, coordinated, and fairly invasive procedures dictated by the urgency and severity of the physical condition. This is a hallmark of medical specialties and their respective services and literature base.

But this model proves awkward and cumbersome as the acute needs are met and behavioral and social issues exert their influence on routine and ongoing activities that affect daily living, and ultimately influence outcomes important in the ICF model. Unfortunately, much of the relevant literature is demarcated by artificial boundaries that define medical specialties, so it is difficult to appreciate the converging evidence supporting the consistency of the underlying behavioral and social processes that affect adjustment across diagnostic conditions.

Indicators of disability severity may be related to specific functional abilities, but key reviews have concluded that participation in meaningful, and rewarding personal and social activities is inconsistently associated with disability severity (Dijkers, 1997; Whiteneck, 1992). This is not surprising, given the well-documented effects of behavioral and social factors in the prediction of self-reported adjustment among persons with disabling conditions (e.g. Elliott and Frank, 1996). For many decades, antiquated and untested stage models of adjustment dominated clinical thinking about initial and subsequent reactions to sudden or gradual physical disability, and the lingering effects of these anecdotal models can still be heard in casual references to 'denial' observed among persons receiving rehabilitative services. However, empirical investigations have consistently demonstrated that persons at risk of depressed moods, depressive symptoms, and episodes of depressive syndromes have unique and measurable psychosocial characteristics that are observed among people in general at risk of depression. Moreover, individuals with physical disability who have more psychosocial assets along these various dimensions are more likely to exhibit optimal adjustment and resume meaningful activities (Elliott et al., 2002a).

These differences have been found on self-report measures of positive and negative adjustment. Persons who have effective problem-solving abilities are more likely to report greater acceptance of disability at discharge from an inpatient rehabilitation program than persons who have ineffective problem-solving skills (Elliott, 1999). Ineffective problem-solving abilities are also associated with higher depression scores and more psychosocial impairment above and beyond variance attributable to disability severity and time since the onset of injury (Elliott et al., 1991). Ineffective problem-solving skills have been associated with greater self-reported disability among persons with chronic low back pain (Witty et al., 2001) and among persons with traumatic brain injury (Rath et al., 2003a). Other psychological characteristics predictive of self-reported disability and functional impairment regardless of disability severity include hope (Snyder et al., 2006), goal orientation (Elliott et al., 2000), and neuroticism (Jang et al., 2002; Rovner and Casten, 2001). Collectively, these findings indicate that psychological characteristics have a pronounced effect on self-report measures of adjustment, function, and disability. The actual mechanisms that are at work in these effects may range from influence on adaptive coping and goal-directed behavior that result in optimal adjustment, to a response bias that contaminates self-report measurement of disability and adjustment.

Compelling evidence from studies integrating objective indicators of severity, symptoms, and outcomes with important psychological constructs has given us insight into several possible mechanisms that influence adjustment following disability. As suggested in the dynamic model, several enduring personality characteristics appear to predispose individuals to certain outcomes. In the chronic pain literature, for example, personality characteristics assessed by Scale 3 of the Minnesota Multiphasic Personality Inventory (MMPI) are predictive of persons who return to work six months (Gatchel et al., 1995a) and one year (Gatchel et al., 1995b) after participating in a pain rehabilitation program (and there is prospective evidence linking these characteristics to persons at risk of pain injuries in the workplace; see Bigos et al., 1991). These studies provide evidence of possible long-term and substantive effects of personality in the rehabilitation process. Generally, the MMPI measures rather pathological behavioral patterns that are often expressed in personality characteristics; of particular importance in these studies is the use of an objective and meaningful adjustment outcome. Employment is associated with greater life satisfaction among persons with disabling conditions and individuals who are not employed are often at risk of secondary complications (Elliott and Leung, 2005).

Pre-disability behavioral patterns emerge as strong predictors of outcomes across other conditions. Pre-injury occupational status is a major determining factor of employment following traumatic brain injury (along with several behavioral, emotional, and neuropsychological indicators; Ownsworth and McKenna, 2004). Among persons with SCIs persons with pre-disability patterns of heavy alcohol consumption display fewer functional gains and longer stays in initial rehabilitation than those without such histories (Bombardier et al., 2004), and they are more likely to develop pressure sores over the first three years of SCI (Elliott *et al.*, 2002b). Certain cognitive-behavioral characteristics have also been associated with health status following disability. These characteristics may be relatively stable and reflect pre-disability behavioral patterns, yet they are amenable to cognitive-behavioral intervention. Effective problem-solving abilities are prospectively predictive of pressure sore occurrence in the first three years of SCI, and this effect occurs independently of disability severity (Elliott *et al.*, 2006). Other data implicate family caregivers' problem-solving abilities in pressure sore development among persons with SCI (Elliott *et al.*, 1999).

The dynamic model posits that subjective appraisal processes are unique mechanisms that influence adjustment, and these often mediate the effects of disability variables, personality characteristics, and behavioral patterns on subsequent adjustment. In this conceptualization, the dynamic model differs from the ICF: The ICF makes no allowance for these important phenomenological activities and these can affect adjustment. Yet cognitive appraisals can directly influence the perception, experience, and reporting of distress, symptoms, and impairment.

Appraisals can be situation- or stress-specific. It is imperative to note that there is considerable variation in the appraisal process between people and we know there can also be considerable consistency over time in the ways a given individual may appraise stress. For example, persons high in neuroticism have a more pessimistic interpretation of routine and stressful events than those low in neuroticism (Watson and Pennebaker, 1989), so we expect persons with high neuroticism to have negatively valenced scores on any self-report measure, including measures of physical symptoms (including pain), environmental constraints, or functional activity. Others may interpret actual physical sensations in a 'catastrophizing' manner, which contributes to greater distress and disability (Turner *et al.*, 2002). Alternatively, persons who report effective problem-solving abilities are less likely to report physical symptoms under routine and stressful conditions (Elliott *et al.*, 2004). Individuals who look inward to find some ability to exert control over their internal states, regulate negative cognitions and moods, identify meaningful personal goals, and restructure their personal values are more likely to experience positive psychological growth following disability (Elliott *et al.*, 2002a).

Specific appraisals of the degree to which a disabling condition interferes with goal-directed and routine activities predict greater distress than objective qualities of the condition (Harkins *et al.*, in press); in contrast, this study also demonstrated that perceived abilities to tolerate symptoms were associated with less distress. Both interference and tolerance appraisals operate in the regulation of distress, and in the process exert an effect on self-reported impairment independent of disability severity (Dreer *et al.*, 2005).

Case vignette 2.1: How psychological therapy can enhance rehabilitation outcomes

'Mike' was a 26-year-old unmarried Caucasian man who was admitted to inpatient rehabilitation nine days after a traumatic SCI. He had sustained an ASIA A L2-3 injury following a motor vehicle accident in which he was the sole passenger. An evaluation was done by the rehabilitation psychologist on the first morning of his admission. Mike presented initially with severely depressed mood and anxious affect. He was tearful when discussing the events of the accident, all of which he remembered, and verbalized feelings of guilt for the circumstances (speeding) that caused the accident to occur. Mike also expressed significant emotional distress over the effect his SCI would have on his sexual functioning. According to Mike, 'My life is completely over, I don't have anything left.' Within a few minutes of the session, he began to verbalize not only thoughts of suicide but plans to end his life after leaving the hospital. The rehabilitation psychologist, in conjunction with the psychiatrist, was able to develop a safety plan for Mike, including consultation with Psychiatry to prescribe an antidepressant. Psychological intervention was provided to Mike on a daily basis to provide cognitive-behavioral therapy for his depression and education on sexuality issues following SCI. This helped him to learn ways to cope with his condition, and to see and understand options for intimacy and sexual expression. Additionally, the rehabilitation psychologist worked with Mike and his girlfriend of two years in couple sessions to help them communicate with each other more effectively when Mike got frustrated over his limitations and projected those frustrations on his girlfriend. Throughout his rehabilitation stay, Mike's coping skills increased dramatically and as his coping skills increased, his verbalizations of hope-lessness and self-harm dramatically decreased. His affect and mood improved on a daily basis. As his psychological state improved, his physical ability to manage his SCI also increased. When Mike reached the end of his inpatient stay, his high anxiety level returned as he prepared for the transition to home with his parents; however, these issues were discussed in depth in individual sessions to help normalize the experience of the transition from inpatient rehabilitation to home. Additionally, the rehabilitation psychologist worked closely with the specialty home-based program that was in place for his continued rehabilitation needs. This allowed the coping skills learned in inpatient rehabilitation to be reinforced by the home-based treatment team. Within two months of discharge to the home setting, Mike was experiencing only occasional episodes of sad mood that appeared to be well within normal limits. He began to attend the outpatient support group for individuals with SCI at the rehabilitation hospital, and was using his own experience to help newly injured patients at the hospital, on both an individual basis and in the inpatient group. Mike also maintained his relationship with his girlfriend and she continued to show her support by encouraging Mike in his new pursuit of driving and his eventual plan to return to college.

Second reason: psychological expertise in measurement and service delivery is essential to rehabilitation

With their scientist-practitioner orientation, psychologists have the particular expertise to develop, study and administer measures and assessments of activities relevant to the rehabilitation enterprise and to the development, implementation and evaluation of services to persons with physical disability.

Given the immense evidence demonstrating the predictive power of psychological variables in the well-being and health of persons receiving rehabilitation services, psychologists have a vital role in the evaluation, assessment, and measurement of these and other activities integral to rehabilitation. Traditionally, psychologists have conducted clinical assessments to identify specific deficits, characteristics, and needs for rehabilitation, and to confer with multidisciplinary teams and various community agencies (e.g. vocational rehabilitation programs, school systems) to maximize therapeutic and community reintegration (Glueckauf et al., 1993). In the early years of rehabilitation, psychologists were involved in the development of relevant norms and the adaptation of popular measures for use with persons with an array of physical or sensory impairments, as these persons were typically underrepresented in normative data and understudied, generally (Elliott and Leung, 2005). These activities remain vibrant aspects of rehabilitation psychology (see Cushman and Scherer, 1995), and clinical practice continues to rely on psychometric instruments for expert assessment in the domains of psychopathology, personality and individual differences, behavioral patterns, cognitive and intellectual abilities, and physical and emotional health. These domains are subsumed in the related components of the dynamic model of adjustment displayed in Figure 2.1.

In the acute inpatient setting, psychologists often receive consultations from attending physicians to assess the psychological and cognitive functioning of a patient within the first few days of the onset of injury. Assessments in the intensive care unit usually include a clinical interview to assess the patient's psychological functioning, complemented by a brief assessment of cognitive abilities or a brief mental status examination. In this assessment the psychologist must take into account current medications and medical procedures that can impact both cognitive and psychological functioning. Assessment techniques are modified as necessary to accommodate physical and communicative impairments, lack of privacy, and multiple distractions in the intensive care unit.

Psychologists have a unique role in developing rapport with an individual in inpatient rehabilitation to help them describe their interpretation of their medical condition and their response to it. Psychologists confer with the multidisciplinary team, and in this process they help staff understand the patient's reaction from the perspective of that individual. This will include some discussion of clinical symptoms that may complicate therapeutic progress and warrant intervention, such as depression or anxiety. Ideally, it will also include discussion of the individual's positive coping mechanisms, personal strengths, and family and social support. The quality of available family support can vary considerably, however, because families have behavioral histories that impinge on the patient's adjustment and family members can experience significant emotional reactions as well. The intensive care and acute trauma environments are often unfamiliar and frightening places for families and they are often attempting to cope with their loved one's injury or illness with limited sleep, limited understanding and limited resources.

Psychologists also play a vital role in the measurement of rehabilitation therapies, functional abilities and gains, and clinical outcomes. For some time, psychologists have expressed concerns about the measurement of clinical outcomes and program evaluation (Keith, 1984). Many psychologists have participated in the development and refinement of measures of functional and cognitive abilities targeted in rehabilitation and for the study of clinical outcomes (Heinemann, 2000). Psychologists were instrumental in the development of the ICF at the WHO (Reed et al., 2005; WHO, 2001) and other relevant instruments that have been used in health care service research (e.g. the SF-36; Ware et al., 1993). Outcome research has also benefited from instrument development in other psychological specialties; for example, the Satisfaction with Life scale (Diener et al., 1985), currently enjoying use in several studies of quality of life among persons with disability, has an extensive history in social psychological research.

Measuring aspects of disability, functional abilities, and clinical outcomes has resulted in a number of empirically based instruments that have advanced the science and practice of health service research (Heinemann, 2005; Mermis, 2005). These instruments are frequently used to (1) evaluate and quantify the extent of physical disability and capacity for self-care, (2) identify limitations for discharge and/or rehabilitation, (3) identify outcomes associated with rehabilitation interventions, and (4) identify goals for rehabilitation.

Case vignette 2.2: How psychological assessment can enhance gains in rehabilitation

David was an 18-year-old Caucasian man who was injured following an unrestrained motor vehicle collision (MVC). As a result of the MVC, David sustained a L3 burst fracture resulting in paralysis and sensory deficits in his lower extremities. He also sustained a mild TBI and had a Glasgow Coma Scale score of 14. A brief psychological assessment of David was done in the intensive care unit (ICU) and included the Galveston Orientation and Amnesia Test (GOAT). David's GOAT score was in the borderline range and indicated the presence of post-traumatic amnesia. David also reported feeling 'depressed,' 'hopeless,' and worried about the future as well as reporting symptoms of insomnia, decreased appetite, and tearfulness. The initial psychological assessment also allowed the rehabilitation psychologist to prepare the inpatient SCI team for David's transition to inpatient rehabilitation.

Once David was admitted to inpatient rehabilitation, he was seen again by the rehabilitation psychologist who conducted the initial evaluation in the ICU. David was given a series of tests to assess both his cognitive and emotional functioning. The purpose of the assessment was to use the results to help the inpatient SCI team to work with David's potential deficits but also to capitalize on his strengths to improve their therapy interventions. David was given the following measures: the Wechsler Adult Intelligence Scale (3rd edition, WAIS-III); the Million Behavioral Medicine Diagnostic (MBMD); a second GOAT; the Rivermead Behavioral Memory Test (2nd edition, RMBT-II); and the Beck Depression Inventory (BDI). The results of David's testing suggested that he had an IQ in the average range and the differences between his verbal and performance scales suggested that he would perform better on visual motor tasks as compared to verbal tasks. This was an important finding to share with the inpatient SCI treatment team. As a consequence of this information, the therapists and physician provided David with visual demon- strations and pictures rather than verbal instruction whenever possible to enhance his comprehension of the SCI education curriculum. David's repeat GOAT showed a shift from a borderline range at the ICU assessment to a normal range at the time of the evaluation in inpatient rehabilitation. How- ever, he still reported retrograde amnesia. Additionally, David's performance on visual memory was in the below average range, as was his performance on auditory non-contextual memory ability. Again, this was critical information for the inpatient SCI team as they found it beneficial to provide him with repetition in a variety of therapy tasks and educational material. It also lessened the frustration on the part of the therapists when David 'didn't seem to be getting it.'

The MBMD and BDI provided an overview of David's socio-emotional and personality functioning as well as suggestions for how the therapy staff could best interact with him in order to meet the treatment goals. David did endorse symptoms of depression as indicated by both the BDI and the MBMD. However, personality testing also indicated that David had always conceptualized his life in a negative way, which was substantiated by the clinical interview. David had experienced many negative life events including the death of his father three months prior to his SCI and an estranged relationship with his mother. He had a very limited social support system which consisted primarily of his current girlfriend, and he feared he would lose this relationship because of the SCI. Personality testing also indicated that he had a historical tendency to be distrustful of others for fear of being hurt and being taken advantage of (which was confirmed by his own perceived minimal social support). Testing also showed David's strengths. He endorsed that he viewed himself as 'tough' and 'smart' and despite his depression he viewed himself as someone with a future. This testing allowed the rehabilitation psychologist to help communicate to the team that the best approach in working with David was to build a strong working alliance to facilitate his trust in them and therefore improve his overall performance in physiotherapy and occupational therapy tasks. Additionally, this testing supported David's need to have a therapy plan at the inpatient rehabilitation hospital that included regular psychological intervention to build his coping skills and provide much-needed support and empathy. As a consequence of the psychological assessment, David's therapy team could help him maximize his rehabilitation and provide him with the tools he needed to cope effectively with his SCI.

Third reason: psychological expertise is essential at all levels of service development, delivery, and evaluation

With their scientist-practitioner orientation, psychologists have the particular expertise to develop, study, administer, and evaluate services provided to persons who live with physical disability.

Rehabilitation provides a series of coordinated, strategic therapies that ideally restore function and facilitate personal health. Psychologists possess unique consultative, measurement, and research skills that can guide and enhance all rehabilitation therapies. Psychologists have particular expertise in recommending, administering, and providing specific behavioral interventions and related services. The extant literature is replete with evidence supporting the appropriateness and effectiveness of psychological interventions in rehabilitation.

Clinical assessment is essential to the determination of appropriate psychological interventions. Issues, characteristics, and behavioral patterns can be assessed along the dimensions delineated in the dynamic model of adjustment. Thus, specific interventions for depression or anxiety would be conducted in the context of pre-disability behavioral patterns or stable personality characteristics. The dynamic model places particular emphasis on the critical issue of *timing*: Interventions are most effective when they are tailored to the problems that occur at specific points in the disability experience. The importance of strategically timing interventions to specific problems is inherent in most rehabilitation therapies in medical settings, but this feature is less obvious in the provision of psychological interventions.

Assessments of both psychological and cognitive functioning allow the psychologist to make recommendations to the attending team. Behavioral recommendations can assist the ICU and trauma staff to effectively respond to 'problem behaviors' such as agitation of a patient with TBI. Understanding behavioral interventions allows the psychologist to develop a behavioral plan for both the patient and the staff. Recommendations are also made with the team and the family to help determine the discharge disposition. With lengths of hospital stays becoming increasingly shorter, and resources of individuals in short supply, it is not uncommon for patients to leave an acute trauma unit even if further specialized care, such as inpatient rehabilitation for a TBI or SCI, is needed.

Many psychological interventions have demonstrable effects in the acute inpatient setting. Some of these interventions alleviate discomfort from symptoms (e.g. hypnosis for pain relief; Patterson and Jensen, 2003). Other formats, such as cognitive-behavioral group therapy, may be effective in providing participants with skills that augment their coping repertoire (King and Kennedy, 1999) and their community reintegration (Rath *et al.*, 2003b). Indeed, the therapeutic effects of group therapy can exert their benefits on phenomenological appraisals of stress, and in fostering a sense of social support among participants (King and Kennedy, 1999). Individual psychotherapy is better suited for detailed problems that require greater confidentiality and tailoring to issues that may at times stem from unique aspects of the disabling condition (Mohr *et al.*, 2001) or for examining issues that may require clinical attention at a later time (e.g. motivational interviewing for substance abuse problems; Bombardier and Rimmele, 1999).

Psychologists play an important role in the development and implementation of patient and family education following injury and subsequent disability. From the onset of an illness or injury, patients and their families often seek answers from a variety of sources, most immediately the medical professionals and then later from sources ranging from the internet to shared experiences with others. Theoretically, early education and information about one's medical condition should result in a reduction of the anxiety and distress that accompany a new and unfamiliar situation. It is logical then that the ICUs and acute trauma units provide a potential opportunity to start early education about an individual's condition to reduce the overall anxiety that commonly occurs.

As observed earlier, however, acute rehabilitation programs do not adequately prepare people for the challenges and issues they face upon their return to live in the community. Therefore, it is critical for the psychologist to help determine what psychological and cognitive resources the individual might need following hospitalization as well as recognize the dynamic issues with the family that can be either barriers or supports to a plan for discharge to home. Many interventions are better suited for persons who have returned to community residence, as certain skills taught in cognitive-behavioral therapies have greater value and generalizability. Social skills training, for example, has been effective for community-residing persons with disability (Dunn et al., 1981; Glueckauf and Quittner, 1992).

In other situations, home- and community-based programs are strategic options. Although these programs are informed by psychological expertise, they are particularly attractive because they may be effectively operated by low-cost service providers. For example, family caregivers report significant benefits from problem-solving training provided in weekly telephone counseling sessions with a nurse (Grant et al., 2002). On a larger scale, structured employment programs, which typically rely on low-cost service providers as on-site job trainers, have demonstrated considerable efficacy in several clinical trials in returning people to competitive work following disability (Bond et al., 2001; Elliott and Leung, 2005).

Other psychological therapies may be required to help persons unlearn 'disabled behavior' that has inadvertently developed over time and compromised adjustment (e.g. pain rehabilitation; Gatchel, 2005). Individual psychotherapy can be useful in helping clients understand ways to *accept* difficult thoughts, feelings, and bodily sensations without struggling with them, and focus on overt activities that contribute to important outcomes (in acceptance and commitment therapy; Hayes et al., 1999). Applications of this model in rehabilitation settings reveal that greater acceptance of chronic pain sensations is associated with less depression and pain-specific anxiety, with less physical and psychosocial disability, and with greater routine activity and work status (McCracken, 1998). Psychologists have also developed disability-affirmative therapy to help individuals find meaning in their circumstances, develop personal goals in the face of stigma and discrimination, and facilitate rewarding significant relationships with others based on acceptance and understanding (Olkin, 1999). In general, cognitive-behavioral therapies have demonstrated considerable utility and flexibility for use with persons who have disabling conditions (Elliott and Jackson, 2005; Radnitz, 2000).

Fourth reason: psychological expertise in research and scientific methods is essential to rehabilitation

Consonant with their scientist-practitioner heritage, psychologists have the particular expertise to advance the empirical and scientific study of rehabilitation with theoretical models of behavior that can expand its knowledge base, develop new therapies, and advance rational alloca-tion of services, generally.

Rehabilitation settings utilize techniques and practices that are often con-sidered the standard of care, but relatively little if any research has been done to determine the true efficacy of the treatment. Psychologists have an important role in working with their colleagues to encourage critical thinking skills and help the development of research studies that directly affect clinical practice. For example, aquatic therapy is routinely utilized in many rehabilitation facilities to improve functional outcomes (e.g. range of motion, gait) but there is relatively no research on its utility, especially in certain conditions such as SCI. Many professions in rehabilitation are moving to research-based practice. However, many standard techniques are a result of clinical expertise rather than true evidence-based practices.

Psychologists possess unique critical thinking skills, grounded in theory and empiricism, that are required to constantly question, examine, refine, and improve the rehabilitation process. Not surprisingly, psychologists have been active in developing standards for evidence-based practice in several areas, and have participated in literature reviews used in clinical standards of care, research agendas, and policy development (Frank and Elliott, 2000). Psychologists have also assumed the lead in critiquing the lack of evidence for routine medical interventions in rehabilitation (e.g. the lack of clinical trials supporting antidepressant therapies in SCI; Elliott and Kennedy, 2004).

Throughout its history, rehabilitation psychology has excelled in prac-tical applications of psychological theories to the understanding and allevi-ation of problems encountered in the clinical setting, including applications of Lewinian field theory (Wright, 1960), operant behavioral principles (Fordyce, 1976), psychophysiology (Ince, 1980), and behavioral neuro-science (Uswatte and Taub, 2005). Constraint-induced movement therapy, developed from a neuroscience perspective and first examined in laboratory models of behavior and disability, provides an instructive case-in-point. The implications of this work are immense, demonstrating the plasticity of neural pathways in learning new neural pathways to effect motor ability following damage incurred in stroke and other brain-related injuries. Although these treatment modalities may currently lack clinical efficacy (in terms of financial costs), the beneficial effects of these interventions raise many possibilities and new avenues for treatment to assist individuals who would otherwise live without certain abilities. In this scenario, the theory and research are essential to developing new interventions that may later result in financial viability in the clinical enterprise.

Similarly, expert use of new statistical methods informs the development, support, and dispersion of clinical services. There are statistical methods that now permit the modeling of an individual's growth and progress during rehabilitation, and these analyses permit a greater understanding of a priori characteristics that predict greater response to rehabilitation therapies, and of those that indicate a poorer prognosis (Warschausky et al., 2001). These tools allow a more precise examination of characteristics of persons at risk of complications following their return to the community, and of those who are likely to adapt well on their own recognizance (see Elliott et al., 2001, for a prospective study of family caregiver adjustment). It should be emphasized, however, that these statistical procedures are more informative when they are guided by an a priori theoretical model that provides a reasonable explanation of anticipated relationships *between* predictor variables that relate to a clinical outcome. In a study germane to this issue, an atheoretical model built primarily on clinically important variables, without specifying a priori relationships between the immutable demographic and disability-specific variables and the psychological constructs in the model, found that demographic and disability severity variables were significantly predictive of pressure sore occurrence in the first three years of SCI (Elliott et al., 2006). This finding was consistent with the extant clinical literature. However, when an a priori model was used to specify the direct paths between the predictor variables, so that the psychological constructs were related to demographic and injury variables in a theoretical and reasonable manner, the psychological constructs were the important contributors to the model, and the demographic and injury variables were no longer significantly related to pressure sore occurrence. The implications for theory in the development of predictive models are considerable: This information is essential for greater precision in identifying persons at risk of complicated adjustment, and for developing cost-effective community-based interventions and prevention programs for these individuals.

Summary

With the advent and international embrace of the ICF as a template for guiding rehabilitative services in contemporary health care, the behavioral and social factors that determine health and well-being following disability will attain recognition. By the very nature of their scientist-practitioner model of training in both clinical application and research expertise, psychologists are critical stakeholders in rehabilitation, and they possess the expertise to influence all levels of rehabilitation service development, provision, and evaluation as systems respond to the needs and concerns of persons living with chronic and disabling health conditions. In this process, psychologists can assume unprecedented leadership roles in practice, research administration, advocacy, and policy development.

Acknowledgements

This chapter was supported in part by funds to the first author from the National Institute on Disability and Rehabilitation Research (Grant #H133N5009 and #H133B980016A), National Institute on Child Health and Human Development (#T32 HD07420), and Centers for Disease Control and Prevention – National Center for Injury Prevention and Control (Grant #R49/CE000191) to the University of Alabama at Birmingham. Its contents are solely the responsibility of the authors and do not necessarily represent the official views of the funding agencies.

References

Bigos, S., Battie, M., Spengler, D., Fisher, L. D., Fordyce, W. E., Hawson, T., Nachemson, A. and Wortley, M. (1991). A prospective study of work perceptions and psychosocial factors affecting the report of back injury. *Spine*, 16, 1–6.

Bombardier, C. H. and Rimmele, C. T. (1999). Motivational interviewing to prevent alcohol abuse after traumatic brain injury: A case series. *Rehabilitation Psychology*, 44, 52–67.

Bombardier, C. H., Stroud, M., Esselman, P. and Rimmele, C. (2004). Do preinjury alcohol problems predict poorer rehabilitation progress in persons with spinal cord injury? *Archives of Physical Medicine and Rehabilitation*, 85, 1488–1492.

Bond, G. R., Resnick, S., Drake, R., Xie, H., McHugo, G. and Bebout, R. (2001). Does competitive employment improve nonvocational outcomes for people with severe mental illness? *Journal of Consulting and Clinical Psychology*, 69, 489–501.

Crews, J. (in press). Neither prepared nor rehearsed: The role of public health in disability and caregiving. In R. C. Talley and J. E. Crews (eds) *Caregiving and disabilities*. New York: Oxford University Press.

Cushman, L. A. and Scherer, M. (eds) (1995). *Psychological assessment in medical rehabilitation settings*. Washington, DC: American Psychological Association.

Diener, E., Emmons, R., Larsen, R. and Griffin, S. (1985). The satisfaction with life scale. *Journal of Personality Assessment*, 49, 71–75.

Dijkers, M. (1997). Quality of life after spinal cord injury: A meta-analysis of the effects of disablement components. *Spinal Cord*, 35, 829–840.

Dreer, L., Elliott, T., Berry, J., Fletcher, D. and Swanson, M. (2005). *Cognitive appraisals, distress and disability among persons in low vision rehabilitation*. Manuscript submitted for publication.

Dunn, D. and Elliott, T. (2005). Revisiting a constructive classic: Wright's *Physical Disability: A Psychosocial Approach*. *Rehabilitation Psychology*, 50, 183–189.

Dunn, M., Van Horn, E. and Herman, S. (1981). Social skills and spinal cord injury: A comparison of three training procedures. *Behavior Therapy*, 12, 153–164.

Elliott, T. (1999). Social problem-solving abilities and adjustment to recent-onset spinal cord injury. *Rehabilitation Psychology*, 44, 315–332.

Elliott, T. and Dreer, L. (in press). Disability. In S. Ayers, A. Baum, C. McManus, S. Newman, K. Wallston, J. Weinman and R. West (eds) *Cambridge handbook of psychology, health and medicine* (2nd edition).

Elliott, T. and Frank, R. G. (1996). Depression following spinal cord injury. *Archives of Physical Medicine and Rehabilitation*, 77, 816–823.

Elliott, T. and Jackson, W. T. (2005). Cognitive-behavioral therapy in rehabilitation psychology. In A. Freeman (Editor-in-Chief), *Encyclopedia of cognitive behavior therapy* (pp. 324–327). New York: Springer Science and Business Media, Inc.

Elliott, T. and Kennedy, P. (2004). Treatment of depression following spinal cord injury: an evidence-based review. *Rehabilitation Psychology*, 49, 134–139.

Elliott, T. and Leung, P. (2005). Vocational rehabilitation: history and practice. In W. B. Walsh and M. Savickas (eds) *Handbook of vocational psychology* (3rd edition) (pp. 319–343). New York: Lawrence Erlbaum Associates.

Elliott, T., Bush, B. and Chen, Y. (2006). Social problem solving abilities predict pressure sore occurrence in the first three years of spinal cord injury. *Rehabilitation Psychology*, 51, 69–77.

Elliott, T., Grant, J. and Miller, D. (2004). Social problem solving abilities and behavioral health. In E. Chang, T. J. D'Zurilla and L. J. Sanna (eds) *Social problem solving: Theory, research, and training* (pp. 117–133). Washington, DC: American Psychological Association.

Elliott, T., Kurylo, M. and Rivera, P. (2002a). Positive growth following an acquired physical disability. In C. R. Snyder and S. Lopez (eds) *Handbook of positive psychology* (pp. 687–699). New York: Oxford University Press.

Elliott, T., Shewchuk, R. and Richards, J. S. (1999). Caregiver social problem solving abilities and family member adjustment to recent-onset physical disability. *Rehabilitation Psychology*, 44, 104–123.

Elliott, T., Shewchuk, R. and Richards, J. S. (2001). Family caregiver problem solving abilities and adjustment during the initial year of the caregiving role. *Journal of Counseling Psychology*, 48, 223–232.

Elliott, T., Kurylo, M., Chen, Y. and Hicken, B. (2002b). Alcohol abuse history and adjustment following spinal cord injury. *Rehabilitation Psychology*, 47, 278–290.

Elliott, T., Uswatte, G., Lewis, L. and Palmatier, A. (2000). Goal instability and adjustment to physical disability. *Journal of Counseling Psychology*, 47, 251–265.

Elliott, T., Godshall, F., Herrick, S., Witty, T. and Spruell, M. (1991). Problem-solving appraisal and psychological adjustment following spinal cord injury. *Cognitive Therapy and Research*, 15, 387–398.

Fordyce, W. E. (1976). *Behavioral methods in chronic pain and illness*. St. Louis, MO: Mosby.

Frank, R. G. and Elliott, T. (2000). Rehabilitation psychology: Hope for a psychology of chronic conditions. In R. G. Frank and T. Elliott (eds) *Handbook of rehabilitation psychology* (pp. 3–8). Washington, DC: American Psychological Association Press.

Frank, R. G., Hagglund, K. and Farmer, J. (2004). Chronic illness management in primary care: The cardinal symptoms model. In R. G. Frank, S. McDaniel, J. Bray and M. Heldring (eds) *Primary care psychology* (pp. 259–275). Washington, DC: American Psychological Association Press.

Gatchel, R. J. (2005). *Clinical essentials of pain management*. Washington, DC: American Psychological Association.

Gatchel, R. J., Polatin, P. B. and Kinney, R. K. (1995a). Predicting outcome of chronic back pain using clinical predictors of psychopathology: A prospective analysis. *Health Psychology*, 14, 415–420.

Gatchel, R. J., Polatin, P. B. and Mayer, T. G. (1995b). The dominant role of psychosocial risk factors in the development of chronic low back pain disability. *Spine*, 20, 2702–2709.

Glueckauf, R. L. and Quittner, A. L. (1992). Assertiveness training for disabled adults in wheelchairs: Self-report, role-play, and activity pattern outcomes. *Journal of Consulting and Clinical Psychology*, 60, 419–425.

Glueckauf, R. L., Sechrest, L., Bond, G. R. and McDonel, E. (1993). *Improving assessment in rehabilitation and health*. Newbury Park, NJ: Sage.

Grant, J., Elliott, T., Weaver, M., Bartolucci, A. and Giger, J. (2002). A telephone intervention with family caregivers of stroke survivors after hospital discharge. *Stroke*, 33, 2060–2065.

Harkins, S., Elliott, T. and Wan, T. (in press). Emotional distress and urinary incontinence among older women. *Rehabilitation Psychology*.

Hayes, S. C., Strosahl, K. D. and Wilson, K. (1999). *Acceptance and commitment therapy: An experiential approach to behavior change*. New York: Guilford Press.

Heinemann, A. (2005). Putting outcome measurement in context: A rehabilitation psychology perspective. *Rehabilitation Psychology*, 50, 6–14.

Heinemann, A. W. (2000). Functional status and quality-of-life measures. In R. G. Frank and T. R. Elliott (eds) *Handbook of rehabilitation psychology* (pp. 261–286). Washington, DC: American Psychological Association.

Ince, L. P. (1980). *Behavioral psychology in rehabilitation medicine*. Baltimore, MD: Williams & Wilkins.

Institute of Medicine (2001). *Crossing the quality chasm: A new health system for the 21st century*. Washington, DC: National Academy Press.

Jang, Y., Mortimer, J. A., Haley, W. and Graves, A. (2002). The role of neuroticism in the association between performance-based and self-reported measures of mobility. *Journal of Aging and Health*, 14, 495–508.

Johnstone, M. (1997). Representations of disability. In J. A. Weinman and K. J. Petrie (eds) *Perceptions of health and illness: Current research and applications* (pp. 189–212). Amsterdam, Netherlands: Harwood Academic Publishers.

Kaplan, R. M. (2002). Quality of life: An outcomes perspective. *Archives of Physical Medicine and Rehabilitation*, 83 (supp 2), S44–S50.

Keith, R. A. (1984). Functional assessment measures in medical rehabilitation: Current status. *Archives of Physical Medicine and Rehabilitation*, 65, 74–78.

King, C. and Kennedy, P. (1999). Coping effectiveness training for people with spinal cord injury: Preliminary results of a controlled trial. *British Journal of Clinical Psychology*, 38, 5–14.

Lazarus, R. and Folkman, S. (1984). *Stress, appraisal, and coping*. New York: Springer Publishing.

McCracken, L. M. (1998). Learning to live with the pain: Acceptance of pain predicts adjustment in persons with chronic pain. *Pain*, 74, 21–27.

Mermis, B. J. (2005). Developing a taxonomy for rehabilitation outcome measurement. *Rehabilitation Psychology*, 50, 15–23.

Mohr, D. C., Boudewyn, A., Goodkin, D., Bostrom, A. and Epstein, L. (2001). Comparative outcomes for individual cognitive-behavioral therapy, supportive-expressive group psychotherapy, and sertraline for the treatment of depression in multiple sclerosis. *Journal of Consulting and Clinical Psychology*, 69, 942–949.

Olkin, R. (1999). *What psychotherapists should know about disability*. New York: Guilford Press.

Ownsworth, T. and McKenna, K. (2004). Investigation of factors related to employment outcome following traumatic brain injury: A critical review and conceptual model. *Disability & Rehabilitation*, 26, 765–783.

Patterson, D. R. and Jensen, M. P. (2003). Hypnosis and clinical pain. *Psychological Bulletin*, 129, 495–521.

Radnitz, C. (ed.) (2000). *Cognitive-behavioral interventions for persons with disabilities*. New York: Jason Aronson, Inc.

Rath, J. F., Hennessy, J. and Diller, L. (2003a). Social problem solving and community integration in postacute rehabilitation outpatients with traumatic brain injury. *Rehabilitation Psychology*, 48, 137–144.

Rath, J. F., Simon, D., Langenbahn, D., Sherr, R. and Diller, L. (2003b). Group treatment of problem-solving deficits in outpatients with traumatic brain injury: A randomized outcome study. *Neuropsychological Rehabilitation*, 13, 461–488.

Reed, G., Lux, J., Bufka, L., Trask, C., Peterson, D., Stark, S., Threats, T., Jacobson, J. and Hawley, J. (2005). Operationalizing the international classification of functioning, disability, and health in clinical settings. *Rehabilitation Psychology*, 50, 122–131.

Rovner, B. W. and Casten, R. (2001). Neuroticism predicts depression and disability in age-related macular degeneration. *Journal of the American Geriatrics Society*, 49, 1097–1100.

Snyder, C. R., Lehman, K. A., Kluck, B. and Monsson, Y. (2006). Hope for rehabilitation and vice versa. *Rehabilitation Psychology*, 51, 89–112.

Turner, J. A., Jensen, M. P., Warms, C. and Cardenas, D. (2002). Catastrophizing is associated with pain intensity, psychological distress, and pain-related disability among individuals with chronic pain after spinal cord injury. *Pain*, 98, 127–134.

US Department of Health and Human Services (2000). *Healthy people 2010: Understanding and improving health* (2nd edition). Washington, DC: US Government Printing Office, November.

Uswatte, G. and Taub, E. (2005). Implications of the learned nonuse formulation for measuring rehabilitation outcomes: Lessons from constraint-induced movement therapy. *Rehabilitation Psychology*, 50, 34–42.

Ware, J., Snow, K., Kosinski, M. and Gandek, B. (1993). *SF-36 health survey: Manual and interpretation guide*. Boston, MA: The Health Institute, New England Medical Center.

Warschausky, S., Kay, J. and Kewman, D. (2001). Hierarchical linear modeling of FIM instrument growth curve characteristics after spinal cord injury. *Archives of Physical Medicine and Rehabilitation*, 82, 329–334.

Watson, D. and Pennebaker, J. (1989). Health complaints, stress and distress:

Exploring the central role of negative affectivity. *Psychological Review*, 96, 234–254.

Whiteneck, G. (1992). Outcome analysis in spinal cord injury. *NeuroRehabilitation*, 2, 31–41.

WHO (World Health Organization) (2001). *International classification of functioning, disability, and health.* Geneva, Switzerland: WHO.

WHO (2002). *Innovative care for chronic conditions: Building blocks for action.* Geneva, Switzerland: WHO.

Witty, T. E., Heppner, P. P., Bernard, C. and Thoreson, R. (2001). Problem solving appraisal and psychological adjustment of persons with chronic low back pain. *Journal of Clinical Psychology in Medical Settings*, 8, 149–160.

Wright, B. A. (1960). *Physical disability: A psychological approach.* New York: Harper & Row.

Chapter 3

Coping and cognitive behavioural models in physical and psychological rehabilitation

Magnus L. Elfström

Coping models

Coping models help to depict people's behaviours, emotions and thoughts when they are under physical, psychological and social stress. A person with a somatic chronic illness or disability (CID) must cope with a variety of potential stressors such as incapacitation, pain and other symptoms, as well as with treatment procedures and hospital environments. Individuals also need to develop and maintain relationships with caregivers and other professional staff. Furthermore, CIDs frequently challenge people's emotional balance, self-image, relationships with family and friends, and often involve preparing for an uncertain future (Moos and Tsu, 1977). Due perhaps in part to the diversity of stressful situations associated with different CIDs and individuals' diverging life situations, the literature on coping has become voluminous. Much research has derived from the Lazarus and Folkman theoretical framework of stress and coping (Folkman, 1997; Folkman and Lazarus, 1988; Lazarus, 1966, 1993, 2000; Lazarus and Folkman, 1984), which is considered the most authoritative theoretical framework in the field.

Basic features of the Lazarus and Folkman stress and coping framework

In the 1960s, Lazarus strongly argued that stress has a psychological dimension, equal in importance to the physiological dimension discovered during the first half of the twentieth century (Lazarus, 1966). He proposed that the strains people experience as stressful depend on characteristics of both the environment and the individual. Briefly, individuals experience stress when they assess their inner and outer resources for dealing with strains to be insufficient and they do not feel good about it. The strain, regardless of the situation, event or symptom, has then become a stressor, that is, a stress-evoking factor. Lazarus and Folkman (1984) used the term 'cognitive appraisal' for the evaluative assessment of situations, events and symptoms. A situation is appraised as stressful if (i) the perceived personal and/or environmental demands threaten the well-being of the individual (primary appraisal) in terms of harm or loss; and (ii) the personal and environmental resources available are judged to be insufficient to meet the demands (secondary appraisal). Appraisals are instant processes that the individual is often not aware of; they help in sorting the continuous perceptual cascade of everyday impressions into what has or has not significance for the individual. Although appraisals are cognitive by nature, there is a good deal of evidence that they are closely linked with affective reactions (Lazarus, 2000; Smith and Lazarus, 1990). Affects, such as fear or sadness, are the subjective cores of emotions, such as anxiety or sorrow (Tomkins, 1962, 1963). Affects help motivate us to take action, and not just cognitively register the meaning of a situation. For example, when a person is faced with functional limitations that restrict his/her ability to engage in a favourite hobby, the appraisal may be that this will seriously hamper his/her well-being. However, it is the sadness, fear or anger about this that motivates the person to take action.

Individuals' coping responses are based on the appraisals and feelings evoked. Coping refers to the efforts in behaviours and thoughts aimed at managing stress (Lazarus and Folkman, 1984). One coping response to being unable to engage in a hobby would be to gather information about feasible alternative activities. Another coping response would be to talk to a close friend or relative about the sadness or anger felt in order to ease the emotional burden of the loss. Both information and support from others are parts of the world outside the individual, that is, the environment; thus, coping is oriented towards the situational context. Coping also changes within this context, in other words coping is process-oriented. For example, the information that is available or the reaction of the friend or relative shapes the events that follow. The interaction between individual efforts to cope with a situation and the external situation itself is sometimes described as 'transactions'; hence, the framework can be labelled a transactional theory of stress and coping.

Coping – what it is not

Coping is different from automatic behaviour because it includes thoughts and behaviours intended to manage situations where the individual feels habitual responses are insufficient (Lazarus and Folkman, 1984). For example, when a newly lesioned person spends a lot of time and energy learning how to use a wheelchair to get around independently this involves coping, whereas smoothly steering the wheelchair in a public setting a couple of years later is automatic behaviour. Routine and automatic modes of getting along are ways to adapt to situations, whereas adapting by coping always involves some sort of stress-induced reaction. Adaptation is a very broad concept that includes virtually all psychological and biological reactions in the individual's interaction with the environment. The more psychosocially oriented term 'adjustment' is also broad in its scope, including emotional, occupational, school and social adjustment.

Coping is sometimes confused with defence mechanisms. However, the former is more or less conscious and the latter are more or less unconscious (Cramer, 2000). An example of coping would be to deliberately suppress thoughts about how sad one feels about not being able to enjoy an activity that was easily performed pre-CID, whereas to show behavioural signs of sorrow and still maintain that everything is just fine is defence (possibly repression or denial).

Coping should not be confused with the outcome of stress and coping (Lazarus, 1993; Lazarus and Folkman, 1984), because efforts to manage a situation may have very different consequences, despite the intention to manage stress that is inherent in the coping behaviours. For example, having a glass of wine may help one to calm down; however, after months or years, wine consumption may have reached a level where the negative effects of alcohol outweigh the initial positive outcome. Outcomes of stress and coping may be physical, psychological and social. Initial physical outcomes concern physical arousal and the level of stress hormones, whereas long-term outcomes involve physical health in general. Psychological outcomes include cognitive functions such as concentration and memory, and emotional states such as generalised anxiety, depression and overall quality of life. Social outcomes include the ability to work or study, engage in leisure activities and have close and distant relations to other persons.

Coping strategies and styles

Coping efforts that have a joint function, for example, different ways of gathering information about alternative hobbies or making plans to overcome obstacles to engaging in a hobby, are labelled 'coping strategies' (i.e. information seeking or planning) (Lazarus and Folkman, 1984). Coping strategies that attempt to solve the actual nature of the stressors are sometimes called 'problem-focused'. In contrast, emotion-focused strategies aim at regulating the emotions evoked by the stress experience. Examples of emotion-focused coping strategies are wishful thinking and seeking emotional support. The division between problem-focused and emotion-focused coping is, however, mainly based on an interpretation of the function of the different coping strategies. The empirical foundation for the division is not overwhelming (Lazarus, 2000), and there are other classifications, such as approach versus avoidance coping and active versus passive coping. Approach-oriented coping strategies aim at closing in on the actual problems, but not necessarily directly solving them. For instance, approaching the problem may imply simply recognising the implications of a CID and the need for new priorities in life (i.e. acceptance). The main function of avoidance-oriented coping is to get away from the problems by intellectual or behavioural distancing. Active coping strategies imply that you do something, but what you do could be merely seeking spiritual support as well as problem solving. Passive coping strategies include such strategies as intellectual distancing and wishful thinking. There are no clear boundaries between the different classifications; hence, a coping strategy such as positive reinterpretation may be classified as emotion-focused, approaching and active.

Behaviours that are similar across different situations, more or less regardless of situational characteristics or degree of stress, are labelled 'coping styles'. Examples of coping styles are generally to relate to other people in a friendly or hostile manner, whether in contact with a health professional or a close relative. A coping style is a reflection of personality. According to Lazarus and Folkman (1984), the treatment of coping as styles or structural traits has had modest predictive value with respect to actual coping processes, and the complexity and variability of actual coping efforts are underestimated. However, since then, other researchers (e.g. (Carver *et al.* 1989; Costa *et al.*, 1996; Parker and Endler, 1992) have extensively advocated the value of the trait approach to the study of coping.

The coping process

Figure 3.1 illustrates the stress and coping process according to Lazarus and Folkman (Folkman, 1997; Lazarus, 1993, 2000; Lazarus and Folkman, 1984). The significant characteristics of a situation, event or symptom are its novelty, predictability, ambiguity and timing in the lifecycle. The experience of a situation, event or symptom is an interaction among perceptions, appraisals and affects. For example, a situation including threats to self-esteem may lead persons to be very sensitive to clues about how other people apprehend them. Coping responses are then chosen to cope with the threats to self-esteem. However, the available coping resources also play a crucial role in influencing coping responses as well as appraisals and affects. Coping resources and constraints against utilising coping resources can be found both in the individual and in the environment. Examples of individual factors are health, energy, beliefs about control, problem-solving skills and social skills. Individual factors also include fundamental commitments and existential beliefs that contribute to motivate an individual. Examples of environmental factors are availability of social support, material resources, legislation, public assistance and attitudes towards people with CIDs. Coping resources contribute to the characteristics of the situation and the outcome. Most coping resources may also serve as constraints, if they are not available or are inimical to the needs of the individual. Furthermore,

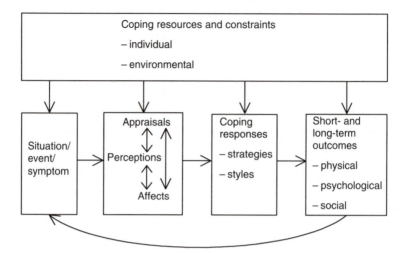

Figure 3.1 Overview of the Lazarus and Folkman stress and coping framework
Sources: Folkman, 1997; Lazarus, 1993, 2000; Lazarus and Folkman, 1984.

what can be viewed as an outcome is in the continued process a part of the situation people perceive, appraise and cope with.

From the perspective of the Lazarus and Folkman framework, appraisals and coping are viewed as mediating factors with regard to outcome. Therefore, they are key concepts in health psychology and other disciplines studying CIDs. Furthermore, a framework for understanding 'normal' adaptive processes as opposed to abnormal behaviour might be provided (de Ridder and Schreurs, 2001) by the study of appraisals and coping. For example, a better understanding of the working mechanisms in psychological interventions and rehabilitation might be provided.

Findings of coping research

Empirical research has shown that appraising stressors as threats or harmful losses is generally associated with negative psychological and physical adjustment (Roesch *et al.*, 2002). However, it is important to note that at intermediate stress levels appraisals of threat and harm may to some extent be linked with the experience of adversarial growth (Linley and Joseph, 2004). Appraising stressors as challenges is associated with positive psychological and physical adjustment (Roesch *et al.*, 2002), whereas appraising stressors as controllable events is related to experiencing positive changes following adversity (i.e. adversarial growth; Linley and Joseph, 2004). There is also some evidence to suggest that the initial appraisal of a stressor indirectly influences adjustment via the elicitation of certain coping methods (Roesch *et al.*, 2002).

Early studies showed evidence suggesting that coping strategies modestly mediate between the confrontation with stressful situations and the consequences for health and well-being (Lazarus and Folkman, 1984). More recent reviews have not found the evidence to be substantially strengthened since the early 1990s (de Ridder and Schreurs, 2001; Penley *et al.*, 2002). Among strategies, problem-focused coping has been associated with beneficial health outcomes (Penley *et al.*, 2002) and adversarial growth (Linley and Joseph, 2004). Approach-oriented and active strategies such as acceptance, positive reinterpretation and positive religious coping have been associated with adversarial growth (Linley and Joseph, 2004). There is some evidence that emotion-focused, avoidance-oriented and passive strategies such as distancing, avoidance and wishful thinking are associated with negative health outcomes (Penley *et al.*, 2002). However, the emotion-focused coping strategy emotional social support has been associated with adversarial growth (Linley and Joseph, 2004). A number of possible reasons for the failure to find stronger empirical links between coping and outcomes are outlined below in the critique of coping research.

Critique of coping research

The most fundamental critique of coping research is the lack of conceptual clarity, in particular what phenomena 'coping' refers to (de Ridder, 1997). Frequently, appraisals, affects, defences, coping strategies and styles, as well as outcomes of stress and coping, have been referred to as 'coping'. Varying and unclear definitions jeopardise the validity and interpretation of research and obstruct clinical applications. Related to conceptual indistinctness is the objection that research has focused on coping responses or strategies, while less attention has been given to other important aspects of the coping process such as the appraisal phase (de Ridder and Schreurs, 2001) or a person's actual goals and commitments (Coyne and Racioppo, 2000; Lazarus, 1993).

Much critique of coping research has been directed at the poor psychometric quality of coping measures, most importantly reliability and validity (de Ridder, 1997; Parker and Endler, 1992). For example, there have been great difficulties in reproducing the factor structure of coping measures derived within the transactional framework (e.g. the Ways of Coping Questionnaire; Folkman and Lazarus, 1988; Parker *et al.*, 1993). It has been argued that many psychometric problems reflect underlying conceptual obscurities (de Ridder, 1997).

In the study of populations with CIDs, it has been argued that general coping measures are not sensitive enough in relation to condition-specific stressors (Coyne and Racioppo, 2000; Maes *et al.*, 1996). A related critique is that general coping scales give too broad results, which may be difficult to interpret in the clinical setting (Coyne and Racioppo, 2000).

Few clinical interventions have been specifically developed based on the Lazarus and Folkman framework for people with CIDs (de Ridder and Schreurs, 2001). Exceptions are coping effectiveness training programmes developed for persons with HIV (Chesney and Folkman, 1994; Folkman *et al.*, 1991) and adapted for traumatic spinal cord lesions (Kennedy *et al.*, 2003). The programmes consist of brief group-based psychological interventions for improving psychological adjustment and enhancing adaptive coping based on the transactional theory of stress and coping, as well as cognitive behavioural therapy techniques.

While coping researchers struggle to meet the critique of their work, there are some simple rules of thumb for the practitioner. First, use a clear rationale. That is, it is important to identify parts of the coping process that are relevant to the case you have in mind. In order to do this, you need a good assessment. Second, the assessment should use more than one source of information and when using questionnaires, make sure they are reliable and valid for the group you work with. Several authors suggest that situation-specific coping strategies and trait-oriented coping-style approaches may supplement each other (de Ridder, 1997; Elfström *et al.*, 2005; Lazarus, 1993; Maes *et al.*, 1996). Third, although the Lazarus and Folkman coping framework is not explicitly tied to any specific theory of personality, the cognitive behavioural approaches share many similarities with the coping framework and may be useful when it comes to intervention. In fact, in a review of 35 controlled studies of psychological interventions for chronically ill persons, it was concluded that coping could be improved by a number of traditional cognitive behavioural techniques (de Ridder and Schreurs, 2001).

Cognitive behavioural framework

Similar to the coping models, the cognitive behavioural framework focuses on people's behaviours, cognitions and emotions. In the last decades there has been a huge development within the field of cognitive behavioural therapy (CBT); a number of approaches now exist and the interested reader should consult more specialised literature (Dobson, 2001; O'Donohue *et al.*, 2003; Simos, 2002). However, common to all CBT approaches is that they are framed within the mediational model. The mediational model assumes that behaviours, cognitions and emotions are interlinked and mutually dependent. This means that if we, for example, want to understand why CID-implied modest restrictions in physical functions may severely limit participation in social and working life for some persons, knowledge about their individual thoughts and feelings about their disabilities is helpful. For instance, thinking that physical activity will worsen the CID leads to fear of movement and eventually incapacitation. The mediational model also implies that a change either in thoughts, behaviours or emotions will affect the other two. For example, there is often a need to help people cope with distressing emotions evoked by the consequences of a CID. The most accessible way to do this, according to the mediational model, is to change the thinking about the distressing situation or to alter the behaviour in the adverse circumstances.

Our point of departure in what will be presented below is the schematic approach developed by Beck and colleagues (Beck, 1976; Beck *et al.*, 1979). In the Beckian approach, the mediational model is complemented with the view that there are three cognition levels besides voluntary conscious thinking, namely automatic thoughts and images, intermediate beliefs (assumptions or conditional beliefs) and schemas (or core beliefs). The different parts of a tree have been used to illustrate the three levels (Morse, 2002). First, like the leaves and branches of a tree, automatic thoughts are relatively easy to access, they are reactive to the environment and can relatively easily be changed. Appraisals, as described in the coping models, are examples of automatic thoughts. Second, like the trunk of the tree, intermediate beliefs are not always visible; they slowly respond to the environment and are harder to change than automatic thoughts. The intermediate beliefs connect the top and bottom of the tree. Third, likened to the roots of a tree, schemas are hidden but they filter all that is passed on to the upper levels. Like the roots, schemas are as old as the organism they are a part of; they have developed over many years and require substantial work to be changed. Schemas are global beliefs about the self and the world, e.g. 'I am helpless' or 'Illness is a punishment'. Intermediate beliefs are more cross-situational and can be described as rules for living, e.g. 'If others do not help me I cannot achieve anything' or 'If you do nothing wrong you stay well'. Automatic thoughts are situation-specific, e.g. 'I could never go back to work again, I am not up to it' or 'Seeing my friends play reminds me of what I unjustly have lost'. As shown in the examples given, schemas, intermediate beliefs and automatic thoughts are thematically interlinked. Also, a critical incident, such as a consequence of a CID, can serve to trigger schemas and intermediate beliefs when congruent with their content.

Principles

CBT is characterised by the following basic principles (Dobson and Dozois, 2001; France and Robson, 1997):

- *Evidence based.* Methods are mainly developed from empirical studies rather than from theory alone. Measures used are known to be reliable and valid. Nevertheless, as a word of caution, it should be pointed out that there is still a lot of work to be done to determine what the necessary and sufficient elements of CBT are.
- *Appropriate for current, repetitive and recordable problems.*

- *Structured and aimed at clearly defined goals.* Attainment of treatment goals is seen as a step-by-step procedure in which progress and setbacks are carefully monitored and discussed with the patient. Treatment success is seen as a gradual change.
- *Main focus on current controlling factors.* However, past history can be of value for understanding which controlling factors are the more important and for choosing management strategy.
- *Use of individual 'tailor-made' problem descriptions*, rather than trying to make the problem fit specific (diagnostic) categories.
- *Emphasis on the positive* in treatment, rather than suppression of the negative. This means focusing on what the patient can do and where and when to do it, instead of dwelling on what the patient should avoid.
- *Collaborative.* The therapist and patient collaborate in a didactic interaction during both assessment and treatment. Patients are seen as active agents in their own lives and have the ability to change their thoughts and actions.

General applications

For healthcare professionals working with persons with CIDs, a cognitive behavioural approach can be used on three levels (France and Robson, 1997; Nichols, 2003). First, a cognitive behavioural approach can facilitate understanding and raise awareness of the role of psychological factors in CIDs. This in turn may help professionals identify problems so that they can refer patients with difficult problems to the appropriate professional agency. Second, a cognitive behavioural approach enables professionals to undertake limited interventions in terms of information, advice, support, counselling and monitoring. Third, psychological therapy, that is CBT, can be given. CBT is appropriate for specific psychological disorders, problems of daily living and problems associated with CIDs. Specific psychological disorders can co-occur or emanate as a result of CIDs, most commonly as anxiety states and depression. Problems of daily living include difficulties in family, marital and sexual relationships, failure to cope at school or work and difficulties adjusting to handicap and disability. General problems associated with CIDs concern adherence to treatment regimen and preparation and recovery from medical procedures. The second part of this book gives several examples of problems associated with specific CIDs.

Assessment

Assessment forms the basis for interventions and therapy (France and Robson, 1997; Persons and Davidson, 2001; White, 2001). The nature of the cognitive behavioural assessment is much like a problem-solving exercise, rather than an effort to find a diagnosis and appropriate treatment. The purpose is to elicit information in order to develop a hypothesis of how a particular problem or symptom emerged, the way it has manifested itself and how it is being maintained. The hypothesis is called a formulation or a conceptualisation and is an attempt to explain the problem in a way that makes sense to both the patient and the therapist. Assessment information also assists with the evaluation of the outcome of interventions. Key elements of the assessment process are that it is structured around the problem at hand, it is performed within a collaborative environment and has a present-oriented focus.

There are several assessment methods (France and Robson, 1997; Persons and Davidson, 2001; White, 2001), including self-report questionnaires, observation, diaries, structural interviews, hospital records and clinical interviews. As a rule, more than one method is used to form valid formulations. Recommended content of the assessment includes information about the referral process, a problem list, a functional analysis with regard to behaviour and cognitions, the history of problem development (including personal, medical and family history), previous coping attempts, psychological symptoms, suicide risk, cognitive mediators (e.g. illness representations and beliefs about illness identity, controllability, time course, consequences, self-efficacy, self-worth), client assets (skills, pleasures and positive characteristics of the patient), the patient's expectation of treatment, suitability for CBT, and treatment goals, including the likely effect of change in the patient. The list of assessment contents may seem a bit lengthy to professionals with little clinical training in CBT; however, it is often helpful to define and structure the problem into its behavioural, cognitive, emotional, physiological and social components. In fact, structuring the problem is a crucial part of the functional analysis, which in turn is at the very heart of assessment. The functional analysis describes how different factors interact to increase or decrease the problem. Some factors are antecedents, some belong to the contextual background and some are consequences. By conducting functional analysis, insurmountable problems take on more manageable proportions.

Some patients have problems in accepting the relevance of assessment. Such patients are more or less questioning whether a biopsychosocial perspective and the mediational model have anything to contribute to their CID-related problems. To deal with such attitudes it is important to acknowledge the patient's viewpoint and that the patient may be correct. It is also important to try to find some common ground; often increasing questions about physical symptoms promote that. Further, the patient can be provided with examples of how psychological factors influence physical health. The patient's reactions to the examples are often rich sources for discussion and assessment.

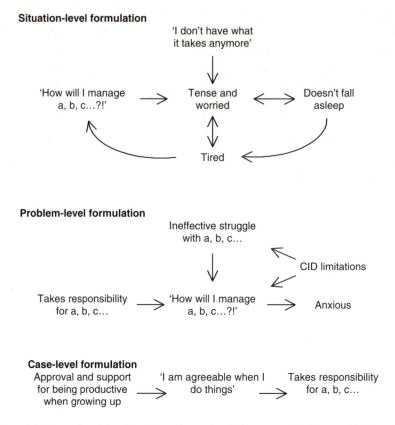

Situation-level formulation

'I don't have what
it takes anymore'

'How will I manage
a, b, c...?!' → Tense and
worried ↔ Doesn't fall
asleep

Tired

Problem-level formulation

Ineffective struggle
with a, b, c...

CID limitations

Takes responsibility
for a, b, c... → 'How will I manage
a, b, c...?!' → Anxious

Case-level formulation

Approval and support
for being productive
when growing up → 'I am agreeable when I
do things' → Takes responsibility
for a, b, c...

Figure 3.2   Example of the three formulation levels (person with sleeping difficulties)

Formulation

Formulations can be made at three levels (Persons and Davidson, 2001; White, 2001), namely the situation level, the problem level and the case level. The following example illustrates the different levels (see Figure 3.2): Anne has severe problems in falling asleep almost every night. In the clinical interview it was found that, when lying in bed, she could not stop thinking about her chores the next day or about not being able to manage work and her children the way she did before her CID worsened. Now, the situation-level formulation is a conceptualisation of a patient's reactions in a particular situation. Anne's difficulties relaxing at night were greatly worsened by a vicious circle where thoughts of the next day kept her awake and worried, which in turn increased her thoughts of how to cope with the demands of the next day. Negative automatic evaluations of herself (e.g. 'I don't have what it takes anymore') increased her worries. The next formulation level, the problem-level formulation, outlines the cognitive, behavioural and emotional components of the specific elements of the problem. Anne had difficulties adjusting her daily priorities to the requirements of her CID and fought more than she had the strength to. At night, Anne was anxious because of all the things she had left undone during the day. The last formulation level, the case-level formulation, outlines the origins of the problem or key events in the course of the problem. In Anne's family history were many instances of approval and support from her close relatives when she had been productive in school and at home. Consequently, she had developed a schema that said she was an agreeable person when performing things. The schema had led Anne to take on great responsibilities at home and at work. The case-level formulation included the schema and how that schema was impossible to live up to given the restrictions Anne's worsened CID imposed.

Formulations help therapists generate hypotheses to plan treatment, including possible outcome variables. For Anne, practising relaxation techniques and meeting negative thoughts with alternative thoughts was helpful (e.g. 'I may not be as physically fit as before, but there are still many things I can do and I am still the same person, and that is what really counts.'). Outcome variables were number of relaxation exercises performed and number of negative thoughts in a self-report questionnaire. Anne rescheduled her night routines and asked her husband to take on more responsibility for the children at night to decrease her stress level. Anne also worked to modify her self-schema by restructuring her life priorities. This was reflected in that she scored higher on an acceptance of disability scale, although she never thought it fair that she had contracted her CID.

Theories and models can assist with the formulation. In Anne's case, the mediational model regarding her difficulties was helpful in relaxing her. Furthermore, the Beckian approach to cognition and findings from coping research on the beneficial associations of acceptance as a coping strategy were used. Other potential models that can assist the formulation are the CBT framework of specific disorders (e.g. panic, generalised anxiety, social anxiety, post-traumatic stress, depression; Simos, 2002) and the transactional stress and coping framework (Folkman, 1997; Lazarus and Folkman, 1984). In fact, findings from clinical health psychology are often integrated into a cognitive behavioural conceptualisation of presenting problems. It is important to note that the formulation is constantly re-evaluated throughout the course of the contact. New information, such as outcomes of treatment goals, may lead to reformulation.

Treatment – general components and considerations

There are a number of key features in all CBT approaches to treatment (France and Robson, 1997; White, 2001). First, treatment sessions are structured by an agenda. This means that every session starts with a brief discussion between the patient and therapist about what items each day's agenda should include. The formulation is an important source of agenda items. Negotiation of agenda items is also an example of another key feature of CBT, namely collaboration between the patient and therapist. The co-operation is often likened to that between two scientists that together try to understand and find ways to solve a problem. The therapist knows a lot about psychological difficulties in general, whereas the patient is the expert on his/her own experience of the particular problem. Thus, feedback from the patient is crucial to a CBT treatment. To test the applicability of hypotheses and treatment strategies discussed during therapy sessions in the patient's real-life circumstances, homework assignments that the patient does between treatment sessions are hallmarks of CBT.

In order to be effective, treatment methods need to be performed in a reasonably stable and safe environment (White, 2001). This means that CBT should be postponed if the patient's living situation does not permit any time or energy for treatment. Neither abusive partners nor extensive childcare facilitate psychological change. A change in the social circumstances must then precede the CBT. Furthermore, in some cases the healthcare environment needs to be more psychosocially sensitive in terms of how test results are reported, the attitudes the staff have to patients and patients' engagement in the treatment process.

The length of a CBT treatment varies. A limited intervention aimed at a newly developed difficulty might require only a few sessions, whereas psychotherapy often ranges between 12 and 16 sessions. Sessions are usually conducted weekly, and progressively decrease as therapy advances. After therapy, follow-up sessions are often offered. Follow-ups may be especially important for persons with CIDs because medical problems are probably lifelong and physical deterioration might arise (White, 2001). Follow-up sessions are also a part of relapse prevention, which is an explicit topic at the end of every CBT. To prevent relapses, the patient and therapist go through future possible difficulties in maintaining therapy results and how the patient can deal with them.

Healthcare professionals' self-care is often a forgotten or neglected topic. However, to meet challenges to empathy in the long run or to the ability to identify alternative ways of thinking when patients see nothing but difficulties, requires that professionals be aware of their own needs. These can be met in several ways, such as through professional and personal networks, supervision, further education and leisure time recreation (White, 2001).

There are many different specific CBT treatment methods, and they are usually combined. In line with the mediational model, one group of methods focuses on behaviour and another focuses on cognitions (O'Donohue *et al.*, 2003; White, 2001).

Behavioural treatment methods

- *Exposure-based treatment strategies.* Persons with CIDs may have had extremely difficult experiences related to their CID or medical treatment. These experiences might have evoked strong fear that later may be easily triggered by something that reminds the patient of the original fear-evoking situation. Fear may also lead patients to avoid certain places or behaviours. The treatment strategy can be performed by gradual or prolonged exposure to the feared situation. A variation is systematic desensitisation in which relaxation, which inhibits fear, is used as patients gradually approach the feared situation.
- *Reinforcement.* This treatment strategy is based on the simple principle that behaviours that lead to a reward tend to be more frequent than behaviours that evoke no response from others. Providing praise when patients adhere to medical treatment regimens or do homework is reinforcement. Unhelpful or dysfunctional responses by patients sometimes receive more attention from medical staff; therefore it may be necessary to refrain from such attention in some instances.
- *Modelling and role-play.* In role-play the therapist can give examples of responses that the patient could use; for example, how to deal with other people's attitudes towards persons with disabilities. The therapist can first play the patient while the patient plays the role of the non-disabled person and then roles can be switched.
- *Activity scheduling.* Planning the amount or type of activity may help patients with depressive symptoms and patients who have limitations in their functional abilities due to medical problems. Activity scheduling gives structure to the patient's daily routine and may increase the extent that activities associated with pleasure or achievement are performed.
- *Behavioural experiments.* Experimenting with different behaviours and then monitoring the consequences may foster more appropriate management of CID symptoms. Behavioural experiments can be helpful when behaviours appropriate for acute symptoms have been transferred to the CID, such as when physical inactivity was an appropriate response to an acute illness but is dysfunctional in response to a CID.

Cognitive treatment methods

- *Identifying, evaluating and modifying automatic thoughts and imagery.* Negative automatic thoughts and images in the patient's interpretation of events or experiences can often easily be accessed by discussing the patient's problems or by reviewing thought records. A thought record is a sheet of paper on which the patient notes characteristics of the situation, mood and thoughts. In discussions, the therapist and the patient often use questions to identify and evaluate automatic thoughts and images. The basic rules are to describe the thoughts and ask the patient for their meaning. When the meaning is found, it is possible to generate alternative ways of thinking.

- *Attentional control.* When experiencing high levels of anxiety over CID symptoms, effective interventions may include selective attention, divided attention and attention switching.
- *Identifying thinking biases/mistakes.* Thinking biases/mistakes are often involved in negative automatic thinking, which in turn evokes negative emotions. Some examples include all or nothing thinking (e.g. 'I am either a successful mother or a total cripple.'), jumping to conclusions (e.g. 'I cannot practise my hobby, hence I will never find another hobby.') and emotional reasoning (e.g. 'I feel worthless, therefore I am worthless.'). As the thinking biases/mistakes are manifested in negative automatic thoughts, the same treatment rules apply.
- *Identifying, evaluating and modifying intermediate beliefs.* Intermediate beliefs are not as easily accessible as automatic thoughts. Nevertheless, by reviewing intermediate beliefs many behaviours, thoughts and emotions may be comprehended. Examples of intermediate beliefs with problematic consequences for persons with CIDs include believing that feeling unwell means CID deterioration, expecting that doctors should always be able to answer all questions and believing a new symptom means that the CID has progressed. Patients are encouraged to think about advantages, disadvantages and origins of their beliefs before alternatives can be considered. To reinforce the alternative beliefs, techniques such as behavioural experiments and role-play can be used.
- *Identifying, evaluating and modifying schemas.* Schema changes require clinical training in CBT and are more time-consuming than the other treatment strategies described. Schema change involves successively weakening the old schemas and strengthening new schemas. This requires that schemas are operationalised, that is, the situations, thoughts, behaviours and emotions following a schema have to be exemplified. Alternatives can then be tested with behavioural experiments, registrations in a positive data log, etc.
- *Addressing 'realistic' cognitions.* In CIDs there are negative thoughts that might be realistic; for example, about deteriorating physical ability. An option may then be to manage the extent that these thoughts influence emotional well-being and activities by, for example, activity scheduling. However, therapists should always be on the lookout for biased thoughts that might accompany the realistic negative thoughts. A passive acceptance that nothing can be done about some medical aspects does not mean that the same is true of all medical aspects and certainly not of the emotional and social impact of CID.
- *Cost-benefit analyses.* Persons with CIDs sometimes have to make complex decisions about treatment, work or whom they should inform

about their problems. The principles of cost-benefit analysis are to generate all possible alternatives, list the short- and long-term advantages and disadvantages and then rank pros and cons in order of importance.

CBT is sometimes misconceived to be equivalent to applying the behavioural and cognitive treatment strategies. However, it is important to understand that a CBT above all is a respectful collaboration between patient and therapist. The collaboration is aimed at achieving clearly defined goals and it is structured by the mediational model and the joint formulation. To achieve the goals, one or more treatment strategies are used.

Acknowledgements

This chapter draws heavily on the author's experiences in working in research projects financed by the Faculty of Medicine at Göteborg University, the Association of Cancer and Road Accidents, the Foundation for Rehabilitation Research, the Norrbacka-Eugenia Foundation, and the Vårdal Foundation.

References

Beck, A. T. (1976). *Cognitive therapy and the emotional disorders*. New York: Penguin.

Beck, A. T., Rush, A. J., Shaw, B. F. and Emery, G. (1979). *Cognitive therapy of depression*. New York: Guilford.

Carver, C. S., Scheier, M. F. and Weintraub, J. K. (1989). Assessing coping strategies: A theoretically based approach. *Journal of Personality and Social Psychology*, 56, 267–283.

Chesney, M. A. and Folkman, S. (1994). Psychological impact of HIV disease and implications for intervention. *Psychiatric Clinics of North America*, 17, 163–182.

Costa, P. T., Jr., Somerfield, M. R. and McCrae, R. R. (1996). Personality and coping: A reconceptualization. In M. Zeidner and N. S. Endler (eds) *Handbook of coping: Theory, research, applications* (pp. 44–61). New York: Wiley.

Coyne, J. C. and Racioppo, M. W. (2000). Never the twain shall meet? Closing the gap between coping research and clinical intervention research. *American Psychologist*, 55, 655–664.

Cramer, P. (2000). Defense mechanisms in psychology today: Further processes for adaptation. *American Psychologist*, 55, 637–646.

de Ridder, D. T. D. (1997). What is wrong with coping assessment? A review of conceptual and methodological issues. *Psychology and Health*, 12, 417–431.

de Ridder, D. T. D. and Schreurs, K. (2001). Developing interventions for chronically ill patients: Is coping a helpful concept? *Clinical Psychology Review*, 21, 205–240.

Dobson, K. S. (ed.) (2001). *Handbook of cognitive-behavioral therapies* (2nd edition). New York: Guilford.

Dobson, K. S. and Dozois, D. J. A. (2001). Historical and philosophical bases of the cognitive-behavioral therapies. In K. S. Dobson (ed.) *Handbook of cognitive-behavioral therapies* (2nd edition, pp. 3–39). New York: Guilford.

Elfström, M. L., Kreuter, M., Persson, L.-O. and Sullivan, M. (2005). General and condition-specific measures of coping strategies in persons with spinal cord lesion. *Psychology, Health & Medicine*, 10, 231–242.

Folkman, S. (1997). Positive psychological states and coping with severe stress. *Social Science and Medicine*, 45, 1207–1221.

Folkman, S. and Lazarus, R. S. (1988). *Manual for the Ways of Coping Questionnaire: Research edition*. Palo Alto, CA: Consulting Psychologists Press.

Folkman, S., Chesney, M. A., McKusick, L., Ironson, G., Johnson, D. S. and Coates, T. J. (1991). Translating coping theory into an intervention. In J. Eckenrode (ed.) *The social context of coping* (pp. 239–261). New York: Plenum.

France, R. and Robson, M. (1997). *Cognitive behavioural therapy in primary care: A practical guide*. London: Jessica Kingsley.

Kennedy, P., Duff, J., Evans, M. and Beedie, A. (2003). Coping effectiveness training reduces depression and anxiety following traumatic spinal cord injuries. *British Journal of Clinical Psychology*, 42, 41–52.

Lazarus, R. S. (1966). *Psychological stress and the coping process*. New York: McGraw-Hill.

Lazarus, R. S. (1993). Coping theory and research: Past, present, and future. *Psychosomatic Medicine*, 55, 234–247.

Lazarus, R. S. (2000). Toward better research on stress and coping. *American Psychologist*, 55, 665–673.

Lazarus, R. S. and Folkman, S. (1984). *Stress, appraisal, and coping*. New York: Springer.

Linley, P. A. and Joseph, S. (2004). Positive change following trauma and adversity: A review. *Journal of Traumatic Stress*, 17, 11–21.

Maes, S., Leventhal, H. and de Ridder, D. T. D. (1996). Coping with chronic diseases. In M. Zeidner and N. S. Endler (eds) *Handbook of coping: Theory, research, applications* (pp. 221–251). New York: Wiley.

Moos, R. H. and Tsu, V. D. (1977). The crisis of physical illness: An overview. In R. H. Moos (ed.) *Coping with physical illness* (pp. 3–21). New York: Plenum.

Morse, S. B. (2002). Letting it go: Using cognitive therapy to treat borderline personality disorder. In G. Simos (ed.) *Cognitive behaviour therapy: A guide for the practising clinican* (pp. 223–241). Hove, UK: Brunner-Routledge.

Nichols, K. (2003). *Psychological care for ill and injured people*. Maidenhead, UK: Open University.

O'Donohue, W., Fisher, J. E. and Hayes, S. C. (eds) (2003). *Cognitive behavior therapy: Applying empirically supported techniques in your practice*. Hoboken, NJ: Wiley.

Parker, D. A. and Endler, N. S. (1992). Coping with coping assessment: A critical review. *European Journal of Personality*, 6, 321–344.

Parker, J. D. A., Endler, N. S. and Bagby, R. M. (1993). If it changes, it might be unstable: Examining the factor structure of the Ways of Coping Questionnaire. *Psychological Assessment*, 5, 361–368.

Penley, J. A., Tomaka, J. and Wiebe, J. S. (2002). The association of coping to physical and psychological health outcomes: A meta-analytic review. *Journal of Behavioral Medicine*, 25, 551–603.

Persons, J. B. and Davidson, J. (2001). Cognitive-behavioral case formulation. In K. S. Dobson (ed.) *Handbook of cognitive-behavioral therapies* (2nd edition, pp. 86–110). New York: Guilford.

Roesch, S. C., Weiner, B. and Vaughn, A. A. (2002). Cognitive approaches to stress and coping. *Current Opinion in Psychiatry*, 15, 627–632.

Simos, G. (ed.) (2002). *Cognitive behaviour therapy: A guide for the practising clinician*. Hove, UK: Brunner-Routledge.

Smith, C. A. and Lazarus, R. S. (1990). Emotion and adaption. In L. A. Pervin (ed.) *Handbook of personality: Theory and research* (pp. 609–637). New York: Guilford.

Tomkins, S. S. (1962). *Affect, imagery, consciousness. Vol 1: The positive affects.* New York: Springer.

Tomkins, S. S. (1963). *Affect, imagery, consciousness. Vol. 2: The negative affects.* New York: Springer.

White, C. A. (2001). *Cognitive behaviour therapy for chronic medical problems: A guide to assessment and treatment in practice*. Chichester, UK: Wiley.

Part 2

Psychological applications and practitioner perspectives

Chapter 4

Psychological aspects of stroke

Jane Barton

Epidemiology and physical impact

A stroke is caused by a disruption of the blood supply to the brain, resulting in brain cells being deprived of oxygen and other essential nutrients. The majority of strokes occur when a blood clot forms and blocks one of the arteries which carries blood to the brain (an ischaemic stroke), but others are caused by a burst blood vessel which results in bleeding within or around the brain (a haemorrhagic stroke). The incidence of stroke is high. Approximately 130,000 people each year in England and Wales will have a first stroke, and of these approximately 10 per cent will probably be under the age of 55 years. It is also estimated that approximately 1000 young people under the age of 20 years will have a stroke every year (Stroke Association, 2002).

The effects of a stroke can be catastrophic, with stroke estimated to be the single largest cause of severe disability in the United Kingdom. While many stroke patients will make a good physical recovery, a significant proportion will have some residual deficit. It is estimated that about one-third of people will remain functionally dependent one year following their stroke, and that approximately 5500 people who are affected by stroke are admitted to long-term residential care each year (Stroke Association, 2002).

A number of physical effects can occur following a stroke, and these will largely depend on the severity and location of the part of the brain that is damaged. Some of the most common include weakness or paralysis, usually on one side of the body (hemiparesis); communication difficulties, which can include difficulties with word finding, reading, writing, and under-standing what is said (aphasia); slurring of speech (dysarthria); and difficulties with swallowing (dysphagia). Other common physical effects include disturbed vision, urinary and faecal incontinence, and loss of sensation. Many people after a stroke complain of an overwhelming tiredness that even a good night's sleep does not cure (Lantin, 2003). Even a small task, such as walking to the kitchen and making a cup of tea, can be totally exhausting. These feelings of fatigue are often very distressing for patients, who often interpret this as their rehabilitation not progressing well and that they are getting worse, or indeed that they are likely to have another stroke.

Emotional, social and psychological impact

Having a stroke is often a traumatic and devastating experience for the stroke patient and their family. It is perhaps not surprising that a range of emotional problems often present, either immediately after the stroke, or at some later point, either during rehabilitation or after it has ended. It should, however, be acknowledged that while emotional difficulties are common, they are by no means universal, and not everyone who has had a stroke will suffer.

Depression

Depression is the most common mood-related problem after a stroke, with estimates suggesting that between 20 to 50 per cent of patients might be clinically depressed at any one time (Gordon and Hibbard, 1997). The course of depression appears to fluctuate. Some people may feel depressed in the early phase after the stroke, whereas for others this might not occur until much later on. Feelings of depression can sometimes emerge towards the end of rehabilitation, often as people start to realise that they may not have made as many gains as they had hoped, and they are left with a sense of 'Is this as good as it is going to get?'

Although it is understood that there is an organic basis for some depression after stroke, it is generally believed that a number of psychosocial variables are relevant, such as perceptions of social support, being younger, and experiencing problems with activities of daily living (Kneebone and Dunmore, 2000). Within this context, depression appears to be related to the losses which people perceive to result from the stroke, and a discrepancy between the real self and the ideal self. In some more extreme cases, patients may develop a pervading sense of hopelessness regarding the future, and feelings of depression can become so severe that people feel they no longer want to continue living. It is estimated that stroke patients are at twice the risk of the general population of committing suicide, and that this risk is greater in younger people if they have already had a previous stroke, and if they only spend a short time in hospital (Stenager *et al.*, 1998; Teasdale and Engberg, 2001). In the majority of cases, suicidal ideation is strongly associated with having a diagnosis of severe depression.

Emotional adjustment

Depression is not an inevitable consequence of having a stroke, and many people will not experience such intense negative feelings. Feelings of distress are, however, common, and are understood to be a part of the natural process of emotional and behavioural adjustment. Emotions experienced often include shock, disbelief, anger, and frustration. Patients often ask: 'Why has this happened to me?', 'What have I done to deserve this?'. These feelings of distress have been likened to the process of grieving following a bereavement, as a stroke too is associated with loss, usually loss of a former life. In the majority of cases, stroke patients and their families are able to work through these feelings, and find a way of adjusting to their new life circumstances. However, for some this remains more of a struggle.

Anxiety

Anxiety following a stroke is also common, with approximately 20–40 per cent of people being affected at any one time (Burvil *et al.*, 1995). The experience of anxiety is often associated with feelings of threat, so this is perhaps not surprising given the enormous threat that a stroke is to a person's life. Anxiety tends to be characterised in terms of the physical experience of anxiety (bodily sensations), how patients think about their situation (cognition), and what they actually do to cope with their worries and concerns (behaviour). Generalised feelings of anxiety are the most common. Patients and their families often express concerns about how they are going to cope in the future, how the stroke will change their lives, the impact of their stroke on their relationships, families and friends, and whether they are likely to have another, potentially life-threatening, stroke in the future. A certain degree of anxiety is, however, expected to occur, as patients and families face the challenge of coping with the crisis of the stroke. In some cases though, these feelings of anxiety can become so intense that they impact negatively on the rehabilitation process, and prevent the patient from engaging fully with their therapy.

Panic is a specific type of anxiety sometimes experienced by stroke patients, and tends to be characterised by very rapid or deep breathing. The effect of this is that the amount of oxygen in the lungs will be reduced, and this can then in turn lead to a range of unpleasant body sensations, such as faintness, dizziness, tingling, headaches, racing heart, flushes, nausea, chest pain, and shakiness. These sensations can be extremely worrying for the patient, and are often misinterpreted as something medically wrong, such as having another stroke. Fears and concerns then intensify, which results in further overbreathing, and hence a vicious circle of panic can develop.

Phobias are another form of anxiety that can develop after a stroke, and are characterised by a sometimes unrealistic fear of a particular object, person or situation, which results in avoidant behaviour. Specific phobias which sometimes develop include: fear of moving, sometimes from the bed to a chair, or from the chair to the toilet; fear of tackling the stairs; and fear of mixing with people and of being in social situations. This last fear, often known as a social phobia, is very common after a stroke. Many patients experience intense negative feelings about reintegrating into their previous social networks. Patients often report that they feel very different to how they did before the stroke, feel that they look very different (even if they do not), and worry about their ability to communicate with people. Patients often report experiencing feelings of shame, and the last thing that they want is for people to feel sorry for them. Hence, they tend to avoid situations which will bring them into contact with often previously known people. The following vignette describes the case of a woman with social phobia.

Case vignette 4.1

Mary was a 68-year-old woman who had had a stroke, and had made a fairly good physical recovery. Even though her speech problems had recovered considerably, Mary thought that she did not sound like she used to do, and that her identity had changed. She worried that her friends and neighbours would think that she was 'daft' if they heard her speak. As a result she tended to stay indoors, and avoid going out, in case she bumped into someone she knew. She stopped going shopping, collecting her pension, and going to the social club on Saturday evenings. She became very isolated, and her worries intensified the longer that she avoided social situations.

Post-traumatic stress is another type of anxiety sometimes seen after a stroke. Post-traumatic stress disorder (PTSD) has traditionally been associated with people who have experienced some extreme threat to their life. Given the potentially life-threatening nature of a stroke, it is perhaps not surprising that a trauma reaction can follow. PTSD is described in the *Diagnostic and statistical manual of mental disorders* (4th edition; DSM-VI) as:

> the development of characteristic symptoms following exposure to an extreme traumatic stressor involving direct personal experience of an event that involves actual or threatened death or serious injury or other threat to one's physical integrity. The characteristic symptoms include persistent re-experiencing through images, nightmares and flashbacks, persistent avoidance of stimuli associated with the trauma, numbing of general responsiveness and persistent symptoms of increased arousal.
>
> (APA, 1994: p. 424)

Recent estimates suggest that between 11 and 15 per cent of people following their stroke might be experiencing PTSD. What is probably more common is that many more people may be experiencing some of these trauma symptoms, but not necessarily sufficiently so to form a clinical diagnosis of PTSD. The following vignette describes the case of a man with PTSD.

Case vignette 4.2

John was a 65-year-old man who had his stroke while he was on the roof of his house doing some repairs. He was fully conscious when the stroke occurred, and called to his wife for help. He was extremely frightened for his safety, and had to be rescued off the roof by the fire brigade. Although John made a good physical recovery, he experienced many intrusive memories and thoughts about being stuck on the roof, fearing that his life was in danger. These flashbacks tended to occur out of the blue, and were extremely distressing.

Emotionalism

Emotionalism after a stroke is characterised by uncontrollable crying or laughing. Traditionally, the cause of this was believed to be organic and unrelated to mood. However, more recent research has suggested a direct link with mood (House *et al.*, 1989; Andersen *et al.*, 1995). People describe that they burst into tears for no apparent reason, and that it is not necessarily a reflection of how they are actually feeling. This can then lead to feelings of embarrassment, particularly if this occurs in the presence of other people. Families may also find it distressing to see their relative upset. In the majority of cases this emotional expression tends to dissipate over time.

Cognitive problems

In the early days following a stroke, the majority of patients will experience some cognitive problems (British Psychological Society, 2002). These typically include:

1　*Confusion and disorientation.* Patients are often unaware of the time, where they are, or what has happened to them.

2   *Memory problems.* These might include remembering important information about themselves and their families, remembering new information, or remembering recent events that have happened.
3   *Concentration.* Problems often manifest during therapy sessions, or when patients are attempting to read a book, or watch a television programme.
4   *Perceptual problems.* These might include problems with the detection of shapes in space, or indeed of themselves in space.
5   *Executive functioning.* Problems are often associated with reasoning and planning, and with the initiation and regulation of behaviour.
6   *Attention.* Problems tend to be characterised in terms of dividing, switching, selecting, or sustaining attention.

Many of these cognitive problems resolve over time, but approximately 35 per cent of those people who survive a stroke will be left with some longer-term cognitive impairment (Tatemichi *et al.*, 1994). The following vignette describes the case of a man with stroke-related cognitive impairment.

Case vignette 4.3

Eric was a 62-year-old man who had made a good recovery from his stroke. However, he described that his relationship with his wife had become increasingly tense, and that there had been a number of occasions when he had lost his temper with her. A full cognitive assessment was undertaken with Eric, which highlighted a very specific problem with switching attention. Although all other cognitive functions appeared to be intact, Eric struggled when he was required to quickly switch his attention from one activity to another. In discussion it transpired that the majority of conflicts which occurred between Eric and his wife, did so when he was interrupted midway through a task, and was asked to do something else by his wife. Eric found it extremely difficult to break off from what he was doing, and to immediately refocus on something else.

Families often report changes in their relatives' behaviour or personality, and these are often related to their cognitive problems. Some of the most typical changes tend to be associated with disinhibition of behaviour and poor control of impulses, which is naturally very distressing for families. In some cases, families report that the changes that have occurred are for the better, and whereas their relative was once quite fiery and argumentative, they are now more placid and easy-going.

Social impact

The social impact of stroke can be enormous. Some of the significant challenges that many people face include: first, the suitability of their housing, and deciding whether they will be able to return to living at home or need to go into residential care. Even for those patients who do return to their own homes, a range of physical adaptations to the home are often necessary. Second, getting out and about can be another challenge, and one which impacts tremendously on quality of life. Some people will be able to mobilise independently, and to re-engage with their previous activities and lifestyles. However, for others, the physical impact of the stroke may prevent people from participating in community activities, such as shopping and attending clubs and societies, which can result in further feelings of dependency and social isolation. Of significance, people's social networks have been shown to reduce substantially following a stroke. While contact with children is often maintained over time, contact with friends and neighbours has been shown to be generally lower than for the general older adult population. Of importance, the maintenance of social networks is associated with more enhanced psychological well-being, and greater life satisfaction (Astrom *et al.*, 1992). Third, a further challenge that often presents is whether or not the person will be able to return to driving, or whether they will need to surrender their driving licence on the basis of being unfit to drive. Many people, particularly older people, rely on using their cars in order to participate socially, and to maintain their chosen lifestyles. Losing the ability to drive may also result in further feelings of dependency, and increasing social isolation. Given the significant numbers of people of working age who have a stroke, return to work and general issues of employment are pertinent. It is not uncommon for patients to retire on the ground of ill-health following their stroke, or to find alternative employment to that which they were doing prior to the stroke. A number of psychological issues are, however, related to retirement, particularly where the occurrence of the stroke is seen as shattering all the planned hopes and aspirations of a post-work lifestyle (Lobeck *et al.*, 2005).

Assessment, formulation and psychological intervention

Assessment

Given the adverse impact of mood on rehabilitation, it is fundamentally important that these problems are assessed and managed effectively. Recent guidance from the Royal College of Physicians (2004) in their *National clinical guidelines for stroke* is that both mood and cognitive problems ought to be assessed as soon as is practicable after the stroke, and that these should be monitored and reviewed and the results and implications built into the rehabilitation programme. There is evidence to suggest that if depression is not treated, then the process of rehabilitation will take longer, and often the outcomes which are achieved will be poorer. In some extreme cases where depression has remained untreated, this has even been shown to be associated with an increased risk of mortality (Pohjasvaara et al., 2001). The exact mechanisms involved are unclear, but it is understandable that if someone is feeling depressed, they are less likely to comply with their treatment, take their medication regularly, and generally adopt the healthy lifestyle behaviours which are recommended. With anxiety, extreme symptoms such as panic, tenseness, and preoccupation with worrying thoughts can also impede the process of rehabilitation. In some cases, patients' anxiety may manifest in avoidance behaviour, and they are reluctant to participate in therapy. With cognitive problems, again, early detection of difficulties, as well as cognitive strengths, is fundamentally important in tailoring rehabilitation programmes to the particular needs of the patient (McKinney et al., 2002).

Assessment of mood

Self-report questionnaire measures are used routinely in hospital and community rehabilitation settings. However, these should be supported by an in-depth clinical interview, in order for a clinical diagnosis to be made. A recent review of mood assessment measures in relation to stroke (Bennett and Lincoln, 2004) highlighted the Hospital Anxiety and Depression Scale (HADS; Zigmond and Snaith, 1983) as the measure of choice for stroke. Although this is not a diagnostic tool, it does give an indication of a person's emotional distress. The HADS was not designed as a tool specifically to be used with stroke patients, but work on the validity of the measure for use with this population has suggested a lower than standard cut-off threshold of 8 for stroke patients.

One of the difficulties with using self-report measures is the possible exclusion of people with aphasia. In cases where someone may suffer from expressive aphasia, it may be possible for the questionnaire to be completed with a trained professional. However, where the problem is one of receptive aphasia, this will not be possible, and alternative measures must be sought. In such cases, clinicians tend to rely on observational methods. A number of observational tools for assessing depression exist, but none are considered to be particularly robust. Two of the most promising measures are the Stroke Aphasic Depression Questionnaire (SADQ; Lincoln et al., 2000), and the Signs of Depression Scale (SODS; Watkins et al., 2001).

Observational methods of assessment can also be useful when assessing anxiety. For patients who become extremely anxious during therapy, possibly showing signs of hyperventilation or panic, much can be gained

Table 4.1 Questions to be answered in a cognitive assessment

1 Is the person understanding what I am saying?
2 Can the person concentrate for a reasonable length of time/attend to a task?
3 Can the person handle more than one task at a time?
4 Is the person able to remember new information?
5 Can the person reason through at a more abstract level?
6 Can the person plan a sequence of steps towards a desired goal?
7 Can the person spontaneously initiate activity?
8 Can the person make accurate perceptual judgements?
9 Can the person make informed judgements?

Source: Kitching (2002).

from the clinical psychologist observing what actually occurs, for example, what triggers the anxiety state, and what seems to help. In such circumstances, simple suggestions based on observation can lead to significant reductions in anxiety.

Assessment of cognitive functioning

Routine assessment of cognitive functioning is usually undertaken with a screening instrument, and followed up with in-depth specialist assessments if problems are detected. Screening instruments vary in their complexity and the range of functions that they assess. The Mini Mental State Examination (MMSE; Folstein and McHugh, 1975) is one such measure, and covers aspects of orientation, short-term memory, attention and concentration, praxis, and writing. In selecting more in-depth assessments, it is important to first define the question to be answered, and to think about what information would actually be helpful. It may be that, rather than administering a whole test battery, specific subtests can be selected in order to answer specific questions. Useful questions to ask are shown in Table 4.1.

Where the patient has a communication problem, the use of standardised measures may not be appropriate, and assessment will need to be undertaken through observation. Using the sorts of questions listed in Table 4.1, evidence can be sought through observation of functional activities during therapy sessions. In some cases, assessments may also be requested in order to answer very specific questions, such as: is the person fit to return to driving?

Formulation

A number of models and theories can be helpful in understanding the emotional experience of people following a stroke. The process of adjustment has been likened to the process of grieving following a bereavement.

Various stage models of grieving exist (e.g. Kubler-Ross, 1975). Patients are often shocked at the actual stroke event, and may find it hard to believe that the stroke has actually happened. This may be followed by feelings of anger and frustration, particularly when simple tasks such as making a cup of tea are a struggle. Feelings of depression often follow, as the person starts to realise how their life has changed, and what they feel they have lost. Adjustment to their new life situation is usually the last stage, as the person starts to adapt and find new ways of doing things. For some people, these feelings of depression become so overwhelming that they find it difficult to reinvest in an alternative lifestyle. While there is little evidence to support this, it may have heuristic value (Wortman and Silver, 1989). Vicious circles of apathy and inactivity can develop, which subsequently impact on mood, and thus lead to further inactivity and disengagement with life. A behavioural model of depression focusing on a lack of positive experiences can sometimes be helpful in understanding this cycle.

Moos and Tsu (1977) offer a framework for understanding the emotional experience of the patient. They describe the experience of a chronic illness as a developmental process. Three distinct phases are identified. First, *the crisis phase*, characterised by the acute phase following the onset of the illness, when the patient and family are trying to make sense of what has happened, are starting to reorganise their lives to cope with the crisis, and are starting to deal with the uncertainty of the future. Second, *the chronic phase*, characterised by the ongoing day-to-day living with the illness, once the initial crisis has been managed. In this phase, patients and families may develop new and adaptive coping skills. Third, *the terminal phase*, characterised by the inevitability of death, and issues surrounding separation and grief. For the majority of stroke patients, the period of rehabilitation is often seen as the crisis phase, when patients and families need to reorganise and restructure their lives to deal with the immediate implications of the stroke. Towards the end of rehabilitation, when the greatest functional gains have been made, patients and families start to settle into a new, longer-term way of coping, and this can be seen as the chronic phase. Barton *et al.* (2002) offer a framework for understanding the emergence of emotional problems after stroke, for both patients and families, over the time course of rehabilitation. These are detailed in Table 4.2.

Individual and personality differences will also play a part in the adjustment process. The degree of disability that the person is left with following the stroke is not necessarily believed to be the crucial factor in determining psychological adjustment. Perhaps the most significant contribution to successful adjustment is related to the meaning that the person attaches to their stroke. Twining (1988) describes the process of adjustment as an interaction between the person and the disability ('handicap'). Table 4.3 shows some of the variables that ought to be considered when understanding how people adjust differently. For example, a keen reader may be

Table 4.2 Stroke-related emotional problems over the time course of rehabilitation

Service	Time	Emotional response (patient)	Emotional response (family)	Time phase
Acute stroke inpatient rehabilitation	A few days to a few months	Anxiety, fear, disorientation, disbelief, shock, 'I'll be fine once I'm home', relief as survived, anxiety about rehabilitation	Shock, disbelief, worries about discharge or maybe feeling home will solve everything	Crisis
Community rehabilitation – 12 weeks in own home (early discharge from hospital)	Approximately 3–6 months post stroke	• Gradual exposure to lost functioning → depression, fatigue at effort of adjustment • Anger	Relief at survival → anxiety about emerging role as 'carer'	Crisis ↓ Chronic
Longer-term rehabilitation (day hospital)	Approximately 6 months onwards	Ongoing struggle between hope for complete recovery and reality of physical limits and losses (role, mobility, speech, job)	Same as patient but may be 'behind' them in terms of balance between unrealistic hopes and adjusting to reality of new life	Chronic

Source: Barton et al. (2002).

Table 4.3 Adjustment as an interaction between the person and the disability

The individual	The disability ('handicap')
Personality	Severity
Attitudes	Extent
Social relationships	History
Interests	Cause
Activities	Prognosis
Expectations	

devastated by a stroke that affects their language, but which leaves their legs unaffected, whereas a keen gardener may feel more distressed by reduced mobility than by problems with communication.

Psychological interventions

Knowing how best to intervene, knowing when it is best to intervene, and knowing who might be the most appropriate person to offer the intervention can be very complex. In clinical practice we are encouraged to base our interventions on the results of evidence-based research, thereby offering the most suitable and valid interventions to address the target problem. One of the difficulties that exists is that the evidence base for the effectiveness of psychological interventions after stroke is minimal. This is not because psychological interventions post stroke are believed to be ineffective, but rather that the necessary systematic research has rarely been conducted. Therefore, the choice of psychological interventions cannot be made on this basis. However, there is an enormous research evidence base on the effectiveness of psychological interventions with other client groups, for example with older adults, and with specific clinical problems, for example depression and anxiety, and it is from these evidence bases that we can draw.

Emotional adjustment and counselling

Talking through the events of the stroke can be crucial in helping both patients and families to emotionally process the trauma of the event. Individual counselling can be undertaken by a range of health professionals. Key aspects of counselling include adopting an empathic approach, listening to what the client is saying, summarising what has been said, and reflecting this back to check out understanding, and to let the patient know that they have been heard. In some cases, bringing patients together in a safe and supportive group to address their experience of loss, their worries and concerns, and to find a way of emotionally moving forward can be extremely helpful. The sharing of experiences, and the mutual support that develops within the group, can have added benefit. The following vignette describes the case of a man who attended a stroke adjustment group.

Case vignette 4.4

Joe was a 77-year-old man who was recovering from a stroke. He had always lived alone, and owned his own house. The rehabilitation team was concerned that Joe's low mood was impeding the progress of his therapy, and that functionally he was not performing at the level that he was physically able to. Joe was initially reluctant to attend the stroke adjustment group, and did not feel that it would be helpful. He did, however, attend, and in the first couple of weeks denied that he was experiencing any difficulties emotionally. As the group progressed Joe started to talk increasingly about how he felt, and how the stroke was impacting on his life. He stated that up until this point he had never felt old! Joe started to make some changes in his life, and started to become more active. He had a telephone installed in his house, started to collect his pension again, and started to make regular trips to the shops. By the end of the group, Joe was functionally much more active, his mood had improved dramatically, and he had a much more positive outlook regarding his future. Overall, Joe reported that he now felt much more in control of his life again.

Anxiety management

Anxiety management includes regulating breathing, physical and mental relaxation, identifying alternative thoughts, and distraction. These approaches can be helpful in tackling most aspects of anxiety, particularly where the anxiety is generalised, and largely related to the person's general rehabilitation and recovery and their plans for the future. Frequently with older people, and people who have had a stroke, pain is an issue in considering what relaxation methods to utilise. Hypnotic or imaginary techniques are less likely to produce or exacerbate pain than those which rely on tensing and relaxing muscles. The psychologist or the occupational therapist can teach the patient basic anxiety management skills, and these can be reinforced by the rest of the therapy team involved. Phobic anxiety is tackled through the process of systematic desensitisation. In this approach the psychologist, working in conjunction with the therapy team, helps the patient to gradually make contact with the feared object or situation, through a series of graded steps. The principle here is of approach rather than avoidance of the feared object or situation. In the case of post-traumatic stress symptoms, cognitive behavioural therapy approaches have been shown to be helpful. A referral to the psychologist should be made in such cases.

Psychological therapy

Although there are mixed results regarding the effectiveness of cognitive behaviour therapy (CBT) with stroke patients (Lincoln *et al.*, 1997), CBT approaches with depressed older people in general are known to be effective

(Gallagher-Thompson and Thompson, 1996). CBT approaches tend to focus on helping clients to challenge and evaluate their negative styles of thinking, and to replace these with more adaptive and realistic thinking patterns. This approach can be helpful with stroke patients who may catastrophise the negative outcome of their stroke and, for example, believe that because they are no longer able to walk independently, they will never be able to leave the house again. This type of psychological therapy is usually undertaken by trained clinical psychologists, in one-to-one or group sessions with the client. Behaviour therapy is another type of psychological therapy which is known to be helpful with depressed older people. The theory underpinning this is that mood is linked to behaviour, and that increasing the positive experiences that people have will lead to an improvement in mood. With stroke patients, building previously enjoyed interests and activities into the day can be extremely helpful. Most patients who are depressed find it difficult to motivate themselves to engage in activities, and this is where professional involvement is helpful. All members of the multidisciplinary team can participate in encouraging patients to participate in activities.

Education and information

Patients and families need to gain some understanding of the stroke experience, and in order to facilitate this there is a need for information and education. Information needs are different for patients and their families, and are known to change over time. How information is given, and in what quantity, are also important factors. Care needs to be taken not to overload patients with information, taking account of the impact of primacy and recency effects in what people remember. Also, targeting particular pieces of information to particular phases in the rehabilitation process is more likely to ensure that information is more meaningful, and hence memorable. Barton (2002) describes a group approach to stroke education, and highlights the importance of timing in the delivery of information.

Cognitive rehabilitation

The purpose of cognitive rehabilitation is not about trying to retrain impaired cognitive functions through drill and exercise, but rather to help to reduce the negative impact of cognitive problems on the person's everyday life and functioning. Wilson (1997) provides an overview of the different approaches to cognitive rehabilitation. In clinical rehabilitation settings, the usual practice is for the results of the cognitive assessment to be used to help inform the rehabilitation programme. This is usually formulated jointly by the psychologist, occupational therapist, physiotherapist, and other members of the multidisciplinary team. Compensatory strategies

Table 4.4 Memory strategies

General principles
- Using multiple sensory modalities, e.g. pictures, writing, audio;
- Physically enacting the task at encoding;
- Providing retrieval cues that are compatible with conditions at encoding, i.e. making the conditions at retrieval as similar as possible to those at the encoding stage, so that learning can initially be made context specific;
- Using participant self-generated cues, i.e. getting the person to generate their own meaningful retrieval cues;
- Elaboration and effortful processing, e.g. writing things down to be remembered, or using photographs.

Specific strategies
- Wear a watch with an alarm that can be used to sound at a particular time. This may be useful as a prompt, especially for remembering regular events, such as taking medication.
- More sophisticated electronic organisers and pagers have the advantage of providing on-screen information.
- Use simple tape recorders or hand-held dictaphones to store new information for later reference and to provide prompts and explanations as to what is to be done.
- Leave things in special or unusual places so that they act as reminders; e.g. placing medication next to the teapot or toothbrush, so that they act as a prompt to be taken each day.
- Ensure that frequently mislaid personal possessions such as a handbag or umbrella are labelled with name and telephone number so that they can be easily returned if left behind.
- Colour-code switches and doors so that they can be easily distinguished.
- Label cupboard doors and drawers to indicate what is kept in each.

are extremely helpful in relation to memory functioning and executive functioning. Errorless learning is an approach which works well with memory-impaired people. When learning new information, the person is prevented from making a mistake, in order that only the correct information is actually encoded. This is different to the trial-and-error approach to learning that is most commonly used. Different strategies and techniques can also be used to help people to remember, and these can be built into the rehabilitation programme. For a comprehensive review of working with memory problems see Clare and Wilson (1997). Table 4.4 lists some strategies which are helpful when working with memory problems.

Working with executive problems can be extremely challenging. Table 4.5 gives a list of principles and strategies which are believed to be helpful, and can be built into the rehabilitation programme (Clare, 2003).

Service and organisational aspects

The number of psychologists currently working in stroke services falls far short of the number ideally recommended, and they tend therefore to be a

Table 4.5 Strategies for working with executive problems

General principles
- The guiding principle is STRUCTURE;
- Planning and talking through a task prior to activity;
- Continual prompting and guiding through a task;
- Encouraging self-reflection of behaviour and activity (e.g. using self-talk);
- Encouraging a problem-solving approach to performing tasks.

Some questions that are useful to ask, and to train the person with executive problems to ask include:

Prior to a task:
- What is it you want to achieve?
- What do you need to be able to move towards that goal?
- What are the steps that you need to take and in what order?
- Are there any alternatives to this plan, and if so what are they?
- How will I know if I have achieved the goal?
- How will I know if I am successful?

On completion of the task:
- Was this a successful outcome?
- Did I achieve what I set out to achieve?
- If I were to carry out the task again, what improvements would I make?

Source: Clare (2003).

scarce resource. The recent Sentinel Audit of stroke services in England and Wales (Royal College of Physicians, 2004) in fact identified that only 17 per cent of stroke services had clinical psychology input. Given the scarcity of psychology input, two important questions need to be considered: first, for those services which do have psychology input, where across the stroke care pathway might this resource be best placed? And second, who else in the multidisciplinary team might be able to perform basic psychological assessments and interventions?

In relation to the first point, the recent guidance from the Royal College of Physicians (2004) has outlined very clearly the psychological implications of stroke which ought to be addressed at different stages of the rehabilitation process. This may help in terms of where best to place scarce resources. In relation to the second point, it is not uncommon for some psychological assessments and interventions to be delivered by members of the multidisciplinary team other than psychologists, and a number of models of service delivery exist. For example, screening assessments for mood and cognition are often undertaken by medical, nursing, and occupational therapy members of staff. More in-depth and specialist assessments can then be followed up by clinical psychologists, or clinical neuropsychologists, in cases of complexity. Such a model of service delivery naturally has training implications, and this is another role for psychologists to undertake. In many cases, services need to think creatively and flexibly in order to address the psychological needs of patients and their carers, and to ensure that ownership of the commitment to deliver psychological care is shared across the multidisciplinary team.

Key areas for future research

Vast opportunities exist for future research into psychological components of stroke and rehabilitation. The following are a few key areas to consider:

- Determining the effectiveness of psychological therapy for treating post-stroke depression or anxiety is a much under-researched area. Although therapeutic interventions have been shown to be effective with older people in general, how these translate to working with stroke patients remains largely unproven. Consideration needs to be given to the particular needs of stroke patients, and the tailoring of therapeutic interventions accordingly.
- Patients with aphasia are often excluded from research studies, and hence the validity of mood-screening assessments which have been designed specifically for people with communication difficulties remains in question.
- An area of research with an increasing profile is the relationship between post-traumatic stress and medical conditions. In the case of stroke, many questions remain to be answered around why some people go on to develop PTSD following a stroke, and why some do not; what are the predictive factors and what are the protective factors?
- From a cognitive abilities perspective, an area of much controversy within healthcare settings centres on determining which patients are most likely to benefit from rehabilitation. Although there is an evidence base for the rehabilitation of memory problems, more clarity about which cognitive abilities or limitations are important in determining outcomes following stroke is much needed, as well as determining where rehabilitation might best be undertaken.
- Perhaps one of the most challenging areas to consider is determining the unique contribution that psychological factors can make to the recovery and rehabilitation of stroke patients. Although it has been shown that successful rehabilitation is a result of a multidisciplinary approach, determining the effectiveness of the unique contribution of psychology remains unknown. In particular, determining the unique contribution that trained clinical or neuropsychologists can make, and differentiating this from the multidisciplinary team delivery of psychological care, is crucial if more resources are to be allocated to developing our under-standing of psychological factors, and our delivery of psychological care in relation to stroke.

References

APA (American Psychiatric Association) (1994). *Diagnostic and statistical manual of mental disorders* (4th edition). Washington, DC: APA.

Andersen, G., Vestergaard, K. and Ingeman-Nielsen, M. (1995). Post-stroke pathological crying: Frequency and correlation to depression. *European Journal of Neurology*, 2, 45–50.

Astrom, M., Asplund, M. D. and Astrom, T. (1992). Psychosocial function and life satisfaction after stroke. *Stroke*, 23(4), 527–531.

Barton, J. (2002). Stroke: A group learning approach. *Nursing Times*, 98(7), 34–35.

Barton, J., Goudie, F. and Scott, S. (2002). Emotional adjustment following stroke: A family affair. *Signpost*, 7(2), 10–12.

Bennett, H. and Lincoln, N. (2004). Screening for depression and anxiety after stroke. Report prepared for the Stroke Association.

British Psychological Society (2002). *Briefing paper 19: Psychological services for stroke survivors and their families.* Leicester: British Psychological Society.

Burvil, P., Johnson, G., Jamrozik, K., Anderson, C., Stewart-Wynne, E. and Chakera, T. (1995). Anxiety disorders after stroke: Results from the Perth Community Stroke Study. *British Journal of Psychiatry*, 166, 328–332.

Clare, L. (2003). Rehabilitation for people with dementia. In B. A. Wilson (ed.) *Neuropsychological rehabilitation: Theory and practice.* Exton, PA: Swets & Zeitlinger.

Clare, L. and Wilson, B. A. (1997). *Coping with memory problems.* Bury St Edmunds: Thames Valley Test Company.

Folstein, S. and McHugh, P. (1975). Mini-Mental State: A practical method for grading the cognitive state of patients for the clinician. *Journal of Psychiatric Research*, 12, 189–198.

Gallager-Thompson, D. and Thompson, L. (1996). Applying cognitive behavioural therapy to the psychological problems of later life. In S. H. Zarit and B. G. Knight (eds) *A guide to psychotherapy and aging.* Washington, DC: American Psychological Association.

Gordon, W. A. and Hibbard, M. R. (1997). Post stroke depression: An examination of the literature. *Archives of Physical Medicine and Rehabilitation*, 78, 658–663.

House, A., Dennis, M., Molyneux, A., Warlow, C. and Hawton, K. (1989). Emotionalism after stroke. *British Medical Journal*, 298, 991–994.

Kitching, N. (2002). Developing a neuropsychological assessment battery on an inpatient stroke rehabilitation unit. Poster presented at The Royal College of Physicians of Edinburgh Consensus Conference on Stroke Treatment and Service Delivery, Edinburgh, 7–9 November 2002.

Kneebone, I. and Dunmore, E. (2000). Psychological management of post stroke depression. *British Journal of Clinical Psychology*, 39, 53–65.

Kubler-Ross, E. (1975). *Death: The final stage of growth.* New York: Prentice-Hall.

Lantin, B. (2003). Fatigue after stroke. *Stroke News*, (Winter), 22–23.

Lincoln, N., Sutcliffe, L. and Unsworth, G. (2000). Validation of the Stroke Aphasic Depression Questionnaire (SADQ) for use with patients in hospital. *Clinical Neuropsychological Assessment*, 1, 88–96.

Lincoln, N., Flannaghan, T., Sutcliffe, L. and Rother, L. (1997). Evaluation of cognitive behavioural treatment for depression after stroke: A pilot study. *Clinical Rehabilitation*, 11, 114–122.

Lobeck, M., Thompson, A. R. and Shankland, M. C. (2005). The importance of social context in adjustment: An exploration of the experience of stroke for men in retirement transition. *Qualitative Health Research*, 15(80), 1022–1037.

McKinney, M., Blake, H., Treece, K., Lincoln, N., Playford, E. and Gladman, J. (2002). Evaluation of cognitive assessment in stroke rehabilitation. *Clinical Rehabilitation*, 16, 129–136.

Moos, R. H. and Tsu, V. D. (1977). The crisis of physical illness. In R. H. Moos (ed.) *Coping with physical illness*. New York: Plenum.

Pohjasvaara, T., Vataja, R., Leppavuori, A., Kaste, M. and Erkihjuntti, T. (2001). Depression is an independent predictor of long-term functional outcome post-stroke. *European Journal of Neurology*, 8(4), 315–319.

Royal College of Physicians (2004). *National clinical guidelines for stroke* (2nd edition). London: Royal College of Physicians.

Stenager, E. N., Madsen, C., Stenager, E. and Boldsen, J. (1998). Suicide in patients with stroke: Epidemiological study. *British Medical Journal*, 316(7139), 1206.

Stroke Association (2002). *Stroke: Good practice in social care*. Northampton: Stroke Association.

Tatemichi, T. K., Desmond, D. W., Stern, Y., Palik, M., Sano, M. and Bagella, E. (1994). Cognitive impairments after stroke: Frequency, patterns, and relationship to functional abilities. *Journal of Neurology, Neurosurgery and Psychiatry*, 57, 202–207.

Teasdale, T. W. and Engberg, A. W. (2001). Suicide after a stroke: A population study. *Journal of Epidemiology and Community Health*, 55, 863–866.

Twining, C. (1988). *Helping older people: A psychological approach*. Chichester: John Wiley.

Watkins, C., Leathley, M., Daniels, L., Dickinson, H., Lightbody, C., van den Broek, M. and Jack, C. (2001). The Signs of Depression Scale in stroke: How useful are nurses' observations? *Clinical Rehabilitation*, 15, 447–457.

Wilson, B. A. (1997). Cognitive rehabilitation: How it is and how it might be. *Journal of the International Neuropsychological Society*, 3, 487–496.

Wortman, C. B. and Silver, R. C. (1989). The myths of coping with loss. *Journal of Consulting and Clinical Psychology*, 57, 349–357.

Zigmond, A. and Snaith, R. (1983). The Hospital Anxiety and Depression Scale. *Acta Psychiatrica Scandinavica*, 67, 361–370.

Chapter 5

The psychological management of persistent (chronic) pain

Zoë Clyde and Amanda C. de C. Williams

Introduction

Fundamental to the management of persistent pain is recognition of the role which psychological factors play in its development and maintenance, and of the profound psychological impact on the individual of having persistent pain. Research evidence is accumulating which demonstrates the centrality of these psychological factors in the transition from acute to persistent pain, in the development and maintenance of disability, and in treatment outcome (Pincus *et al.*, 2001; Turk and Monarch, 2003). However, this is not to underplay the role of physiological processes, but rather to emphasise the importance of understanding the integration of the two, and that the neglect of either may compromise treatment (Turk and Monarch, 2003). The term 'persistent pain' will be used in preference to 'chronic pain', consistent with current usage.

Historically, theories of persistent pain tended to be unidimensional (Turk and Monarch, 2003), favouring explanations in either physical or psychological domains. The gate control model (Melzack and Wall, 1965; Wall, 1999) provided a credible rationale for the integration of psychological factors in the transmission and processing of pain events, and was an important step in explaining individual differences in pain experience. Research since then has elaborated the functional changes brought about by pain from first synapse to cortical representation, the latter being far more plastic than previously thought (Flor *et al.*, 1997), and integrated models are emerging (e.g. Suzuki *et al.*, 2004). Biopsychosocial models build on these by considering wider influences on the individual that might contribute to his/her experience of pain, although the social dimension currently remains underdeveloped. The International Association for the Study of Pain (IASP) definition of pain, as 'an unpleasant sensory and emotional experience associated with actual or potential tissue damage or described in terms of such damage' (IASP, 1979: 249), relies on subjective report.

Optimal management of persistent pain involves taking a perspective which incorporates the patient's viewpoint, however inaccurate and idiosyncratic, and truly integrating physical and psychological intervention. Consequently, the management of persistent pain often involves many health professionals working, in an integrated way, in collaboration with the patient. The interrelationship between the physical, psychological and the social is such that it is often hard, if not impossible, for an individual health care professional to work in isolation, particularly in more complex cases. Further, those health care professionals who are dismayed at the too-frequent failure of well-intended physical interventions are keen to extend their understanding of the psychological dimensions of persistent pain (Harding and Williams, 1995). Therefore, the dominant theme in this chapter is the psychological management of persistent pain in its physical and social contexts.

Understanding the difference between acute and persistent pain is essential to their management. Acute pain signals a threat to physical integrity, dominating attention and prompting responses which prioritise escape or minimisation of the pain, facilitate learning of cues and context, and then prioritise recovery and avoidance of further exposure to pain. This latter phase of rest and conservation of resources is also curiously characteristic of humans in persistent pain. Unfortunately, many patients, as well as health professionals, make little distinction between acute and persistent pain. Consequently, years after an injury, concern is still expressed about 'healing' of putative lesions. In fact, prolonged rest has adverse consequences for recovery of function and for the pain itself, but it is not surprising that the person who is fearful about the pain, distressed by it and its impact on life, who is poorly advised and has little support, may well get stuck in this phase. Factors which may increase the possibility of developing persistent pain following an acute musculoskeletal problem include high levels of current and average pain intensity, pain in several body sites, impairment across multiple activities, increased stress and depressed mood, and greater belief that physical activity will cause further damage and/or pain (Linton, 1999). Recovery from an episode of acute low back pain is an active process that involves correcting misconceptions about harm, physical activity, medical diagnosis and cure (Goubert et al., 2004).

Persistent pain is classified as that which is experienced beyond the time expected for healing to have occurred, so excluding pain experienced due to ongoing pathology such as cancer. It cannot, however, be assumed that this distinction will have been made clear to the person with persistent pain, and it may fall to the psychologist to do this. Until relatively recently, the psychological management of persistent pain was offered as a 'last resort' (Hadjistavropoulos and Williams, 2004), once other approaches had failed to reduce the pain and/or to enable the patient to return to a more normal life. Currently, the point at which psychological management is initiated in the course of treatment varies enormously. We argue that physical, psychological and social factors should be considered from the beginning of treatment, with the aim of minimising persistence and providing optimal management.

The aim of rehabilitation of persistent pain is (informed) management of the pain, such that the person with pain feels more in control, more able to lead the life s/he wishes, and empowered in handling pain problems. This chapter aims to provide an overview of the psychological management of persistent pain.

Epidemiology

For several reasons, it is difficult to obtain a clear estimate of the prevalence of persistent pain. First, the diagnosis is problematic, as it crosses disease categories and boundaries of medical specialisms, being regarded as a symptom rather than as a diagnosis within many. It can be described by (putative) mechanism (e.g. neuropathic pain), by site (e.g. low back pain), by presumed cause (e.g. discogenic pain), or by symptom clusters (as in fibromyalgia). Many people with persistent pain experience it in multiple sites, complicating diagnosis. There are also issues concerning the population sampled and the questions asked. Although recent estimates have suggested that as many as 30 per cent of the population suffer from persistent pain, this does not imply that all require clinical care. Pain is such a common experience, and recurrent or longer-lasting pain is so much more prevalent with increasing age, that questions are needed about its impact on functioning and mood in order to identify those who are more severely affected. In terms of quality of life, pain may have a greater negative impact than a wide variety of other physical diseases and psychiatric disorders (Sprangers et al., 2000). While some people with persistent painful disorders rarely or never seek health care, accepting the pain (correctly or not) as unchangeable (Reitsma and Meijler, 1997), a small group uses a very large proportion of health care resources (CSAG, 1994). Those in this group are more likely to have multiple sites of pain, to be subject to many investigations and treatments, and to be supported by informal carers and welfare provision. Differences between those who present to services and those who do not may be predominantly psychological, rather than physical.

While the psychological and social cost of persistent pain to the individual is emphasised in this chapter, the financial cost of pain is striking. Twenty-five per cent of those with persistent pain lose their jobs and suffer a substantial drop in household income (Kemler and Furnee, 2002). For those who continue to work, pain is the second most common reason for sickness leave, and this amounts to 203 million days a year. The Department for Work and Pensions estimates that £3.8 billion is paid annually as disability benefits for pain-associated conditions.

Physical impact

While higher levels of pain are generally associated with greater disability, the relationship is by no means simple. Headache provides one of the best examples: a person who avoids bright light, loud noise, crowds, and other stressful stimuli on the grounds that these precipitate headaches, may suffer headaches relatively rarely or mildly but nevertheless be very restricted. The belief that pain warns of danger, and the aversiveness of pain itself, tend to elicit avoidance, escape, and resource-conservation behaviours. As a consequence of these strategies, intended by the person with pain to promote health, secondary physical problems such as reduction in fitness and guarded or restricted movement may further contribute to decreased functioning. Additionally, effects on function can be mediated by poor-quality sleep and daytime fatigue, or by the adverse effects of analgesic drugs, such as the morning lethargy felt by many people who take antidepressants for pain.

Work demands, both physical and mental (particularly concentration), can also be hard to meet when pain persists. Loss of work is common, with low likelihood of returning after six months' absence, yet at six months the individual with pain may still be undergoing tests and specialist consultations and hoping for a diagnosis and full pain relief. Psychosocial factors within the first month or two predict return to work better than do medical characteristics of the individual or work demands. For those who continue to work, pain can affect job satisfaction, performance, and therefore their career prospects (Blyth et al., 2003).

The cumulative effect of these direct and indirect influences on daily physical functioning is that persistent pain can invade most or all areas of an individual's life: work, leisure, interpersonal, and social activities. This has been described as a psychological cascade (Morley and Eccleston, 2004) of interruption and interference with ongoing activities, ultimately impacting on identity.

Psychological, emotional, and social impact

Clinically, individuals describe a wide range of emotions associated with pain, often a combination of anxiety, depression, frustration, anger, and fear, with frustration being the most commonly reported (Price, 1999). Although not inevitable, an emotional response is understandable in the experience of persistent pain, particularly in relation to certain beliefs about the pain. It is important to acknowledge and validate the emotional as well as the physical experience. There is poor support for the commonly held belief that people who struggle with persistent pain also find it hard to cope with other challenges, in health or in other aspects of life. There are problems with measuring affect in persistent pain populations due to reliance on models and instruments developed for mental health or community populations excluding those with physical illness or disability. Somatic items are therefore ambiguous and cannot uncritically be counted as symptomatic of mood disorder (Pincus and Williams, 1999).

Frustration

Frustration described by people in pain represents anger, disappointment, and perhaps confusion and demoralisation, usually when pain prevents the completion of goal-directed activity. For many people with pain, everyday life is full of difficulties carrying out activities which they used to do without needing to consider the cost in pain and energy, but which now exacerbate pain to the extent that they may not seem worth those costs: sitting through a meal, standing in a queue, walking the dog, or cuddling a partner or child. Although there is almost no work on frustration in persistent pain, what emerges from casework is a consistent picture of confidence being steadily undermined by repeated experience of failure, and a conviction that pain stands in the way of all that is worthwhile or necessary for a reasonable existence.

Anxiety and fear

Anxiety is a common response to the experience of pain and the search for its meaning. A recent review (Symreng and Fishman, 2004) highlights the overlap of anxiety and pain in terms of the interplay of physical and psychological factors, their roles in alarm systems – therefore primarily adaptive – and the similarities in their treatment, both pharmacological and psychological. There is often uncertainty around the cause of the pain, and around the prognosis and treatment demands. Less inevitably, anxiety may also be generated by explanations offered for the pain, because implicit or explicit models describe damage, or are misunderstood by the patient to do so. Patients try to make sense of what is wrong with them, to the best of their abilities, but, in lay models, pain is a signal of damage which it is risky to ignore; tingling or 'pins and needles' and talk of nerve damage may presage paralysis. Too little time is spent, even by psychologists, in trying to understand the patient's framework before attributing motives such as secondary gain to low levels of activity and distortions of movement and gait. Fears are widespread and individual and need to be elicited within a setting where the patient feels heard and respected. Morley and Eccleston (2004) describe the object of fear in pain as even broader than the physical domain, often multiple, and sometimes abstract and difficult to verbalise, such as, for example, fear of altered identity, or of feeling worthless.

Over recent years, the cognitive-behavioural model of fear of movement/ (re)injury (Vlaeyen et al., 1995) has been developed for certain individuals in whom decreased functioning and increased suffering are maintained by fear of pain and its consequences, rather than by pain itself (Vlaeyen et al., 2001, 2002). Fear of pain is driven by cognitions and cognitive-processing biases which exaggerate expectation of harm. For example, a man who experienced a sharp sudden onset of pain, rendering him unable to move and to attend to his young child, remained alert to possible repetition and was keen to avoid it. Believing that his back was precarious, any twinge of pain ('like the muscles are strangling the bone structure') was alarming and stopped him in his tracks. His preoccupation with moving in the 'right way' and avoidance of risky activities precluded playing spontaneously with his children, and necessitated a change of work.

Fear and avoidance are often bracketed together but we would argue that this may not be helpful as patients do not necessarily experience much fear if avoiding feared activities. Nor does it fit well with the model of phobia (Vlaeyen et al., 2004), since rather than seeming excessive or even irrational to the individual, his or her fear often relates to events which the individual believes are genuine threats or recurrences of previous crises. The object of the fear is the physical threat and possibility of (re)injury, fear of the pain itself, the psychological threat (feeling unable to cope with it), and fear of the effects of the pain on life ('If I end up in a wheelchair then my partner will leave me').

Safety behaviours, paradoxically, worsen the situation. By avoiding the anticipated disaster, they also prevent the individual from learning that the disaster would, in fact, not happen (Salkovskis et al., 1999; Thwaites and Freeston, 2005). Safety behaviours can be difficult to identify as they may be mistaken for coping strategies when actually they serve to maintain pain-related fear, for example, only making very gradual increments in exercise in order to avoid the feared exacerbation of pain, but thereby delaying recovery of function. Safety behaviours may also be unwittingly encouraged by over-elaborate manoeuvres to minimise pain, including those activities with official sanction, such as 'manual handling' and 'back protection'.

Catastrophising

This construct, originally part of a coping strategy questionnaire with both 'positive' and 'negative' strategies (Rosenstiel and Keefe, 1983), has emerged as robust and of widespread relevance (Sullivan et al., 2001). It is defined as attention or vigilance to threatening information, whether from the body or from external sources such as health care professionals; over-interpretation of that threat; and underestimation of the capacity to cope, i.e. helplessness. It is clear from these descriptions of processing biases that people who catastrophise are likely also to express anxieties or fears, and may become depressed. It predicts poorer physical and psychological health and function, and less response to treatments, in both acute and persistent pain. It has recently been reconceptualised (the 'communal model of coping') as an attempt to elicit help from others (Sullivan et al., 2004), and this reformulation is the subject of some lively debate and empirical work.

Depression

Given the enormous potential physical and psychological losses that persistent pain can cause, it is not surprising that considerable levels of distress are reported. Estimates of the prevalence of depression in persistent pain vary enormously, though the rate appears higher than found in the general population and in other chronic illness populations (Romano and Turner, 1985; Banks and Kerns, 1996; Pincus and Williams, 1999). However, while it is generally recognised that depression and depressed mood are common, it is not an inevitable response to persistent pain. As it may be those who are more distressed who seek treatment services and therefore are more likely to be sampled in research, we know less about those with persistent pain who are minimally distressed and disabled by it. Many examples can be found in the literature of attempts to understand further the causal relationship between persistent pain and depression. The Banks and Kerns (1996) diathesis-stress model of depression in persistent pain is a widely accepted conceptualisation of the relationship, highlighting the interaction between underlying vulnerability (diathesis) and the situation of chronic pain. The focus, not just on vulnerability, but also on the nature of the stressor, directs attention to what it is about persistent pain that heightens its potential to cause distress. Such characteristics include the ability of pain to capture attention; its persistent, constant, unrelenting nature; the uncertainty associated with cause and prognosis; its ability to dominate activity and seemingly take control; and the isolation resulting from other people's scepticism or lack of understanding of the experience.

It is likely that there is heterogeneity within the depressed persistent pain population, and that pain and depression are related via several pathways (Pincus and Morley, 2001). The population of people with persistent pain includes those who have experienced depression in the past and for whom the pain, and associated difficulties and losses, may trigger a further episode; those with a vulnerability to depression for whom the pain as stressor precipitates a first episode of clinical depression; and a large proportion whose psychological distress does not reach the criteria for clinical depression but may be disabling and bring them into treatment. This is borne out by studies of the content of depressed mood in pain (Pincus and Morley, 2001; Clyde and Williams, 2002), and there are obvious implications for treatment in making these distinctions.

Cognitive content

Beliefs about pain and its meaning to the individual and the wider social context have been described already and are a central psychological component in the management of persistent pain. Patients presenting with persistent pain represent a cross-section of the population, with varied

Table 5.1 Examples of patients' beliefs about pain and its implications

- I was told it's 'wear and tear' from heavy work when I was younger, so I'm as careful as I can be not to wear it out. I feel old before my time.
- The surgeon said he couldn't operate to free the nerve as it was too risky – I might be paralysed.
- Now every time I feel a sharp pain I think maybe that is it – and I hardly dare try to move in case I can't any longer.
- I'm sure my muscles are just tearing apart. I try to be careful, but I can't just sit around and do nothing.
- I'm afraid that if I get any worse my family will leave me – I'm no use to them since this happened – but I can't control it or stop it getting worse.
- What happens if I can't cope with the pain anymore? I'll go mad with it, day and night, never ending.

beliefs about the causes of pain and appropriate solutions. Rather than judging patients' beliefs by their approximation to expert physiology and anatomy, it is more helpful to enter into their understanding, since this often provides a logical explanation for their behaviour (see Table 5.1). Their beliefs may be expressed as much in images and sensations as in words, and working with images can provide a richer understanding of the distress associated with the problem (Hackmann, 1997).

Identity

The onset of persistent pain can occur at any time of life and, while its impact on individuals depends to a certain extent on life stage, its meaning is determined by a wider range of variables, so that adjustment varies considerably between people. Pain interrupts many roles and presents an obstacle to goals, present and future, such as career progression, active parenthood or grandparenthood, travel, or further learning or skills development for pleasure. In particular, those responsible for the welfare of others feel that they cannot afford to be unreliable in or prevented from carrying out those duties by pain, and so may see themselves as completely unable to be an adequate parent, grandparent, or carer.

Morley and Eccleston (2004) describe the impact of persistent pain on the individual as a 'psychological cascade' in terms of its impact at three levels: interruption, interference, and identity. Interruption by pain commands attention, disrupting ongoing tasks and concentration, and thus impairs cognitive functioning. The personal meaning of the pain then partly determines whether the interruption can be terminated and attention re/turned to other matters, or whether ruminative and catastrophic thoughts and images prevail. Interference of pain with activity may take the form of chronic interruption, physical limitations, fatigue, distress, and fears, affecting not only performance of desired activities, but also the degree of shortfall between that performance and what is necessary for satisfaction or enjoyment. There is also the cost in pain, which undermines the gains of managing an activity. The deepest level of impact is that on an individual's identity.

Acceptance of persistent pain, being able to live a meaningful life with the pain without fighting it or seeking to be rid of it, is an area of increasing interest. A qualitative analysis of participants' accounts of learning to live with pain (Ridson et al., 2003) uncovered three features: acknowledgement that cure is unlikely so that the task is to adapt; a shift in focus away from pain-centred activities to non-pain activities; and the assertion that persistent pain is not a sign of personal weakness or failure.

Social impact

Persistent pain impacts on both the individual's personal relationships with friends and family and his/her wider social contact, particularly through altered roles and difficulty in communicating to others the experience of persistent pain. The complex relationships between pain, disability, mood, impact on the carer, the carer's own mood and limitations, and the ways in which the person with pain and carer interact are far from understood. Most studies are cross-sectional and cast no light on causal relationships or development over time, while gender is often disregarded although it emerges as an important variable when examined. In addition, an operant model has dominated design and interpretation of results, in direct contrast to the neglect of instrumental and emotional support in the literature on stress, health, and social support.

The facial expression of acute pain, and quite possibly other expressions, can be understood on brief exposure not only by those close to the person but by strangers such as health service staff (Williams, 2002a). However, the observer's judgements of others' pain and behaviour are affected by contextual variables and by their beliefs (Williams, 2002a). In health professionals, judgements of others' pain are informed by expectations, such as of the acute pain face in all pain; by contextual variables such as the presence or absence of medical findings; and by beliefs such as of the likelihood of malingering. For gross motor behaviour, despite efforts to define certain spontaneous behaviours or pain responses to physical investigations as signs of distress, the behaviours are widely interpreted as signs of exaggeration or faking (Waddell et al., 1980; Main and Spanswick, 1995).

Assessment

Please see this 48-year-old lady who has experienced a gradual onset of low back pain over the past five years. CT scans have not revealed any underlying

structural abnormality. She has been a frequent visitor to her general practitioner over this time and has tried several treatments, none of which she
feels has helped. Initially, she was encouraged to rest, use a TENS machine,
and take painkillers and has since been referred to the pain clinic where she
has had physiotherapy, acupuncture, and nerve blocks. She has two young
children and tries to keep going but is finding it harder and harder. She
reports difficulties in sleeping and feels hopeless and helpless about her
situation. She describes feeling like she has the body of a 70-year-old. She is
taking increasing amounts of painkillers and has recently started antidepressants. We would welcome your assistance with the care of this lady.

The referral above highlights the journey common to many patients who
finally end up being referred for psychological management of persistent
pain. The experience of pain can be further compounded by the treatment
process and the search for a cure.

The form and content of assessment depend on its purpose, but it is
essential to convey to the patient belief in his or her pain, to dispel fears of
being thought weak, or of imagining pain, or even of malingering. All these
are common lay models of the complaint of pain, and variously represented
within the health system. By contrast, an elaborated biopsychosocial model
provides the basis for making sense of patients' psychological, emotional,
and social difficulties related to the pain, facilitating engagement and
establishing shared ground for concordance in treatment. This socialisation
of the individual into the 'expert patient' role is a key feature of psychological management and differs from most patients' previous experiences of
health care for pain. The earlier in the patient journey this occurs, the
better, in terms of preventing feelings of helplessness and lack of control
and 'being done to' by health care professionals. It is important to convey
the notion that the individual needs to play an active and ongoing role in
managing pain: this requires identification of worthwhile goals, willingness
to attempt and to integrate new strategies into daily life, and mobilisation
of support.

Content of assessment

In clinical settings, information about the physical, psychological, emotional, and social aspects of the individual's pain experience is all-important
and often best obtained through interview. Asking about the pain experience engages the patient. While it is not essential to have the person with
pain give his or her narrative in full, some details of pain onset, treatment

attempts, and the patient's own ideas about what might be wrong are an essential background to the present situation: where the pain is, its quality, variations in intensity, what exacerbates and eases it, and how the pain affects intended or actual activities. Questionnaires, checklists, pain diaries, and pain drawings may all supplement the interview and help assessment.

A central part of the individual's account is the personal meaning of the pain: beliefs and attributions about the pain, its cause, its consequences, and expectations of treatment and of the future. These beliefs and attributions may then be related to current decisions by the patient about what is safe to do, and what is not worth doing because of the cost in pain. They also provide the basis for discussion of treatment aims, and barriers to these. While litigation and the expectation of compensation are not necessarily obstacles to treatment, they can put the patient in a difficult position where he or she will suffer significant financial losses with improvement in pain and function. Much welfare benefit is allotted on the same basis: to exclude all patients in such a position is inequitable and not justified by available evidence.

Formal assessment is detailed in many texts on pain, including Main and Spanswick (2000) and Williams (2002b). Briefly, the following domains should be considered: biomedical information, including pain experience; psychosocial function; behaviour and activity, including disability or quality-of-life measures; an account of qualitative or quantitative effects on work; and an account of health care use, from analgesic intake to hospital visits and interventions. While no published measures will provide all that is required, they are likely to be better developed and to have more information on their interpretation than home-grown ones. Attention to the standardisation population is important, in order to avoid floor or ceiling effects, but it is always worth checking the questions for suitability and to prepare explanatory information.

Biopsychosocial formulation

The information from assessment serves to construct a formulation, preferably in collaboration with the patient or subsequently shared with him or her. Combining physical and psychological aspects highlights their interaction and allows focus on what can be changed, rather than on what cannot. The distinction between what can be changed, using problem-based coping, and what cannot be changed, and may therefore be addressed using emotion-based coping, can be very useful (see Chapter 6 for a fuller account). It also helps to normalise the multiple problems reported by most patients and can link apparently unrelated difficulties, prefiguring the introduction of treatment strategies applicable across these difficulties. The focus thus shifts from removing the putative cause of pain to managing its present deleterious effects on the patient's life and well-being, and modifying

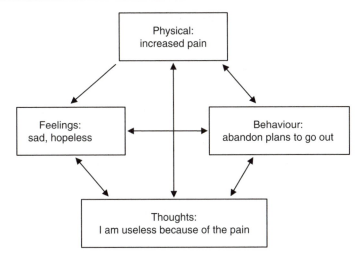

Figure 5.1 Model for formulation

Source: Padesky and Greenberg (1995).

maintaining factors. Finally, it can pave the way for the key task of identifying realistic and meaningful goals.

Formulation at its simplest may involve use of the generic model shown in Figure 5.1.

In certain cases, a more specific model may be added, for example, that of pain-related fear and avoidance (Vlaeyen and Linton, 2000; Williams and McCracken, 2004). Alternatively, where there are long-standing or multiple psychological issues, or the pain impacts on a core belief, formulation needs to identify cognitions beyond automatic negative thoughts. This brings the current pain problem into the broader context of an individual's life history. The example in Figure 5.2 concerns a woman with disabling neck pain following a car accident which was not her fault; she had experienced depression in the past for which she had been sent to mental health services, before being referred to a pain clinic. She described feeling very depressed and hopeless about her situation.

Eliciting the full picture in this way does not imply that every level must be addressed in treatment: it may be that pain management addresses part of the picture, and the patient is encouraged to seek help elsewhere with longer-standing problems. However, it allows treatment expectations to be clarified, since the interaction between problems may mean that symptom relief is only partial until further interventions have been made. The order or combination of treatments, particularly where there is marked depression or post-traumatic symptomatology, often needs careful consideration so that the patient does not feel shuttled between services, each of which rejects him or her until other problems are resolved.

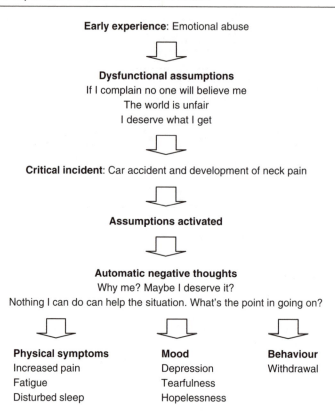

Early experience: Emotional abuse

Dysfunctional assumptions
If I complain no one will believe me
The world is unfair
I deserve what I get

Critical incident: Car accident and development of neck pain

Assumptions activated

Automatic negative thoughts
Why me? Maybe I deserve it?
Nothing I can do can help the situation. What's the point in going on?

Physical symptoms	Mood	Behaviour
Increased pain	Depression	Withdrawal
Fatigue	Tearfulness	
Disturbed sleep	Hopelessness	

Figure 5.2 CBT formulation of patient with long-standing depression

Goal setting

Goal setting is a bridge between assessment and treatment, clarifying the aim of treatment as recovery of (more) normal function despite pain, rather than predicating recovery of function on relief of pain, as medical interventions tend to do. Information about valued goals and guidance from medical or physiotherapy colleagues about the physical requirements to be considered underpin the specification of priorities, discussion of rate of progress and milestones, and the balance of duties and chores to pleasurable, social, or creative pursuits. It can be appropriate to raise possible goals which the patient fears are beyond his or her reach: work, particularly, may be prevented by psychosocial rather than physical factors (Linton, 1999; Pincus *et al.*, 2001). Employers may also discriminate against job applicants with long medical histories. Discussion of return to work can proceed without pressure, exploring the psychological, social, and financial gains and losses from working or not working.

Treatment

Early psychological theories of persistent pain and its management were based on behavioural assessment and treatment; the later addition of cognitive therapy followed mainstream psychological practice, and their combination, with many minor variations, constitutes the foremost treatment since the early 1980s (Main and Spanswick, 2000; Nicholas *et al.*, 2003; Keefe *et al.*, 2004). Cognitive-behavioural approaches within the broader biopsychosocial framework will be the main focus of this chapter, not least because they have been subjected most to empirical scrutiny, providing sufficient trial data for several systematic reviews with meta-analyses (e.g. Morley *et al.*, 1999). Pooling studies with somewhat heterogeneous populations, different measures, and varying quantity and content of treatment, provides evidence of gain (over no treatment or routine medical treatment) in physical function, psychological state, and pain experience. Unfortunately, too few studies assess changes in work status or use of health care resources for entry into the meta-analyses, although individual trials show improvement in these outcomes.

Less is known about the mechanisms of treatment and what works for whom. Better-specified and heuristic theoretical models, such as that of Vlaeyen *et al.* (1995), are urgently needed. It is mistaken to assume that disability can only be remedied by physical means or that psychological change only comes about through psychological therapy, and no reliable predictors of treatment success have yet emerged from the attempts to elucidate them (see Morley and Williams, 2002). It therefore makes economic and practical sense to provide a group-based multicomponent cognitive-behavioural treatment from which patients are encouraged to try everything and to adopt and refine those approaches which best match their needs and resources.

Common components of CBT for persistent pain

Education about pain

There are fundamental facts about persistent pain which are key to the management of pain. These include its distinction from acute pain, the lack of a reliable relationship with damage or pathology, and pain mechanisms which are disorders of function rather than structure (therefore not appearing in imaging). The opportunity to discuss the history of the problem and treatment attempts with an informed person can result in a helpful 'rewriting' of the individual's personal medical history; it can change the meaning of the pain, and open the way for experimenting with new ways of managing it.

Behavioural activation

Goal setting, described above, is an ongoing process, keeping in focus what is important to the individual, with improvements in physical and/or psychological state allowing review and extension of, or addition to, existing goals. Cost-benefit analyses can be used to explore the possibility of activity with more pain versus the status quo, alongside a non-catastrophic reinterpretation of the implications of more pain. Pleasurable activities should not be delayed until all chores can be performed, despite social pressure, since they are important for mood and for the availability of reinforcement.

In addition, the spread of activity through the day, week, or month should be monitored and pacing strategies implemented to regulate activity levels. Pacing strategies involve changing the contingency parameters of activity. The individual who tends to stop activities because pain (or associated thoughts and emotions) becomes intolerable, learns instead to stop on completion of a set amount of the activity, often measured by time. With realistic goals and good use of breaks (such as relaxation or alternative activity), pacing provides more reliable activity levels, with greater satisfaction and less sense of defeat by pain. However, it can be very difficult for some people to break off from tasks before completing them, and they may need to challenge their beliefs about that. It may also be that overcautious patients develop rigid patterns which amount to avoidance of increasing activity, or in which safety behaviours counteract the development of confidence. Pacing is effectively a behavioural experiment with changing parameters, not a recipe for minimising pain.

Where fears impede progress, the fear-avoidance model suggests that graded exposure in vivo can disconfirm expectations of pain and harm from specific activities (Vlaeyen *et al.*, 2001, 2002). This involves activating the fear by confronting the activity in manageable steps, generating catastrophic expectations which are then challenged cognitively and disconfirmed by the activity successfully undertaken. This process may only take one session, but more usually involves a hierarchy of steps, carefully planned, often with repeated stages to reduce anxiety. Increases in activity are determined not by quota but by anxiety reduction to a tolerable level.

Exercise and fitness

Exercise fulfils multiple aims: establishing a healthy maintenance strategy; building fitness, stamina, or flexibility in pursuit of particular activity goals; correcting posture, movement, or muscle wasting. Even among pain-free people, only a minority maintain exercise routines, so it is unrealistic to expect it of people with pain, unless they bring tangible gains, subserve goals, or become part of a pleasant pastime (such as a dance class in which new friends are made).

Relaxation

Exploring the links between tension and pain can highlight the relevance of relaxation training, in particular in the context of movement and anticipation of pain. If tension is linked to the pain, relaxation can result in a greater sense of control over the pain. Learning relaxation skills may also provide a useful tool for dealing with the demands of persistent pain, in aiding stress management and improving the quality of rests, breaks, and sleep. Relaxation skills, once learned, are applied to stressful situations, such as driving, queuing in shops, etc., for maximum benefit.

Attention control

While distraction of attention is commonly attempted by patients, its efficacy (whether by anecdotal report or formal test) is low for persistent pain. By contrast, methods which direct attention towards the pain, counter-intuitively, can be used to change both the aversiveness of pain and its intensity. These methods include manipulation of imagery from unpleasant to neutral, and cultivating a dispassionate observational stance (as in meditation) towards the pain.

Cognitive therapy or restructuring

The use of cognitive therapy techniques such as identifying and challenging beliefs, combined with the use of behavioural experiments, has been alluded to several times in relation to a variety of goals. Depending on the formulation (see p. 91), treatment may or may not require cognitive therapy beyond the level of the maintenance cycle. Explanation of the role of beliefs in influencing activity, mood, and pain can draw on patients' experience (see Figure 5.1). Most cognitive work focuses on automatic negative thoughts, including the identification of thoughts that are inaccurate, unfair, or unhelpful in the current situation. It is important not to overlook automatic negative imagery, which can be subject to similar restructuring (Wells and Hackmann, 1993; Hackmann, 1997).

Problem-solving

In their attempts to cope with their situation, people with persistent pain may use a restricted range of strategies, which, however successful in other settings, may not work for them in the context of pain. Generating a wider range of possible approaches to problems, then being able to select them and experiment with them in a systematic way, are valuable skills which can be practised on everyday problems, practical or personal/social, and on obstacles to goal achievement.

Contingency management

Discussion of habits as automatic responses and their relationship to cues and consequences can introduce self-management of contingencies to break unhelpful habits and establish ones which support pain management; self-reinforcement (or reinforcement by supportive family members or friends) can also be demonstrated to mark goal achievement or progress in the use of pain management strategies. Recognising small achievements is particularly important for patients who write them off against 'what I used to be able to do' when pain free.

Generalisation

While methods of relapse prevention are not straightforwardly applicable to the management of pain, since there are multiple goals or end points and therefore many possible infractions, it is valuable to spend some time anticipating vulnerabilities and stresses which will make continuing use of pain management methods difficult. Breaks during the course of a pain management programme often provide good material for such discussion; patients who have become accustomed to pacing activities, and changing positions which are painful when sustained, can find these hard to do when in public places and without the support of the pain group.

In relation to this, some pain management programmes include development of communication skills for use within the family or within wider social contexts, such as work or further education. Finding and practising an explanation for limitations, for instance, can help patients to prepare for social encounters with others who may be sceptical about their pain and/or about the wisdom of pain management methods. This may extend to role-playing job interviews, visits to the general practitioner, or responses to others' well-meaning insistence on 'helping'.

Drug reduction

Analgesic and/or psychotropic drugs which deliver little benefit or which have a high cost in adverse effects, particularly sedation, are reviewed in CBT for persistent pain (with an educational input) and reduction is planned. As with other changes, reduction is carried out in the spirit of experiment, observing changes and reviewing end points, as abstinence does not always provide the best cost-benefit balance.

Outcome

The vignette below is an excerpt from the discharge letter of the lady discussed in the referral letter at the beginning of the assessment section.

Case vignette 5.1

Thank you for referring this 48-year-old lady for pain management. In general, she reports that she still experiences the pain, but that she is able to lead a more active life and feels more in control of the pain, less distressed by it and has more hope for the future.

Specifically, she benefited from explanation of chronic pain and what it means in terms of her physical capabilities and future health. She understands why other treatments were tried and why they may fail to resolve the pain. Making more sense of the pain has enabled her to establish a regular routine of stretching and exercising without fear of doing damage. She feels she is more flexible and fitter as a result and this has helped to strengthen her belief that pain does not signal damage. Return to physical activity has been achieved by taking a paced approach to all daily activities and she reports being able to do more than before. At the same time, she has surprised herself by reducing the number and dose of analgesics that she was taking. She has learned relaxation skills which she uses to cope with increased pain, in taking breaks in activity, and to help sleep. She has also experimented with more direct and less emotional ways of communicating her pain to others and has mostly found the responses more helpful. Finally, she feels that she has come to accept that, while she will most likely continue to experience the pain, it does not have to restrict her life as it did before. We will invite her to attend for further follow-up appointments.

Service and organisational aspects

While these components are usually delivered by the staff who are specialists in that area (doctors for education on pain and treatments; psychologists or cognitive-behavioural therapists for behavioural and cognitive change and emotional issues; doctors or nurses for reduction of drugs; physiotherapists for improving physical functioning; occupational therapists for some practical issues, and/or employment advisors for work-related activities), good liaison between team members allows some overlap and frequent reference to other components. Despite the apparently extravagant staffing, group treatment allows an approach based on models of adult education, at least as much as on group therapy, and which draws strongly on experience and expertise among group members. Unfortunately, skills in working inter-actively within such a group may be underemphasised in selection of staff, and a didactic approach which overlooks participants' shared experience and individual concerns risks alienating them.

Recent developments have emphasised self-management and, while this is an important outcome of any treatment, as a method of treatment it has too often been equated with low-level staff/trainer skills, a didactic approach, and brevity, often mixing pain with other chronic disorders and recommending very general coping strategies. Evidence for specific benefits of this approach is not yet available, although participants often feel better for being part of a group in which their problems are acknowledged and shared. Nor is there yet evidence for the effectiveness of self-help texts, often used as an adjunct to individual or group treatment.

By contrast, individualised treatment within a group requires a reason-able level of therapist skill and the active participation of the person with pain. The use of formulation-led specific treatment for particular fears, or for depression, or for post-traumatic symptomatology, alongside pain management, urgently requires testing to resolve issues about the sequence and depth of treatment.

Persistent pain often starts as a recurrent episodic condition, or with an acute episode, first presenting in primary care. It has become increasingly clear that, both initially and in the short term, psychosocial factors predict more variance in functional outcome than do physical indicators (Waddell, 1992; Linton, 1999), once 'red flag' medical problems have been ruled out. More effective treatment at an early stage can prevent recurrence or per-sistence, and there are successful trials of written intervention (Burton et al., 1999) and of short psychoeducational and exercise programmes; there is also an important role for general practitioner advice to help patients understand that the pain is not in this case a signal of danger and work towards full activity again. Identification of psychosocial risk factors using 'yellow flags' is under continuing development (Kendall et al., 1997). A model of 'stepped care' has been described and evaluated by Von Korff (1999) and Von Korff and Moore (2001), and, although developed within the US health service, it is applicable in other settings. It proposes three levels of care offered in ascending order of intervention level (Table 5.2), with the aim of delivering the least care necessary to benefit the patient.

A significant obstacle to providing early intervention is the widespread misunderstanding of pain among medical and health care staff. For instance, one study showed that two-thirds of general practitioners and physiotherapists advised patients to avoid painful movements; one-third believed that pain reduction was necessary for return to work; and one-quarter believed that sick leave was a good treatment for back pain (Linton et al., 2002). Such beliefs can serve to maintain the problems associated

Table 5.2 Stepped care

Patients	Objectives	Resource
All	Identify worries Promote normal activity	Primary care clinician + educational materials
Still limited at 6–8 weeks	Identify problems Set and help to work to functional goals; support return to activities	Case manager (e.g. nurse) + educational materials Individual or group intervention
Disabled at work or home	Intervention to restore function; graded exercise Psychological help where needed	Refer to rehabilitation Provide psychological care at primary or specialty level

Source: Adapted from Von Korff and Moore (2001).

with persistent pain and to foster fearful beliefs in patients. Professionals' fear of litigation can add to their caution in advising patients to return to activity.

Future directions

A number of areas of developing interest in mainstream clinical psychological practice, such as interpersonal therapy, have not yet appeared in the pain literature; others, such as mindfulness (McCracken, 1998; Hayes et al., 1999), a meta-cognitive dispassionate stance taken to bodily experience and to thoughts and emotion, show promise (McCracken et al., 2004). The same questions arise for these newer therapies as for longer-established practices: for whom do they work, and how? Single case and multiple baseline studies are sorely needed to cast some light on these questions.

Further burgeoning areas include early intervention and secondary prevention, as described; the integration of psychological with ongoing medical approaches; and primary care and community provision, the latter driven as much by politics and economics as by theory.

References

Banks, S. M. and Kerns, R. D. (1996). Explaining high rates of depression in chronic pain: A diathesis-stress framework. *Psychological Bulletin*, 199, 95–110.

Blyth, F. M., March, L. M., Nicholas, M. K. and Cousins, M. J. (2003). Chronic pain, work performance and litigation. *Pain*, 103, 41–47.

Burton, K., Waddell, G., Tillotson, M. and Summerton, N. (1999). Information and advice to patients with back pain can have a positive effect: A randomized trial of a novel education booklet in primary care. *Spine*, 24, 2484–2491.

Clyde, Z. and Williams, A. C. de C. (2002). Depression and mood. In S. J. Linton (ed.) *New avenues for the prevention of chronic musculoskeletal pain and disability.* Pain Research and Clinical Management Series, vol. 12, pp. 105–121. Amsterdam: Elsevier Science.

CSAG (Clinical Standards Advisory Group) (1994). *Clinical Standards Advisory Group report on back pain.* London: HMSO.

Flor, H., Braun, C., Elbert, T. and Birbaumer, N. (1997). Extensive reorganization of primary somatosensory cortex in chronic back pain patients. *Neuroscience Letters*, 224, 5–8.

Goubert, L., Crombez, G. and De-Bourdeaudhuij, I. (2004). Low back pain, disability and back pain myths in a community sample: Prevalence and interrelationships. *European Journal of Pain*, 8(4), 385–394.

Hackmann, A. (1997). The transformation of meaning in cognitive therapy. In M. Power and C. Brewin (eds) *The transformation of meaning in psychological therapies: Integrating theory and practice.* Chichester: John Wiley and Sons.

Hadjistavropoulos, H. and Williams, A. C. de C. (2004). Psychological interventions and chronic pain. In T. Hadjistavropoulos and K. D. Craig (eds) *Pain: Psychological perspectives* (pp. 271–301). Hillsdale, NJ: Lawrence Erlbaum Associates, Inc.

Harding, V. and Williams, A. C. de C. (1995). Editorial: Applying psychology to enhance physiotherapy outcome. *Physiotherapy Research and Practice*, 11, 129–132.

Hayes, S. C., Strosahl, K. D. and Wilson, K. G. (1999). *Acceptance and commitment therapy: An experiential approach to behavior change.* New York: Guilford Press.

IASP (International Association for the Study of Pain) (1979). Pain terms: A list with definitions and notes on usage. *Pain*, 6, 249–252.

Keefe, F. J., Rumble, M. E., Scipio, C. D., Giordano, L. A. and Perri, L. M. (2004). Psychological aspects of persistent pain: Current state of the science. *Journal of Pain*, 5, 195–211.

Kemler, M. A. and Furnee, C. A. (2002). The impact of chronic pain on life in the household. *Journal of Pain Symptom Management*, 23(5), 433–441.

Kendall, N. A. S., Linton, S. J. and Main, C. J. (1997). *Guide to assessing psychosocial yellow flags in acute low back pain: Risk factors for long term disability and work loss.* Wellington, NZ: Accident Rehabilitation and Compensation Insurance Corporation of New Zealand and the National Health Committee.

Linton, S. J. (1999). Prevention with special reference to chronic musculo-skeletal disorders. In R. J. Gatchel and D. C. Turk (eds) *Psychosocial factors in pain: Critical perspectives.* New York: Guilford Press.

Linton, S. J., Vlaeyen, J. and Ostelo, R. (2002). The back pain beliefs of health care providers: Are we fear-avoidant? *Journal of Occupational Rehabilitation*, 12, 223–232.

McCracken, L. M. (1998). Learning to live with the pain: Acceptance of pain predicts adjustment in persons with chronic pain. *Pain*, 74, 21–27.

McCracken, L., Carson, J. W., Eccleston, C. and Keefe, F. J. (2004). Acceptance and change in the context of chronic pain. *Pain*, 109, 4–7.

Main, C. J. and Spanswick, C. C. (1995). 'Functional overlay', and illness behaviour in chronic pain: Distress or malingering? *Journal of Psychosomatic Research*, 39, 737–753.

Main, C. J. and Spanswick, C. C. (2000). *Pain management: An interdisciplinary approach.* Edinburgh: Harcourt Publishers Limited.

Melzack, R. and Wall, P. (1965). Pain mechanisms: A new theory. *Science*, 150, 971–979.

Morley, S. and Eccleston, C. (2004). The object of fear in pain. In G. J. G. Asmundson, J. W. S. Vlaeyen and G. Crombez (eds) *Understanding and treating fear of pain* (pp. 163–188). New York: Oxford University Press.

Morley, S. and Williams, A. C. de C. (2002). Conducting and evaluating treatment outcome studies. In D. C. Turk and R. Gatchel (eds) *Psychological approaches to pain management: A practitioner's handbook* (2nd edition, pp. 52–68). New York: Guilford Press.

Morley, S., Eccleston, C. and Williams, A. (1999). Systematic review and meta-analysis of randomized controlled trials of cognitive behaviour therapy and behaviour therapy for chronic pain in adults, excluding headache. *Pain*, 80(1–2), 1–13.

Nicholas, M., Molloy, A., Tonkin, L. and Beeston, L. (2003). *Manage your pain: Practical and positive ways of adapting to persistent pain* (2nd edition). London: Souvenir Press Limited.

Padesky, C. and Greenberg, D. (1995). *Mind over mood: Cognitive treatment therapy manual for clients.* New York: Guilford Press.

Pincus, T. and Morley, S. (2001). Cognitive processing and bias in chronic pain: A review and integration. *Psychological Bulletin*, 127, 599–617.

Pincus, T. and Williams, A. (1999). Models and measurements of depression in chronic pain. *Journal of Psychosomatic Research*, 47, 211–219.

Pincus, T., Burton, A. K., Vogel, S. and Field, A. P. (2001). A systematic review of psychological factors as predictors of disability in prospective cohorts of low back pain. *Spine*, 27, 109–120.

Price, D. D. (1999). *Psychological mechanisms of pain and analgesia.* Seattle, WA: IASP Press.

Reitsma, B. and Meijler, W. J. (1997). Pain and patienthood. *Clinical Journal of Pain*, 13, 9–21.

Ridson, A., Eccleston, C., Crombez, G. and McCracken, L. M. (2003). How can we learn to live with pain? A Q-methodological analysis of the diverse understandings of acceptance of chronic pain. *Social Science and Medicine*, 56, 375–386.

Romano, J. M. and Turner, J. A. (1985). Chronic pain and depression: Does the evidence support a relationship? *Psychological Bulletin*, 97, 18–34.

Rosenstiel, A. K. and Keefe, F. J. (1983). The use of coping strategies in chronic low back pain patients: Relationship to patient characteristics and current adjustment. *Pain*, 17, 33–44.

Salkovskis, P. M., Clark, D. M., Hackmann, A., Wells, A. and Gelder, M. G. (1999). An experimental investigation of the role of safety-behaviours in the maintenance of panic disorder with agoraphobia. *Behaviour Research and Therapy*, 137, 559–574.

Sprangers, M. A., de Regt, E. B., Andries, F., van Agt, H. M., Bijl, R. V., de Boer, J. B., Foets, M., Hoeymans, N., Jacobs, A. E., Kempen, G. I., Miedema, H. S., Tijhuis, M. A. and de Haes, H. C. (2000). Which chronic conditions are associated with better or poorer quality of life? *Journal of Clinical Epidemiology*, 53(9), 895–907.

Sullivan, M. J. L., Adams, H. and Sullivan, M. E. (2004). Communicative dimensions of pain catastrophising: Social cueing effects on pain behaviour and coping. *Pain*, 107, 230–236.

Sullivan, M. J. L., Thorn, B., Haythornthwaite, J. A., Keefe, F., Martin, M., Bradley, L. A. and Lefevre, J. C. (2001). Theoretical perspectives on the relation between catastrophising and pain. *Clinical Journal of Pain*, 17, 53–61.

Suzuki, R., Rygh, L. J. and Dickenson, A. H. (2004). Bad news from the brain: Descending 5-HT pathways that control spinal pain processing. *Trends in Pharmacological Sciences*, 25, 613–617.

Symreng, I. and Fishman, S. M. (2004). Anxiety and pain. *Pain: Clinical update.* Seattle, WA: IASP.

Thwaites, R. and Freeston, M. (2005). Safety-seeking behaviours: Fact or fiction? How can we clinically differentiate between safety behaviours and adaptive coping strategies across anxiety disorders? *Behavioural and Cognitive Psychotherapy*, 33, 177–188.

Turk, D. C. and Monarch, E. S. (2003). Chronic pain. In S. Llewelyn and P. Kennedy (eds) *Handbook of clinical health psychology*. Chichester: Wiley.

Vlaeyen, J. W. and Linton, S. J. (2000). Fear-avoidance and its consequences in chronic musculoskeletal pain: A state of the art. *Pain*, 85, 317–332.

Vlaeyen, J. W., Kole-Snijders, A. M., Boeren, R. G. and van Eek, H. (1995). Fear of movement/(re)injury in chronic low back pain and its relation to behavioural performance. *Pain*, 62(3), 363–372.

Vlaeyen, J. W., de Jong, J., Geilen, M., Heuts, P. H. and van Breukelen, G. (2001). Graded exposure in vivo in the treatment of pain-related fear: A replicated single case experimental design in four patients with chronic low back pain. *Behavioural Research and Therapy*, 39, 151–166.

Vlaeyen, J. W., de Jong, J., Geilen, M., Heuts, P. H. and van Breukelen, G. (2002). The treatment of fear of movement/(re)injury in chronic low back pain: Further evidence on the effectiveness of exposure in vivo. *Clinical Journal of Pain*, 18, 251–261.

Vlaeyen, J. W. S., de Jong, J., Leeuw, M. and Crombez, G. (2004). Fear reduction in chronic pain: Graded exposure in vivo with behavioural experiments. In G. Asmundson, J. Vlaeyen and G. Crombez (eds) *Understanding fear and treating fear of pain*. Oxford: Oxford University Press.

Von Korff, M. (1999). Pain management in primary care: An individualised stepped-care approach. In R. J. Gatchel and D. C. Turk (eds) *Psychosocial factors in pain* (pp. 360–373). New York: Guilford Press.

Von Korff, M. and Moore, J. (2001). Stepped care for back pain: Activating approaches for primary care. *Annuals of Internal Medicine*, 121, 187–195.

Waddell, G. (1992). Biopsychosocial analysis of low back pain. *Baillieres Clinical Rheumatology*, 6(3), 523–557.

Waddell, G., McCulloch, J. A., Kummel, E. and Venner, R. M. (1980). Non-organic physical signs in low back pain. *Spine*, 5(2), 117–125.

Wall, P. D. (1999). *Pain: The science of suffering*. London: Weidenfeld & Nicolson.

Wells, A. and Hackmann, A. (1993). Imagery and core beliefs in health anxiety: Content and origins. *Behavioural and Cognitive Psychotherapy*, 21, 265–273.

Williams, A. C. de C. (2002a). Facial expression of pain: An evolutionary account. *Behavioural Brain Sciences*, 25, 439–488.

Williams, A. C. de C. (2002b). Selecting and applying pain measures. In H. Breivik, W. Campbell and C. Eccleston (eds) *Clinical pain management: Practical applications and procedures* (pp. 3–14). London: Arnold Publications.

Williams, A. C. de C. and McCracken, L. (2004). Cognitive-behavioural therapy for chronic pain: An overview with specific reference to fear and avoidance. In G. J. G Asmundson, J. W. S. Vlaeyen and G. Crombez (eds) *Understanding and treating fear of pain* (pp. 293–312). New York: Oxford University Press.

Chapter 6

Spinal cord injuries

Guinevere Webster and Paul Kennedy

A spinal cord injury only ceased being a mortal condition in the mid-1940s. Sir Ludwig Guttmann, who pioneered rehabilitation for people with spinal cord injuries, was given the brief to establish a spinal unit at Stoke Mandeville Hospital in England in preparation for the D-Day landings. Guttmann invented nothing new, but effectively challenged the attitude and assumption that nothing could be done for people with spinal cord injuries. Up until then, over 90 per cent of people died within the first year post injury. He systematically assessed patients' needs and worked back from causes of mortality to the introduction of life-maintaining procedures. For example, many people died from septicaemia as a consequence of acquiring pressure sores. To prevent pressure sores, patients need to be turned. With nursing staff, Guttmann organised a very strict regime of turning, which reduced the frequency of pressure sores. This model of rehabilitation was emulated in North America and other spinal centres within the UK and Guttmann's early work has provided a blueprint for the comprehensive rehabilitation of people with spinal cord injuries (Guttmann, 1976).

Guttmann's first psychological intervention highlights how important psychological issues are in the management of spinal cord injuries. Clearly, a spinal cord injury has an impact on many aspects of a person's life, affecting personal attitudes and mood, general psychosocial functioning with respect to employment, managing responsibilities and relationships, as well as the consequences of the physical changes. There are also different psychological challenges throughout the various phases post injury, ranging from dealing with initial pain, discomfort and sensory loss, to coping with prolonged hospitalisation and lack of contact with family and friends.

Disability often presents significant challenges with respect to access, social integration and coping. Psychological factors are also important because much research demonstrates that it is not the extent of the physical disability that predicts longer-term overall adjustment, but psychological factors. Such psychological factors are also important in and have a role in mediating changes within roles and responsibilities for individuals, their families and social contexts. Most industrialised economies provide comprehensive treatment and rehabilitation care for people with traumatic and non-traumatic injuries.

Aetiology, incidence and prevalence

Almost half (47 per cent) of traumatic spinal cord injuries are caused by road traffic accidents. Domestic and industrial falls cause 27 per cent, and between 15 and 20 per cent are from sporting injuries. In the UK, 5 per cent are caused by self-harm and 0.5 per cent by acts of violence. In the USA, 15 per cent of injuries are caused by criminal assault (Duff and Kennedy, 2003; Go et al., 1995). Causes of non-traumatic injuries include infective diseases, ischaemic insults, neoplastic disorders and multiple sclerosis.

There are four male injuries for every female spinal cord injury. The mean age is 28 and the mode is 19. The annual incidence of spinal cord injury in the UK, like most other European countries, is between 10 and 15 per million; in the USA it is thought to be between 30 and 40 per million, and in Japan, 27 per million. There are an estimated 40,000 people in the UK and 200,000 in the USA with spinal cord injury. Life expectancy estimates vary: for a young person with an incomplete injury the relative (to normal population) survival is 96 per cent, but for complete tetraplegics over the age of 50, it is estimated to be 33 per cent. A reasonably good life expectancy is probable for most people. Primary causes of early mortality include pneumonia, septicaemia, heart disease and pulmonary emboli. A recent Australian study (O'Connor, 2005) suggests that the incidence of spinal cord injury is likely to increase, with a greater proportion of older people accounting for almost half of new injuries by 2021.

The physical impact

An injury to the spinal cord occurs when sufficient force causes the cord to be compressed, lacerated or stretched and may be associated with a fracture or fracture-dislocation of the vertebral column and displacement of the intervertebral discs. These hyper-extension injuries are often the consequence of sudden impact as with car accidents and falls. The neurological losses will depend upon completeness of the injury. Cervical (neck) injury may result in tetraplegia (quadriplegia). Injuries to the thoracic, lumbar and sacral levels (upper, middle and lower back) may result in paraplegia. Of injuries, 53 per cent are neck injuries and 47 per cent are back injuries. A complete injury is one in which all motor and sensory functions are lost below the level of the injury, as well as the loss of control of visceral functions, such as bladder, bowel and sexual function. In paraplegia, lower trunk muscles are impaired while cervical injuries result in loss of function in the hands, arms, shoulder and diaphragm, as well as the lower thorax. Complete injuries above the seventh cervical segment may preclude the possibility of independent living. Sensory losses are similar to the areas of motor loss, and include loss of touch, pressure, temperature regulation and position. The loss of sexual sensation and responsivity and control of bladder and bowel function is common to all complete lesions above the sacral roots. Incomplete injuries may result in partial damage of the cord. Complications post-discharge include pressure sores, urinary tract infections, muscular spasm and chronic pain.

Rehabilitation

Most people are transferred to a specialist spinal cord injury treatment and rehabilitation centre shortly after the onset of the injury. Once any fracture is stabilised, generally through internal fixation, or more rarely external fixation or postural reduction, the person begins a period of rehabilitation which can last between three and six months, depending on the level of the injury and social circumstances. Rehabilitation enables the person to acquire new skills to address their needs and adjust physically, socially and psychologically to their physical disability. This includes learning to manage bladder and bowel functions, use a wheelchair and develop and maintain functional independence skills. Exploring adaptations to accommodation, financial independence and personal assistance needs may also be necessary. People also require information about their new needs and emotional support in maintaining general psychosocial well-being.

The impact of spinal cord injury

Emotional responses

Spinal cord injury is a devastating event that usually occurs suddenly and unexpectedly. Without warning, the person is plunged into a trauma that will have far-reaching consequences for most aspects of life. It is not surprising, then, that spinal cord injury is something the injured person needs to adjust to psychologically as well as physically. In the same way as physical adjustment following spinal cord injury, psychological adjustment involves a period of recovery following the initial trauma, a gradual process of working out what has changed or been lost as a result of the injury, and how these changes can be compensated for or accommodated.

Previously it was thought that the process of psychological adjustment in spinal cord injury followed a set path through several different phases. This model comes from the literature on coping with bereavement and suggests that, for example, first the person is in shock, then there might be a period of denial when it is difficult to acknowledge the reality of what has happened. This is followed by depression, then anger, until finally the person reaches a resolution and acceptance of the situation (Tucker, 1980).

Research into psychological adjustment after spinal cord injury has shown that there is little support for the existence of this type of set pattern of adjustment. Instead, what is clear is that people adjust in different ways. People may experience a wide range of different emotions, including shock, fear and anxiety, anger, and sadness or depression. But not everyone experiences all of these, and they do not occur in any fixed order or at specific time phases post-injury (Frank et al., 1987).

Although it is common to feel a range of negative emotions following spinal cord injury, in only a minority (roughly 25–30 per cent) does this develop into a clinically significant level of anxiety or depression (Duff and Kennedy, 2003). Also, negative emotions such as fear and sadness may be mixed with positive ones such as relief at having survived, gratitude at being given a 'second chance', or appreciation of personal relationships.

Coping and adjustment in detail

So what distinguishes those people who appear to cope well with the trauma of spinal cord injury from those who do not? It is a common but mistaken assumption that the severity of injury is what determines how effectively people cope with the situation. Many people think that a person who sustains a more severe injury, for example becoming tetraplegic, will find it more difficult to cope than someone who sustains a less severe injury, for example someone who has an incomplete injury and recovers the ability to walk.

In fact research has shown repeatedly that injury severity is not clearly associated with coping (Duff and Kennedy, 2003). The person who regains walking ability may experience greater difficulties with psychosocial adjustment than the tetraplegic person. At first this may seem counter-intuitive – surely a worse situation would be harder to cope with? But the key is the injured person's perception of the situation: although from the outside becoming tetraplegic may appear a more severe situation than becoming paraplegic or sustaining an incomplete injury, what counts is the individual's response to his or her particular situation. One person with tetraplegia may have difficulty coping and become depressed, but another may adjust well and go on to gain much satisfaction from life. Rehabilitation staff who are new to spinal cord injury may not be aware of this, and because many newly injured people may also assume that sustaining a severe injury will make it impossible to have a good quality of life, it is essential that staff are able to correct this assumption and give a positive message about the future.

Stress and coping theory (Lazarus and Folkman, 1984) suggests that when people are faced with an event such as a spinal cord injury, their response is mediated by the cognitive process of appraisal. This means that the person assesses the situation, first in terms of the impact and threat involved (what has happened? what effect will it have?) – this is known as primary appraisal. Second, the person then considers how this situation can be managed – what resources does the person have, and what strategies would help? This is known as secondary appraisal.

The results of this thought process will influence the person's emotional reaction, and the type of coping strategy used to attempt to manage the situation. For instance, somebody who thinks that the situation threatens everything that makes life worth living (primary appraisal), and that s/he is powerless to cope with this (secondary appraisal), is likely to feel sad, demoralised and hopeless about the future. This person, in believing that s/he cannot do anything to improve the situation, will tend to use coping strategies that try to avoid the problem (avoidance-focused coping). Examples of these are denying the problems, avoiding situations or activities that highlight issues raised by the injury and abusing drugs or alcohol. This helps the person to feel better in the short term but because it does not improve the situation the problems remain; if this continues over time the person may become depressed, withdraw from others around him and disengage from rehabilitation. This of course will prevent him/her from learning the new skills that will enable him/her to manage his/her spinal cord injury successfully, and over time will make him/her vulnerable to a poor psychosocial outcome with chronic emotional disorders, self-neglect and substance use problems.

Case vignette 6.1

Ben sustained a T6 spinal cord injury as a result of a motorbike accident. Initially he was motivated with his rehabilitation, and spent as much time as possible in the physiotherapy gym. His goal was to walk again, and he was distressed when his physiotherapist explained that he was unlikely to gain any further recovery. He thought: 'This is the worst possible situation – I've lost everything' (primary appraisal) and 'I can't cope with it – there's nothing I can do to make things better' (secondary appraisal). Ben felt hopeless and terrified about the future. He started to avoid rehabilitation activities, believing there was no point in them when he would never again be able to walk or ride a motorbike. Instead, he spent more and more time on his own, refusing to take part in therapy sessions or see visitors. His relationship with his girlfriend ended, and staff were concerned that he was drinking excessive amounts of alcohol. Because he was neglecting to care for his skin he developed a pressure sore requiring a period of bed rest. He became more isolated and depressed, saying that he just wished to be left to die.

Alternatively, someone may appraise the situation as severe, but manageable. This will result in more positive emotions and hope for the future, and a corresponding motivation to tackle the situation using positive coping strategies (approach-focused coping) such as problem-solving, acceptance (accepting the situation and working out how to accommodate it into the person's life) and positive reframing (focusing on positive possibilities of the situation). Because this person is tackling the problems caused by the spinal cord injury, s/he will learn how to manage them and will work out a way of continuing to lead a satisfying life. In the long run, this person's sense of self-efficacy (seeing her/himself as someone who can cope) will be enhanced and s/he will develop in her/her ability to tackle future situations.

Case vignette 6.2

Sarah sustained a complete C5 spinal cord injury during a diving accident while on holiday. After her doctor had explained the prognosis, she thought: 'This is the worst thing that's ever happened to me – it's changed every area of my life' (primary appraisal). She could no longer carry out her job as a nurse in a children's hospital, or her favourite activities which included country walks and knitting. She was concerned about how her injury would affect her relationships with her husband and two children. But she had a strong belief in her ability to cope, thinking: 'I'll get through it – I'm tough and I always pull through somehow' (secondary appraisal). Although at times she felt sad about the way her life had changed, and worried about the future, she resolved to put all her efforts into her rehabilitation to get the best she could out of it. This helped her to learn how to manage the practical problems caused by her injury, and prompted her to think about what activities she could still do that would give her the same enjoyment and satisfaction as her previous job and interests. A few years later Sarah completed an Open University course in child development, and went on to gain a job as a counsellor with a children's charity. In her spare time she enjoyed painting and socialising with friends. She was proud of the way that she and her family had coped, and believed they had all grown stronger as a result.

Other factors that research has shown to be important in how well people adjust post-spinal cord injury include age (younger people adjust better), gender (women adjust better), internal locus of control (people who believe they have more control over events adjust better than those who feel at the mercy of events beyond their control), social support (those who have many supportive relationships adjust better) and experience of chronic pain

(North, 1999). These factors may be important in determining people's ability to cope because they are linked to the appraisal process. For instance, younger people may be more flexible in their ability to imagine living with spinal cord injury and generate coping strategies; people with an internal locus of control are more likely to view themselves as able to cope with a situation and to come up with problem-solving strategies; while greater social support provides people with both practical and emotional coping resources, facilitating their perception that the situation is manageable.

Coping and adjustment through the phases of rehabilitation

Coping and adjustment is not a single event, but a process that unfolds over time. The injured person's appraisals, emotional responses and coping behaviours change and develop according to the changing situation during acute medical care, rehabilitation and reintegration into the community. In the acute phase, the emphasis is on physical stabilisation. The injured person is physically dependent on medical and nursing care, and may be experiencing shock or acute stress following the trauma of the injury. The individual needs to make sense of what has happened and work out what effects the situation will have.

During the rehabilitation phase, the focus is on regaining independence, and moving from treatment being guided by hospital staff to becoming more involved and in control of treatment decisions and rehabilitation activities. The injured person will gradually be gaining more information about his or her functional abilities in the long term, and may need to accept that a hoped-for goal (such as walking again) will not be possible. Initially the person is concerned with the minutiae of rehabilitation activities, with the many new skills that must be learned in order to self-care effectively (or become verbally independent in self-care). This can seem overwhelming and people may wonder how they will manage to complete the rehabilitation programme. Setbacks, such as a period of bedrest due to a urinary tract infection or pressure area, are often demoralising and may lead people to feel they are making no progress. It is often difficult for people to remember their achievements since these happen gradually, and many feel that the pace of rehabilitation is slow. Sometimes this can be beneficial, because when rehabilitation proceeds more quickly (for instance with incomplete or low-level injuries) people may experience a sense that their psychological adjustment has not 'caught up' with their physical recovery, and may not feel ready to tackle the new challenges in the community despite being physically fit for discharge.

Towards the end of rehabilitation the day-to-day tasks of living with spinal cord injury have been mastered and the focus shifts to preparation for life in the community. Issues such as housing, work and renewing family relationships come to the fore. It is common for people to experience greater mood disturbance in the weeks leading up to discharge from the rehabilitation centre (Kennedy *et al.*, 2000). People may have concerns about managing the practical problems associated with the injury outside the relatively protected environment of the hospital, and may be feeling acutely the loss of their previous circumstances or hoped-for recovery.

For people living with spinal cord injury in the community, quality of life improves with time (Krause, 1998). Most people gradually accommodate the injury into a lifestyle that they find satisfying. Certain aspects may become important during the community phase, for instance re-establishing a social network, relationships and sexuality, and combating societal issues such as discrimination and physical access problems. A minority of spinal cord-injured individuals continue to experience problems with psychosocial adjustment, which may start to become chronic and entrenched. As mentioned earlier, this can lead to problems caused by self-neglect, resulting in physical complications.

Sexual relationships

Sexual issues are important to people with spinal cord injury and are often neglected by rehabilitation staff. Some injured people may place more importance on the ability to have a sexual relationship than walking. Men with spinal cord injury are rarely able to have a psychogenic erection (in response to thinking about sex); although many retain the ability to have a reflex erection most do not experience orgasm, and fertility is affected (Sipski and Alexander, 1992). In women, vaginal responsiveness and orgasm are affected; women with spinal cord injury value kissing, hugging and touching more than sexual intercourse (Sipski and Alexander, 1993). The keys to satisfying sexual relationships following spinal cord injury for both men and women are the willingness to experiment, and believing that they can satisfy their partner (Kreuter *et al.*, 1996).

Chronic pain

Chronic neuropathic pain affects between 25 per cent and 45 per cent of people with spinal cord injury and is responsible for poorer overall adjustment, with increased depression and lower life satisfaction (Duff and Kennedy, 2003). Neuropathic pain occurs as a result of disruption to the signalling of nerve fibres that were damaged during the injury, so that they constantly signal pain in the absence of a painful stimulus. This pain can be intense and highly unpleasant. Many people report that pain is a more important factor than the spinal cord injury itself in preventing them from returning to work.

Cognitive dysfunction

A significant number of people with spinal cord injury also experience cognitive problems – as many as 40–50 per cent may be affected (Davidoff *et al.*, 1992). This may be due to traumatic brain injury sustained at the time of the spinal cord injury, or hypoxic brain damage due to respiratory problems. Alternatively, cognitive problems may predate the spinal cord injury, caused, for instance, by stroke or substance abuse. Cognitive problems include difficulties with learning and memory, attention and concentration, flexible thinking and problem solving, and planning and organisational skills. Clearly these problems will interfere with rehabilitation activities, which rely on the ability to learn new skills and remember to carry out activities such as pressure relief regularly. The problems may also make it harder to adjust well, as they can interfere with the use of adaptive coping strategies such as problem-solving and cognitive restructuring (changing negative thought patterns).

Spinal cord injury and the family

In supporting the spinal cord-injured person through rehabilitation, it is important not to overlook the impact of the injury on the injured person's family members. Although the research in this area is more limited, studies have found that family members such as spouses go through an adjustment process in the same way as the injured person. Similarly, family members may be vulnerable to maladaptive coping styles and poor psychosocial adjustment (Kreuter, 2000). The rates of emotional disorders may actually be higher in relatives compared to spinal cord-injured individuals; one study found that 28 per cent of spouses and partners experienced depression and 38 per cent anxiety (Chandler, 2003). Family members who act as caregivers are especially at risk of emotional and health problems (Weitzenkamp *et al.*, 1997).

Even fewer research studies have looked at how children cope when a parent or other close family member sustains a spinal cord injury. Again, there is some evidence that a minority of children experience difficulty coping and are at risk of developing emotional and behavioural problems (Webster and Hindson, 2004). The picture is different, however, for children who are born to parents who already have a spinal cord injury. In this situation children do not experience the stresses associated with the injury, such as separation from the parent during hospitalisation, and changes in family roles and circumstances. Studies have found that being spinal cord injured does not negatively affect parental ability, and that children born to spinal cord-injured parents grow up to be psychologically well adjusted (Alexander *et al.*, 2002).

Psychological assessment, formulation and intervention

Assessments are carried out to answer specific questions, and formulation and intervention provide the rationale for these questions. Assessments which help in formulation may include identification of behavioural risk factors as in the acquisition of pressure sores and the identification of negative assumptions following acquired disability. Questionnaires, self-report and self-monitoring techniques are helpful in assessing antecedent conditions, responses and consequences in a traditional cognitive-behavioural therapy formulation. The assessment of individual appraisal and coping responses also helps by identifying propensities to engage in emotion-focused and problem-focused coping strategies. These assessments can help identify adaptive coping strategies which are useful in many chronic conditions. In general, strategies that include the processes of acceptance, reframing, planning and utilisation of social support have been found to be adaptive, while behavioural disengagement, mental disengagement and alcohol and drug use ideation are associated with increased distress and disability. Many formulations require multi-factorial assessments. This is not surprising given the comprehensiveness of the biopsychosocial perspective. These assessment techniques can help in the prediction of problems and in some cases help in the prediction of morbidity and, indeed, mortality. The model of adjustment shown in Figure 6.1 has been developed from Folkman and Lazarus's (1980) model and highlights the key psychological factors associated with adjustment post-spinal cord injury (Duff and Kennedy, 2003).

The aims of psychological interventions are to enable the individual to manage the consequences of their disability, to maximise their potential to benefit and engage in the rehabilitation process and to provide the person with ongoing psychological support throughout their adjustment. Depression has received more attention than any other psychological issue post-spinal cord injury. Elliott and Kennedy (2004) reviewed the evidence base for the treatment of depression post-injury and concluded that while nine studies met the inclusion criteria, only one was randomised, highlighting the need for further multi-centre, randomised research.

Cognitive behavioural techniques are utilised to work with the patient in redefining their difficulty and decatastrophising. It is clear that many aspects of the injury may seem catastrophic and the psychologist will be involved in encouraging the patient to understand the more manageable aspects of the consequences and affirm them in their personal capacity to respond to these challenges. The provision of clear information about the nature, extent and consequences of the injury is important. Information has been shown to reduce anxiety. This information needs to be clear, comprehensive and consistent.

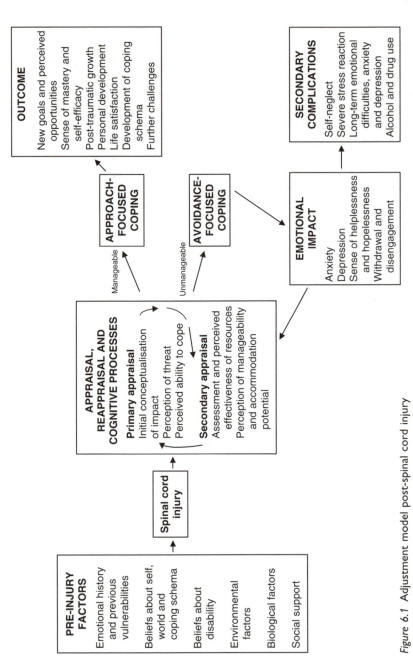

Figure 6.1 Adjustment model post-spinal cord injury

Source: Duff and Kennedy (2003).

Psychological care pathways

One of the most important factors to establish in the early acute period is to convey the idea of safety. The patient has been through a major trauma where many of their assumptions about life and security have been challenged. In the early stages the patient will often complain of being in shock and may exhibit early symptoms of acute stress disorder. During this time it is important for all involved to communicate to the individual that the spinal cord injury is a manageable situation, and that the consequences are manageable. This may be difficult to accept initially. It is essential to get the right balance at this time by providing sensible, objective reassurance rather than making platitudinal comments. During this assessment the clinical psychologist may assess the individual's general psychological well-being with respect to their history of coping and effective functioning and ascertain whether they have had any premorbid mental health, psychiatric or psychological difficulties.

Again, further work may be required to enable the patient to talk about their situation. It is important to develop a collaborative framework with the client and support them in constructing a new reality that is both helpful and credible. Managing significant distress is often done on a one-to-one basis using cognitive behavioural therapeutic techniques that include appraisal training, challenging negative beliefs, acknowledging strengths and fostering social support. Work to increase and reconstruct the individual's reality may also include increasing engagement, increasing a sense of self-efficacy and internal attributions regarding competency and encouraging the patient to look for opportunities of exerting and experiencing a sense of control.

Rehabilitation is also about fostering engagement and managing the physical consequences of the spinal cord injury. There are a number of rehabilitation planning and goal planning frameworks that ensure psychological principles are incorporated into rehabilitation programmes. These are fully described in Chapter 12.

Individual therapy

Not surprisingly, people with a spinal cord injury will face challenges that they have not previously experienced. If these demands are perceived to be greater than the resources the person has available to deal with them, the person may encounter an increased level of distress. A small amount of stress can motivate us to do something about a problem, but excessive stress can lead to stress reactions. This can often reduce the person's confidence in their ability to cope and can result in feelings of helplessness and depression.

The coping strategies people mobilise in response to the consequences of a spinal cord injury are important in determining the extent of the psychological distress experienced. There is a growing body of evidence that highlights the strong predictive relationship between the coping strategies people use and the level of psychological distress. Depression and anxiety are often the consequences of escape avoidance strategies, while positive affective states are associated with coping strategies such as acceptance, positive reappraisal and problem-solving (Reidy *et al.*, 1991; Kennedy *et al.*, 2000). As previously mentioned, Duff and Kennedy's (2003) adjustment model emphasises the importance of acknowledging pre-injury factors such as emotional history and previous vulnerabilities, as well as the beliefs that the individual has about disability and their capacity to cope.

Cognitive behavioural therapy

Cognitive behavioural therapies are common psychological interventions for the management of a variety of emotional disorders, including depression, anxiety and panic disorder. Clinical psychologists integrate the cognitive behavioural therapy perspective with coping effectiveness training to enable successful adjustment to the consequences of spinal cord injury. The cognitive behavioural therapy perspective examines the reciprocal interdependence of feelings, thoughts and behaviours. The primary appraisal of a new situation will determine whether it is a threat, a challenge or benign. Spinal cord injury results in many new situations that precipitate considerable uncertainty and fear about the future. If the individual has a belief that a situation can be managed, they are more likely to adopt a problem-focused solution which facilitates coping and adjustment. Individuals who appraise their spinal cord injury to be unmanageable have a low expectation of coping, which may precipitate unhelpful attempts at adaptation. Folkman and Lazarus (1980) make a distinction between problem- and emotion-focused coping. Clinically, much coping involves both processes. In therapy, the patient is encouraged to develop emotion-focused strategies, such as positive reframing and acceptance, for those aspects of the disability that are unchangeable. Problem-focused strategies are utilised to manage those consequences of the disability that are capable of being changed (such as problem-solving and engagement). Working with primary and secondary appraisal processes, i.e. realistically what is the threat and what resources do I have to deal with it, can help promote approach-coping strategies which are associated with positive outcomes such as increasing a sense of mastery, self-control and the development of a coping schema.

Once rapport has been established and the patient's beliefs about the disability have been identified, together with the appraisal processes, the individual may be encouraged to challenge cognitive distortions, negative beliefs and reappraise threats in light of available resources. Most individual cognitive behavioural therapy sessions last for one hour and are usually not more than once or twice per week. This enables the individual to work on a variety of homework tasks, such as keeping a diary of negative thoughts, and set up behavioural experiments such as monitoring mastery of feared situations. Tirch and Radnitz (2000) suggest six categories of cognitive distortions following spinal cord injury. These are: (1) an overly negative view of the self and others; (2) appraisals about self-worth following injury; (3) expectations of rejection from others and inadequacy; (4) the expectation of consistent failure; (5) development of excessive personal entitlement; and (6) an over-developed sense of vulnerability.

It is critically important to provide people with newly acquired injuries accurate information and the likely course of the spinal cord injury, both physically and psychologically. Research results indicate that between 65 and 75 per cent of people with spinal cord injuries do not experience clinical levels of anxiety and depression (Kennedy and Rogers, 2000; Woolrich *et al.*, 2006). It is therefore important to provide those with clinical levels of distress appropriate treatment, but also to recognise that there is no fixed pattern of adjustment.

Interventions with families

Families play a critical role in supporting the individual throughout the life-span. Spinal cord injury occurs within a social context and more often than not the primary social context consists of the family. Families may require support because of the distress they experience as a result of the change in function, well-being and capacity of an injured family member. Families may also have to renegotiate roles and responsibilities, which in some cases may be non-traditional. Occasionally there is the prospect of financial hardship because of the impact on employment and reduced earning capacity. In some cases, the level of psychological distress is higher within family members than the injured person. For example, approximately 40 per cent of parents of children with spinal cord injury display post-traumatic distress symptomatology (Boyer *et al.*, 2000).

Group coping effectiveness training

Coping effectiveness training (CET) consists of a series of group learning sessions aimed at helping people deal with the demands resulting from a spinal cord injury. King and Kennedy (1999) and Kennedy *et al.* (2003) undertook a series of controlled trials comparing spinal cord injury patients who received a CET intervention with matched controls. They found a decrease in depression and anxiety post-intervention and at six-week follow-up, but not in the control group. CET is generally based on the idea that coping has two functions: (1) to alter the problem causing distress, and

(2) to regulate the emotional response to the problem. Once changeable aspects have been identified, the individual is trained to utilise problem-focused strategies. For those which are unchangeable, the person is trained to utilise emotion-focused strategies.

Kennedy *et al.* (2000) identified a number of coping strategies that were associated with positive adjustment that included accepting the reality of the injury occurring, having available high levels of quality social support, having the capacity to engage in positive reappraisal and engagement in planned problem-solving. Maladaptive coping strategies associated with poor adjustment included behavioural and mental disengagement, alcohol and drug use ideation, denial, escape-avoidant coping strategies, focusing on and venting of emotions and low social support.

CET aims to improve skills for assessing stress, teach a range of coping skills that can be used to tackle stress and provide an opportunity for interaction with others who have similar experiences of spinal cord injury. The intervention consists of seven, 60–75 minute sessions run twice a week in small groups of six to nine people. The concept of stress is introduced in the first session and attempts are made to normalise stress reactions. The need to develop the ability to think critically about how one appraises and copes with situations is also emphasised. The second session covers appraisal skills and the third session problem-solving, which includes working through several realistically based scenarios commonly experienced by people with a spinal cord injury. In the fourth session, the connections and distinctions between thoughts, feelings and behaviour are examined with the inclusion of work on pleasant activity scheduling and relaxation. Session five is concerned with increasing awareness of negative assumptions, thoughts and expectations and how to challenge them. The final two sessions describe the meta-strategy for choosing appropriate ways of coping and increasing social support. The provision of a meta-strategy for choosing the optimum coping response for a particular situation is important because research suggests that the effectiveness of individual coping strategies can vary at different times following injury (Reidy and Caplan, 1994).

Everyone at some point responds inappropriately to stress, which can exacerbate the situation. CET includes the identification of effective and ineffective responses to stress, especially those that are particularly unhelpful, such as disengagement, general avoidance, long-term denial and the expression of extreme emotion. By encouraging individuals to think critically about their behaviour in response to stressors, CET helps people avoid unproductive ways of coping. As mentioned, in trials undertaken by King and Kennedy (1999) and Kennedy *et al.* (2003), CET successfully reduced levels of depression and anxiety and also resulted in changes in negative self-perception and improved self-efficacy in coping with spinal cord injury. It was also effective in promoting and socially validating the belief that many aspects of the spinal cord injury are indeed manageable. Kennedy *et al.* (2005) revisited the psychological characteristics of people who benefited from CET and found that time since injury was predictive, suggesting that to maximise positive responses from CET, the earlier it is introduced the better.

Organising services for people with spinal cord injury

User involvement and empowerment

User involvement in health services has become a priority for healthcare providers. In practical terms this means giving people a more active role in making decisions about and shaping the structure of the healthcare services that they use. This can be done through, for example, informing users about proposed changes to the service and asking for feedback, asking users about their priorities for new developments in service provision or research, establishing positions on decision-making groups and committees for user representatives, or initiatives such as the Expert Patient (discussed in more detail in Chapter 1).

Service provider strategies for involving users with spinal cord injuries may take advantage of organisations set up to represent and promote the needs of people with spinal cord injury (such as the Spinal Injuries Association in the UK), by including representatives from such organisations on management committees and special interest groups. At a basic level, user involvement includes interactions with individuals who are accessing services in order to promote their involvement in their treatment, for instance through programmes such as goal planning (Chapter 12) or established ways of gaining feedback from current service users, such as a regular discussion forum.

Psychologically, user involvement benefits people with spinal cord injury by increasing their sense of control over and choice in their treatment and rehabilitation. This is important in promoting people's ability to take positive action in solving the problems that arise as a consequence of spinal cord injury, and enabling people to see these problems as manageable. As discussed above, a proactive, problem-solving approach is linked to better psychosocial adjustment in the long term, so services which foster this approach in their users will help to maximise psychosocial adjustment.

Teamwork

Working as an interdisciplinary team is often a more effective way to provide a service that is in tune with the rehabilitation needs of people with spinal cord injury. Interdisciplinary team working involves the different professional disciplines working closely together on rehabilitation aims that are more relevant and specific to individual users. This differs from multi-disciplinary teamwork, where each discipline carries out tasks related to their area of expertise in parallel, so that a user's rehabilitation needs are divided into separate categories, such as physiotherapy and nursing goals.

Most people's lives are not divided into professional categories, and the personal goals of people with spinal cord injury are more likely to require the input of several members of the professional team. For instance, one person may wish to return to her previous employment, which might require the input of the physiotherapist for wheelchair mobility, the occupational therapist for advice on adaptive equipment in the office, and the nurse for training in self-intermittent catheterisation. Another person may wish to drive his/her son to school, requiring advice from the occupational therapist about appropriate vehicles, training from a driving instructor on driving an adapted car, and learning car transfers in physiotherapy.

The most efficient way of addressing the personal goals of people with spinal cord injury is for the rehabilitation staff to work closely together as an interdisciplinary team, using the injured person's needs as a starting point. This ensures that the rehabilitation goals the person is working on are directly relevant to his or her priorities in life, helping to engage and motivate the person in the rehabilitation programme.

Psychological interventions may also be included in the interdisciplinary approach to rehabilitation, depending on the needs of the injured person. For instance, someone who is experiencing severe pain during physiotherapy sessions could benefit from a psychological pain management programme that includes practising techniques during physiotherapy. Alternatively, someone who is anxious about venturing outside the rehabilitation centre could be helped by the clinical psychologist and occupational therapist to construct a 'graded hierarchy' of community skills to practise in a gradual way that is manageable. Someone with memory problems may have difficulty with learning tasks such as self-intermittent catheterisation. The clinical psychologist could work with the nurse on compensatory strategies, such as using prompt sheets that are gradually faded out as the skill is learned and a reminder alarm on the person's watch.

When the staff team works closely together, this results in improved cooperation and communication among the team. Clearly this has benefits for the service user, with a smoother and more efficient delivery of the rehabilitation programme. It also benefits the staff team, as different professional disciplines are more aware of the ways in which each discipline works and how they contribute to the service overall. Staff members who are in closer communication and more aware of each other's working practices are likely to be better able to support each other practically and emotionally. This can be especially important in spinal cord injury rehabilitation, which involves working over an extended period of time with people who are going through a traumatic period in their lives. Such work can be emotionally draining, and staff require support in order to avoid problems with burn-out (North, 1999).

Key areas for future research

Psychological research has gained a good understanding of how people react and cope following a spinal cord injury. But the details of this process still remain to be explored further. Specifically, research is now looking at appraisal – how people think about their spinal cord injury, and how this shapes their reactions. Threat appraisal (thinking about the injury as something that could severely threaten the person's life goals) appears to be particularly important in limiting people's ability to adjust well (Pakenham, 1999; Chandler, 2003). Research needs to look more closely at this process, with a view to investigating how threat appraisals could be targeted by psychological interventions in order to promote positive adjustment. Another important area for research into psychological treatments is to explore interventions that foster acceptance, as this appears to be beneficial for positive adjustment (Kennedy et al., 2000).

Finally, one area that requires further research is the impact of spinal cord injury on families. This has been researched more extensively in other areas of disability, such as traumatic brain injury, but the literature on spinal cord injury and families is small. Research done so far suggests that a significant minority of family members are severely affected by a relative's spinal cord injury. Further research is required to focus on the details of the appraisal and coping process in family members, including whether there are links between the coping styles of different family members, and how the family's adjustment affects the injured person. There is some evidence that better family adjustment results in a better rehabilitation outcome for the injured person (Kreuter, 2000). Further research is needed to investigate the details of this, which would underline the importance of involving and supporting family members as well as the injured person in living with spinal cord injury.

References

Alexander, C. J., Hwang, K. and Sipski, M. L. (2002). Mothers with spinal cord injuries: Impact on marital, family, and children's adjustment. *Archives of Physical Medicine and Rehabilitation*, 83, 24–30.

Boyer, B. A., Knolls, M., Kafkalas, B. and Tollen, L. (2000). What is the trauma? Mothers' and fathers' fear and helplessness related to posttraumatic aspects of paediatric SCI. *Topics in Spinal Cord Injury Rehabilitation*, 6(51), 135–147.

Chandler, M. (2003). The psychological impact on partners of people with spinal cord injuries: The role of social support, coping strategies and appraisals associated with adjustment. Unpublished doctoral dissertation, University of Oxford.

Davidoff, G. N., Roth, E. J. and Richards, J. S. (1992). Cognitive deficits in spinal cord injury: Epidemiology and outcome. *Archives of Physical Medicine and Rehabilitation*, 73, 275–284.

Duff, J. and Kennedy, P. (2003). Spinal cord injury. In S. Llewelyn and P. Kennedy (eds) *Handbook of clinical health psychology*, pp. 251–275. Chichester: John Wiley & Sons.

Elliott, T. R. and Kennedy, P. (2004). Treatment of depression following spinal cord injury: An evidence-based review. *Rehabilitation Psychology*, 49(2), 134–139.

Folkman, S. and Lazarus, R. S. (1980). An analysis of coping in a middle-aged community sample. *Journal of Health and Social Behaviour*, 21, 219–239.

Frank, R. G., Elliott, T. R., Corcoran, J. R. and Wonderlich, S. A. (1987). Depression after spinal cord injury: Is it necessary? *Clinical Psychology Review*, 7, 611–630.

Go, B. K., DeVivo, N. J. and Richards, J. S. (1995). The epidemiology of spinal cord injury. In S. L. Stover, J. L. DeLisa and G. G. Whiteneck (eds) *Spinal cord injury: Clinical outcomes from the model systems*, pp. 21–55. Gaithersburg, MD: Aspen Publishers.

Guttmann, L. (1976). *Spinal cord injuries: Comprehensive management and research* (2nd edition). Oxford: Blackwell Scientific.

Kennedy, P. and Rogers, B. (2000). Anxiety and depression after spinal cord injury: A longitudinal analysis. *Archives of Physical Medicine and Rehabilitation*, 81, 932–937.

Kennedy, P., Taylor, N. M. and Duff, J. (2005). Characteristics predicting effective outcomes after coping effectiveness training. *Journal of Clinical Psychology in Medical Settings*, 12(1), 93–98.

Kennedy, P., Duff, J., Evans, M. and Beedie, A. (2003). Coping effectiveness training reduces depression and anxiety following traumatic spinal cord injuries. *British Journal of Clinical Psychology*, 42, 41–52.

Kennedy, P., Marsh, N., Lowe, R., Grey, N., Short, E. and Rogers, B. (2000). A longitudinal analysis of psychological impact and coping strategies following spinal cord injury. *British Journal of Health Psychology*, 5, 157–172.

King, C. and Kennedy, P. (1999). Coping effectiveness training for people with spinal cord injury: Preliminary results of a controlled trial. *British Journal of Clinical Psychology*, 38, 5–14.

Krause, J. S. (1998). Changes in adjustment after spinal cord injury: A 20-year longitudinal study. *Rehabilitation Psychology*, 43(1), 41–55.

Kreuter, M. (2000). Spinal cord injury and partner relationships. *Spinal Cord*, 38, 2–6.

Kreuter, M., Sullivan, M. and Siosteen, A. (1996). Sexual adjustment and quality of relationship in spinal paraplegia: A controlled study. *Archives of Physical Medicine and Rehabilitation*, 77(6), 541–548.

Lazarus, R. S. and Folkman, S. (1984). *Stress, appraisal and coping*. New York: Springer.

North, N. T. (1999). The psychological effects of spinal cord injury: A review. *Spinal Cord*, 37, 671–679.

O'Connor, P. J. (2005). Forecasting of spinal cord injury annual case numbers in Australia. *Archives of Physical Medicine and Rehabilitation*, 86(1), 48–51.

Pakenham, K. I. (1999). Adjustment to multiple sclerosis: Application of a stress and coping model. *Health Psychology*, 18(4), 383–392.

Reidy, K. and Caplan, B. (1994). Causal factors in spinal cord injury: Patients' evolving perceptions and association with depression. *Archives of Physical Medicine and Rehabilitation*, 75, 837–842.

Reidy, K., Caplan, B. and Shawaryn, M. (1991). *Coping strategies following spinal cord injury: Accommodation to trauma and disability*. Paper presented at the 68th Annual Meeting of the American Congress of Rehabilitation Medicine, Washington, 27–31 October.

Sipski, M. and Alexander, C. J. (1992). Sexual function and dysfunction after spinal cord injury. *Physical Medicine and Rehabilitation Clinics of North America*, 3, 811–828.

Sipski, M. L. and Alexander, C. J. (1993). Sexual activities, response and satisfaction in women pre- and post-spinal cord injury. *Archives of Physical Medicine & Rehabilitation*, 74(10), 1025–1029.

Tirch, D. D. and Radnitz, C. L. (2000). Spinal cord injury. In C. L. Radnitz (ed.) *Cognitive behavior therapy for persons with disabilities*. Northvale, NJ: Jason Aronson, Inc.

Tucker, S. J. (1980). The psychology of spinal cord injury: Patient–staff interaction. *Rehabilitation Literature*, 41, 114–121.

Webster, G. and Hindson, L. M. (2004). The adaptation of children to spinal cord injury of a family member: The individual's perspective. *SCI Nursing*, 21(2), 82–87.

Weitzenkamp, D. A., Gerhart, K. A., Charlifue, S. W., Whiteneck, G. G. and Savic, G. (1997). Spouses of spinal cord injury survivors: The added impact of caregiving. *Archives of Physical Medicine and Rehabilitation*, 78, 822–827.

Woolrich, R. A, Kennedy, P. and Tasiemski, T. (2006). A preliminary psychometric evaluation of the Hospital Anxiety and Depression Scale (HADS) in 963 people living with a spinal cord injury. *Psychology, Health and Medicine*, 11(1), 80–90.

Chapter 7

Respiratory rehabilitation

*Maarten Fischer, Margreet Scharloo, John Weinman
and Ad Kaptein*

Introduction

Over the last decades, quality of life has become one of the main outcomes
by which the effectiveness of medical treatment is determined. This development recognises the multidimensional character of illness. Especially in
chronic illnesses, this multidimensional character is visible, as many patients
have to deal with the behavioural, emotional, cognitive and social consequences of their disease. Rehabilitation programmes have been designed to
address these consequences. In the field of respiratory diseases, comprehensive rehabilitation programmes (which comprise educational and pharmacological elements, breathing retraining and physical reconditioning)
have been developed since the end of the 1960s (see Petty, 1993, for a
historical review) and are now accepted by many respiratory physicians as a
beneficial treatment for patients suffering from chronic airway obstruction
(American Thoracic Society, 1999).

This chapter will focus on rehabilitation programmes for patients with
chronic obstructive pulmonary disease (COPD). The first reason for this is
that most patients who attend pulmonary rehabilitation programmes suffer
from COPD (American Thoracic Society, 1999). Consequently, most research
has been conducted on the effects of rehabilitation programmes for patients
with COPD. The second reason is that benefits of pulmonary rehabilitation
for patients with COPD and for patients with other respiratory disorders
(such as cystic fibrosis, asthma and lung cancer) appear to be comparable
(British Thoracic Society, 2001; American Thoracic Society, 1999).

This chapter will start with a description of COPD and its physical
impact, followed by a discussion of the emotional, social and psychological
consequences of COPD. The background, content and effects of respiratory
rehabilitation will be described along with a few comments with regard to
the assessment of patients' physical and psychosocial functioning and the
effects of intervention. Service and organisational aspects within the context
of respiratory rehabilitation will be reviewed and the chapter will end with
suggestions for future research.

Epidemiology and physical impact

Definition of COPD

COPD entails chronic bronchitis and emphysema. Together, these two disorders are characterised by 'expiratory airflow limitation that is not fully reversible. This limitation is usually progressive and is related to inflammatory reaction of the lungs to noxious particles or gases' (Global Initiative for Chronic Obstructive Lung Disease (GOLD), 2004). Typical of chronic bronchitis are symptoms of persistent cough and sputum production. The large airways are inflamed and swollen. Breathing problems arise mainly as a consequence of the production of large amounts of mucus by the lining of the air tubes. For a clinical diagnosis, these symptoms must last for three months during two or more years.

Patients with emphysema suffer from chronic dyspnoea, especially during physical exercise, as a result of damage to the walls of the air sacs (alveoli). This reduces the lungs' elasticity and decreases the ability to exchange oxygen and carbon dioxide. Epidemiological data (2003) indicate that most cases of COPD concern chronic bronchitis (approximately 75 per cent). Sixteen per cent of COPD patients suffer from emphysema and less than 10 per cent are diagnosed with both emphysema and chronic bronchitis (National Institutes of Health, 2003).

Prevalence

There is much variation in prevalence rates across the world, but most well-designed epidemiological studies in the Western world find a prevalence between 4 and 10 per cent among the adult population (Halbert et al., 2003). These differences may be a result of actual variations in the occurrence of COPD, different definitions of COPD, characteristics of study samples (e.g. age of participants) and the use of spirometry to confirm COPD diagnosis. American statistics indicate that in 2000 an estimated 10 million persons were clinically diagnosed with COPD. However, spirometry tests among nearly 14,000 survey participants suggested that actual COPD prevalence exceeded 24 million, indicating that COPD may be highly underdiagnosed (Mannino et al., 2002). Prevalence rates in Europe (UK, Italy, France, the Netherlands, Spain and Germany), among adults over 45 years of age, appear to vary between 6 and 8 per cent (Rennard et al., 2002).

Risk factors

Tobacco smoke is the most important risk factor for the development of COPD. Studies show that approximately 80–90 per cent of the patients with COPD have been smoking and approximately 15 per cent of all smokers will develop COPD (Halbert *et al.*, 2003). In those genetically susceptible to COPD, usually the disease will develop after smoking one pack of cigarettes (20 cigarettes) a day for 20 years (Stratelis *et al.*, 2004). More women than men have started smoking since the second half of the twentieth century. This has led to an increasing prevalence rate of COPD in women. Apart from smoking behaviour, women may be at risk of COPD because of a potentially higher susceptibility to the effects of tobacco smoke compared to men (Varkey, 2004).

Non-smokers may be at risk as a consequence of passive smoking (Jaakkola, 2002). Other environmental factors that may contribute to the onset of COPD are air pollution, cooking on biomass fuels (e.g. wood, crop residues), occupational dusts and chemicals, and infections such as HIV and tuberculosis (GOLD, 2004).

Mortality

According to the 2004 *World Health Report*, COPD is the fifth leading cause of death behind ischaemic heart disease, cardiovascular disease, lower respiratory infections and HIV/AIDS (WHO, 2004). In 2002, COPD was accountable for nearly 2.75 million deaths worldwide (261,000 in Europe). These worldwide mortality rates are more than twice as high as mortality rates resulting from lung cancer. Mortality rates resulting from COPD for men have been higher than for women in the past, but the increase in mortality has been higher for women over the last decades. In 2000, for the first time more women than men in the US died as a result of COPD (Mannino *et al.*, 2002).

Morbidity and co-morbidity

The global burden of COPD in terms of disability-adjusted life years (DALYs), as an indicator of time lived with disability and the time lost due to premature mortality, is high and steadily increasing. Future health scenarios estimate that in 2020 COPD will be one of the most prominent causes of worldwide chronic morbidity, ranking fifth after ischaemic heart disease, unipolar major depression, road traffic accidents and cerebrovascular disease (Murray and Lopez, 1997). The high burden of COPD is also apparent from a healthcare system perspective. In the US, COPD was responsible for over 13 million physician office visits in 2001 and 670,000 hospital admissions in 2002 (National Institutes of Health, 2004). In 2000, over one-and-a-half million emergency department visits for COPD were registered in the US (Mannino *et al.*, 2002).

Patients with COPD are at risk for quite a range of concomitant diseases. Van Manen and co-workers have explored the co-morbidity in patients with chronic airway obstruction (COPD and chronic asthma) older than 40 years of age, comparing them to age-matched controls without chronic airway obstruction. They found that patients with chronic airway obstruction suffer more often from ulcers, sinusitis, migraine, depression and cancer. High blood pressure and heart disease also appear to occur frequently in patients with airway obstruction, but not more often than in controls (van Manen et al., 2001).

Patients with COPD are particularly vulnerable to sleep problems. However, these problems remain largely unreported. Insomnia in COPD has many causes such as the presence of physical symptoms like sputum and cough, hypoventilation, disturbed gas exchange, and sleep deprivation caused by depression. Since many hypnotics also affect respiratory functioning, pharmacotherapy for sleep problems in patients with COPD needs to be applied with caution. Another often occurring dyssomnia is sleep apnoea. Together with hypoventilation, this may cause shortness of oxygen in the cardiovascular system and may be related to premature mortality (Kutty, 2004).

Physical impact of COPD

COPD is often diagnosed at an advanced stage. A reason for this is that patients in the first stages do not necessarily experience symptoms. One of the first symptoms is a cough, with or without sputum production. These symptoms are easily overlooked or considered not important. Dyspnoea is usually the first symptom that leads patients to consult a physician (Pauwels and Rabe, 2004). Dyspnoea is highly related to fatigue and these two are the most important symptoms experienced by patients with COPD (Meek and Lareau, 2004). In one study, nearly half of the patients with COPD stated that they had problems with fatigue every day, compared to 13 per cent of the age- and sex-matched control group. Furthermore, the fatigue lasted for more than six hours per day in 53 per cent of the patients with COPD, compared to 19 per cent of the healthy controls (Theander and Unosson, 2004).

COPD is considered to be a systemic disease, which means that its effects can be found beyond pulmonary malfunctioning. The most frequent effects are abnormal systemic inflammation, nutritional abnormalities (changes in metabolism), weight loss and skeletal muscle dysfunction (Agustí et al., 2003). Osteoporosis is also frequently found in patients with COPD. As it increases the chance of fractures, it is a secondary cause of disability and mortality in COPD patients (Ionescu and Schoon, 2003).

Review of key emotional, social and psychological impacts of COPD

Emotional impact of COPD

As COPD is a progressive disabling disease with little reversibility, it is not surprising that this disease is accompanied by a considerable psychological burden. In her review of studies about anxiety in patients with COPD, Brenes found that anxiety disorders occur more frequently in patients with COPD compared to the general population. The prevalence of generalised anxiety disorders (GAD) in patients with COPD appears to vary between 10 and 16 per cent, while prevalence of GAD in the normal population usually does not exceed 5 per cent. The occurrence of anxiety symptoms without a specific diagnosis is even higher (between 13 and 51 per cent). Panic attacks also occur often in patients with COPD. Prevalence rates of panic attacks appear to vary between 8 and 37 per cent (Brenes, 2003).

Although it is often said that COPD is a disease that is characterised by a high prevalence of depression, van Ede and colleagues, in their review of the literature, were unable to reach a definitive conclusion about the exact prevalence of depression, due to the many differences in the published studies (power/sample size, control group, screening instrument for depression and cut-off score). Ten epidemiological studies had a satisfactory methodological quality. These studies showed a large variation in prevalence rates (between 6 and 42 per cent) for depression among patients with COPD. Only two of the ten reviewed studies were able to show a significantly higher prevalence of depression in comparison to matched controls (van Ede *et al.*, 1999). It appears that living alone, physical impairment and severity of airway obstruction are risk factors for depression in patients with COPD (van Manen *et al.*, 2002). Not only do depression and anxiety have a negative effect on experienced quality of life but they also affect the patient's motivation to quit smoking. It is therefore important for healthcare providers to be aware of signs of psychological problems when smoking abstinence is advised.

The occurrence of anxiety and depression does not only affect psychological well-being, it may also be strongly related to functional limitations. It appears that disease severity, as measured by forced expiratory volume (FEV_1) is not a strong predictor of functional status (e.g. general health, role functioning, social functioning, pain and vitality). However, patients' levels of anxiety and depression (measured without somatic items) show strong associations with these indices of functional health (Kim *et al.*, 2000).

Social impact of COPD

Like many progressive chronic diseases, COPD affects patients as well as their social system. Patients' roles within their family, as a partner, parent or grandparent may change, and family members and friends may be involved in caretaking over a long period of time. Withdrawal from the labour force has its impact on the financial situation of the patient and his/her family, especially when the patient is the family's main source of income. Symptoms such as productive cough, dyspnoea and the use of supplemental oxygen may lead to embarrassment which affects patients' social interactions. In a large survey, over 60 per cent of the respondents with COPD indicated that their disease restricts them in their recreational activities and social outings (Rennard *et al.*, 2002). Scharloo and colleagues also demonstrated that patients with COPD experience more limitations in social functioning, compared to a sample of healthy citizens over 60 years of age (Scharloo *et al.*, 2000). At the same time, patients appear to be concerned that others do not take their situation seriously (Oliver, 2001). Some are anxious about speaking openly about their disease, because they anticipate the public's opinion that COPD is a self-inflicted disease. The absence of visible symptoms may create the fear of others seeing them as 'frauds', taking advantage of the situation (Nicolson and Anderson, 2003).

Although less studied, sexual activity may be hindered as a consequence of COPD. As a result of dyspnoea, cough, reduced muscle strength or anxiety, quality and/or frequency of sexual activity often decreases. In a qualitative study, nearly 70 per cent of the male patients with COPD indicated some type of sexual problem (i.e. reduced libido or erectile problems). Most partners were less satisfied with the relationship than patients. Dissatisfaction in partners appeared to be a result of communication problems (e.g. irritability on the part of the patient and continuous arguments), rather than of patients' sexual dysfunction (Ibañez *et al.*, 2001).

Psychological impact of COPD

The systemic effects of impaired oxygen exchange affect neurological and cognitive functioning. Antonelli Incalzi and colleagues found that patients with COPD, as compared to age-matched controls, showed significant impairments in immediate and delayed recall of information (i.e. short- and long term-memory), attention span and recognition. Additionally, it was demonstrated that impairments in long-term memory and overall cognitive functioning were both associated with lower medication adherence (forgetting to take prescribed medications at least twice a week) (Antonelli Incalzi *et al.*, 1997).

The psychological effects of COPD may also be apparent from patients' self-concept. Becoming dependent (e.g. on medication or the support and understanding of others) has serious consequences for the patients' self-esteem. Patients tend to gradually experience themselves as different from the person they were before, which is often accompanied by feelings of loss and distress. In addition, self-esteem may be undermined by feelings of self-blame and the sense of being a burden to others (Nicolson and Anderson, 2003).

Another important psychological concept that is seriously compromised in COPD is patients' self-efficacy (i.e. the subjective judgement of capability to perform functional activities). As a consequence of physical symptoms (mainly dyspnoea), patients' confidence to perform desired activities without experiencing breathing problems often declines (Scherer and Schmieder, 1997). Self-efficacy appears to be closely related to perceived quality of life, even when controlling for the effect of medical (pulmonary function, respiratory symptoms, duration of illness) and sociodemographic variables (age, previous occupation) (McCathie et al., 2002).

Background, content and benefits of pulmonary rehabilitation

Definition of pulmonary rehabilitation

No cure for COPD exists at this time. Therefore, increasing or maintaining quality of life is one of the most prominent goals in healthcare. According to the GOLD recommendations, pulmonary rehabilitation is one of the main non-pharmacological treatment modalities. Besides oxygen therapy and lung volume reduction surgery or lung transplantation, rehabilitation plays an important role in the management of stable COPD (GOLD, 2004).

Pulmonary rehabilitation can be described as 'a multidisciplinary program of care for patients with chronic respiratory impairment that is individually tailored and designed to optimize physical and social performance and autonomy' (American Thoracic Society, 1999: 1666). As stated by GOLD (2004), the goal of rehabilitation is to reduce symptoms, improve quality of life and increase physical and emotional participation in everyday life.

Components of rehabilitation

The emphasis on a comprehensive approach is the reason for the many components that are present in a rehabilitation programme. Physical exercise and education are core components of such a programme. Other components such as smoking cessation modules, relaxation and energy conservation exercises, cognitive-behavioural interventions and nutritional advice and support are less frequently added (British Thoracic Society, 2001). Below, the individual components in pulmonary rehabilitation are described in detail.

Physical training

The most frequently applied exercises in rehabilitation are lower and upper extremity endurance training, (respiratory) muscle strength training and breathing exercise. The endurance training includes walking or cycling and lifting weights or stretching elastic bands (American Thoracic Society, 1999). These exercises usually are performed at a percentage (>60 per cent) of the maximum capacity. Over the course of rehabilitation, duration or intensity of the exercises can be gradually increased (British Thoracic Society, 2001).

Respiratory muscle strength training aims to reverse deterioration of muscle strength, which is a cause of dyspnoea and exercise limitation. Breathing techniques, such as pursed-lip breathing and diaphragmatic breathing, aim to increase tidal volume and to reduce breathing frequency.

Education

Education in rehabilitation aims to increase patients' comprehension of the physical and psychosocial consequences of their disease. Increased knowledge is thought to facilitate patients' active participation in the management of their disease. Most rehabilitation programmes comprise an educational component. However, the content of the educational classes may vary. A classification can be made in medical/physiological topics (e.g. pathology and pharmacology, breathing techniques, nutritional advice, exacerbation management) and psychosocial or behavioural topics (e.g. smoking cessation, energy conservation, goal-setting, coping, relaxation, self-management, social and intimate relationships) (American Thoracic Society, 1999; British Thoracic Society, 2001).

Psychosocial interventions

Besides the provision of psycho-education, specific cognitive or behavioural interventions can be part of a rehabilitation programme. Different from the education component, these interventions are individually tailored depending on the patients' needs. A treatment strategy is formulated during the intake to the rehabilitation clinic on the basis of a formal assessment of psychological and social well-being. There is a wide array of interventions that are applied in the context of pulmonary rehabilitation. Frequently-used techniques are cognitive and behavioural interventions, self-management techniques (monitoring, realistic goal-setting, contracting and stimulus control), relaxation training (aimed at reducing stress and conserving energy) and coping skills training (promoting a positive and problem-focused way of handling their condition). An example of assessment and psychosocial interventions within the context of pulmonary rehabilitation is described in the following vignette.

Case vignette 7.1

Mr Jones, a widower of 64 years, has been referred to an outpatient pulmonary rehabilitation clinic by his respiratory physician. Three years ago he was diagnosed with emphysema. Complaints about fatigue and reduction in activities were the main indication for referral. Standard psychological assessment during the intake includes the Symptom Checklist (SCL-90) questionnaire, from which it became apparent that Mr Jones quite often suffers from depressive thoughts. In the intake interview with the social worker, Mr Jones explains he is, to a large extent, house-bound as a result of lack of energy. The decrease in mobility and reduction in social activities turned out to be the cause of his depressive feelings. Furthermore, he has trouble doing household chores by himself, such as cleaning and cooking. He experiences feelings of guilt and self-blame as he has been a heavy smoker. At the same time he admits he finds it hard to express these feelings to other people.

It is agreed that during the rehabilitation the clinical psychologist will have a few sessions with Mr Jones about the origins of guilt and self-blame. The aim is to educate Mr Jones about the destructive nature of these negative thoughts, as they influence his motivation and outlook. In collaboration with Mr Jones, the training staff will formulate realistic and achievable goals for the rehabilitation programme in terms of functional capacity, in order to boost his self-confidence. The social worker will apply for home-care services as well as a private parking lot near to Mr Jones' home. Group sessions on self-management are a standard element in the programme. It is expected that Mr Jones may learn how others cope with practical and psychosocial difficulties. One session specifically deals with problems and solutions in maintaining social contacts. In these sessions Mr Jones will be encouraged to express his concerns in a safe environment, but also to share his self-developed strategies for self-care.

As part of a smoking cessation intervention, Mr Jones is asked to sign a 'no-smoking contract'. Additionally, he will be assisted in his attempt with nicotine replacement therapy and counselling by the social worker during the programme. After the end of the programme, Mr Jones' family physician will continue the provision of support and counselling in relapse prevention.

Patient selection

Patients eligible for rehabilitation are those who suffer from dyspnoea, reduced exercise tolerance and/or a restriction in activities. The need for rehabilitation should be determined by the level of impairment and subjective burden rather than by physiological indices of pulmonary functioning (American Thoracic Society, 1999). This indicates that pulmonary rehabilitation programmes are not designed for one type of pulmonary disease. Donner and Lusuardi (2000) state that patients with severe deconditioning, muscle weakness and exercise intolerance are prime candidates for participation.

Rehabilitation programmes are not recommended for patients who suffer from serious co-morbidity (severe heart failure, non-respiratory cancer or neuromuscular disorders) and limited ability to learn/cognitive impairment (American Thoracic Society, 1999). The discussion about whether to include or exclude smokers is still ongoing. However, there is no evidence that smokers would not benefit. Most programmes include smokers if they are prepared to quit or follow a smoking cessation programme (American Thoracic Society, 1999; British Thoracic Society, 2001).

Setting and duration of pulmonary rehabilitation

Three different settings for rehabilitation programmes are usually distinguished. In an outpatient setting, patients visit a hospital or community centre a few (usually two to three) times a week for exercise and education sessions. When travelling is too difficult, home-based programmes may be an alternative. Physiotherapists provide patients with exercise and education in their own environment. Inpatient settings are used for patients with the most profound physical impairments who need intensive nursing and monitoring (American Thoracic Society, 1999). Outpatient programmes are usually less expensive than inpatient or home-based programmes. However, they require additional motivation and resources with regard to transport.

The optimal duration of a pulmonary rehabilitation programme is not yet determined, but most programmes take between six and twelve weeks. There is some evidence that a longer duration is associated with greater improvements in physical and psychological functioning (Rossi *et al.*, 2005).

Impact of rehabilitation on physical disabilities

Pulmonary functioning, as measured by the maximal volume of air that can be forcibly exhaled (forced vital capacity, FVC) and the maximum amount of air exhaled in one second (forced expiratory volume, FEV_1), does not improve as a result of pulmonary rehabilitation (Devine and Pearcy, 1996; Emery *et al.*, 1998). Still, in the absence of improvement of lung function, rehabilitation leads to many improvements in the functional domain. Lacasse and co-workers conducted a meta-analysis on the short-term effects of 23 pulmonary rehabilitation programmes on quality of life and exercise capacity. Their review included only randomised controlled studies comparing rehabilitation programmes (inpatient, outpatient or home-based) with conventional care. Interventions were included in the review if they consisted of exercise training with or without education or psychosocial support. Maximal exercise capacity (14 reviewed studies measuring improvements on the cycle ergometer test) and functional exercise capacity (10 reviewed studies measuring outcomes on six-minute walk distance) showed significantly greater improvement in rehabilitation groups compared to the control groups. Also, a larger decrease in feelings of fatigue and dyspnoea was found in patients who had attended rehabilitation programmes, compared to patients who had received usual care (Lacasse *et al.*, 2001). Another meta-analysis showed that pulmonary rehabilitation improved exercise endurance (time and/or distance patients are able to walk or cycle) and reduced the restrictions that patients experience in activities of daily living (Devine and Pearcy, 1996).

To date, there is no convincing evidence that disease-related aspects, such as number and severity of exacerbations and healthcare use, are affected by education or self-management programmes as a single intervention (outside the context of comprehensive pulmonary rehabilitation) (Monninkhof *et al.*, 2002).

It is also still unclear whether pulmonary rehabilitation affects survival of patients with COPD (Troosters *et al.*, 2005). However, the important effects of rehabilitation on functional status and walking ability may be related to longer survival, as these indices are stronger predictors of survival than traditional measures of disease severity, such as one-second FEV_1 or need for supplemental oxygen (Bowen *et al.*, 2000).

Impact of rehabilitation on emotional well-being

Besides positive effects on exercise capacity, comprehensive rehabilitation programmes have demonstrated beneficial effects on psychosocial well-being. Withers *et al.* (1999) showed that a six-week outpatient pulmonary rehabilitation programme, consisting of exercise training, education, psychosocial support and stress management, decreased depression and anxiety scores among patients with COPD. Moreover, at six-month follow-up these improvements were still present (Withers *et al.*, 1999). Similar improvements in depression and anxiety scores were found in patients who had completed a rehabilitation programme that comprised physical exercise, educational lectures (e.g. regarding anatomy of lungs and pathophysiology of COPD) and stress management (which included relaxation techniques and cognitive restructuring). Patients who had completed an education plus stress-management intervention without the physical exercise did not show improvements in psychological well-being, indicating the importance of exercise (Emery *et al.*, 1998). Interestingly, their results indicate that in the groups of patients who had received education without exercise, greater disease knowledge was associated with increased anxiety. The finding that a combination of education plus exercise yields positive results for well-being and emotional functioning was further supported by the meta-analysis by Devine and Pearcy (1996).

In their review of randomised controlled studies of psychosocial interventions as part of pulmonary rehabilitation, Kaptein and Dekker (2000) conclude that most of the applied psychosocial interventions consist of relaxation training. Only on a few occasions, cognitive-behavioural modification, coping training and stress management were offered. All 10 reviewed studies showed significant improvements in the psychosocial domain (e.g. self-reported quality of life, dyspnoea, well-being, reduced social disability and increased self-efficacy) (Kaptein and Dekker, 2000). The popularity of relaxation training may be explained by the fact that the techniques are easy to learn and are inexpensive to deliver (e.g. on CD or audiocassette) (Devine and Pearcy, 1996).

Atkins and colleagues (1984) tested the effectiveness of behavioural and cognitive interventions in promoting adherence to an individual exercise regimen in patients with COPD. After patients had received a personal walking programme, they were assigned to one of three intervention conditions, an attention-only condition or a no-treatment control condition. In the cognitive intervention, patients were instructed to monitor negative thoughts and feelings and were taught to replace these by positive ones in order to motivate them during exercising. The behavioural intervention consisted of several self-management techniques (keeping a daily schedule, signing a contract and self-reinforcement) as well as relaxation training and breathing exercises. A third intervention combined both behavioural and cognitive interventions. This approach enabled the researchers to determine the individual contribution of each intervention to patients' adherence, perceived self-efficacy and well-being. The results showed that adherence to exercise regimen (as measured by time spent walking) greatly improved after a combined cognitive-behavioural intervention. Furthermore, patients' self-reported quality of well-being (representing mobility, physical activity and social activity) increased in patients who had undergone a behavioural, a cognitive or a combined cognitive-behavioural intervention. Patients in an attention-only control or no-intervention condition reported a decrease in well-being scores after three months (Atkins et al., 1984).

De Godoy and de Godoy (2003) have studied the benefits of an additional cognitive psychotherapy module (addressing patients' psychosocial needs and thoughts about marriage, work, health and interpersonal relations) in a 12-week rehabilitation programme. Although the sample was very small (intervention n=14 vs. control n=16), the experimental group showed a significant reduction in anxiety (Beck Anxiety Inventory: BAI) and depression (Beck Depression Inventory: BDI) scores, which was not apparent in controls who followed the same rehabilitation programme without the psychotherapy sessions.

Kunik and colleagues (2001) designed a two-hour group therapy session for older patients with COPD. This session comprised psycho-education (the role of anxiety and depression in chronic illness), relaxation exercises and cognitive-behaviour interventions (redirecting maladaptive thoughts, and encouraging exposure to anxiety-provoking situations/reducing behaviour that maintains anxiety). Patients received a booklet with practice exercises regarding coping skills and an audiotape containing the educational material. Additionally, these patients were called weekly by the staff to provide an opportunity to ask questions and to monitor and enhance compliance with the coping skill exercises. After six weeks, anxiety and depression had been reduced, compared to patients who had been assigned to an education-only control group.

However, not all studies on psychotherapy for patients with COPD yield positive results. For instance, a pilot study consisting of six 90-minute sessions of cognitive-behavioural therapy, focusing on the origin of anxiety, the development of psychological coping styles and instruction of relaxation and distraction techniques, did not affect anxiety and depression (Hospital Anxiety and Depression Scale: HADS) or quality of life of 10 participants (St. George's Hospital Respiratory Questionnaire) (Eiser *et al.*, 1997). After three sessions, a different therapist took over the sessions, which may have reduced the potential effect of the intervention.

Blake and colleagues (1990) studied the effects of a psychosocial intervention for patients who had been referred to a pulmonary clinic. Stress reduction techniques included relaxation, breathing exercises, visual imagery and cognitive restructuring. By making a plan for increasing social and (recreational) activities with family members and friends, the intervention aimed to increase patients' perceived social support and social participation. Unfortunately, compared to the control condition, the intervention was not able to effect a significant improvement in morbidity outcomes (e.g. hospital days, restricted activity days) after six and twelve months. Psychosocial and physical functioning (Sickness Impact Profile: SIP) did not improve after six months. However, after 12 months the intervention group showed a higher physical function status than the control group (SIP). According to the authors, insufficient sample size may have been responsible for the lack of effect. Table 7.1 provides an overview of psychosocial interventions for patients with COPD.

Impact of rehabilitation on social well-being

The effects of pulmonary rehabilitation on social functioning are largely understudied. In a review by Maillé and colleagues on quality of life studies in chronic lung diseases, none of the included 43 studies from 1980 to 1994 evaluated the effects of rehabilitation on social functioning (Maillé *et al.*, 1996). One major problem is that only a limited proportion of the empirical studies have used a measurement instrument which included a specific social functioning subscale.

One study that reported effects on social functioning was conducted by Fuchs-Climent and co-workers (1999). In this study a three-week inpatient pulmonary rehabilitation programme for patients with COPD was organised. The programme consisted of health education (information about the

Table 7.1 Effect of psychosocial interventions for patients with COPD

Authors	Intervention	Results
Atkins et al., 1984	Walking regimen + behaviour modification (BM) or cognitive modification (CM) or cognitive + behaviour modification (CBM)	For all three interventions: Health status (QWB) ↑ Efficacy expectations (walking distance) ↑ Adherence (time spent walking) ↑ Exercise tolerance ↑ CBM shows more improvement than BM or CM for time spent walking
	Control groups: attention only and no intervention	Control groups: QWB ↓
Blake et al., 1990	Stress management (relaxation techniques, breathing exercises, visual imagery, cognitive restructuring), follow-up telephone contact	No improvement in morbidity, psychosocial and physical functioning after 6 months After 12 months: physical function and total function (SIP) ↑
	Control group: no intervention	Control group: no improvement
Eiser et al., 1997	Exploration of roots of anxiety. Deep breathing techniques, muscle relaxation, distraction techniques	6MWD ↑ No improvement in anxiety and depression (HADS), dyspnoea (VAS) or quality of life (SGRQ)
	Control group: no intervention	Control group: no improvement
Emery et al., 1998	Exercise (EX) + education (E) + stress management (SM)	Depression (SCL-D) ↓ Anxiety (SCL anxiety) ↓ Quality of Life (SIP) ↑ Verbal fluency (Halstead-Reitan) ↑
	Control group: E + SM	Control group: no improvement
De Godoy and de Godoy, 2003	Standard programme (physical exercise, education, relaxation techniques, breathing exercises) + psychotherapy (assessment of psychosocial needs, cognitive therapy and logotherapy)	Anxiety (BA) ↓ Depression (BDI) ↓ 6MWD ↑
	Control group: standard programme	Control group: 6MWD ↑

continues overleaf

Table 7.1 continued

Authors	Intervention	Results
Kunik *et al.*, 2001	CBT: psycho-education, skills training (relaxation, thought stopping, recognising maladaptive thoughts), exposure and practice exercises. Follow-up telephone contact	Anxiety (BAI) ↓ Depression (GDS) ↓ Mental health (SF-36) ↑ Other seven dimensions of SF-36 did not improve
	Control group: education	Control group: no improvement
Withers *et al.*, 1999	Exercise training, education, psychosocial support, stress management	Depression (HADS) ↓ Anxiety (HADS) ↓

Notes: ↓: reduction, ↑: improvement. 6MWD - Six Minute Walking Distance; GDS = Geriatric Depression Scale; SCL-A = Symptom Checklist Anxiety subscale; SCL-D = Symptom Checklist Depression subscale; SF-36 = Medical Outcomes Study, 36-item Short Form; SGRQ = St. George's Respiratory Questionnaire; QWB = Quality of Well-being; VAS = Visual Analogue Scale.

disease, discussions about healthy daily living strategies and psychosocial problems linked to the disease), respiratory therapy with aerosol and/or drainage and physical exercise. Apart from improvements in mobility, energy and emotional reactions, participants reported a decrease in feelings of social isolation (measured by the Nottingham Health Profile).

Increased physical health as a result of rehabilitation may pave the way for restoration of social functioning. However, social interactions within the programme may also be valuable for patients, especially for those who live alone. Monninkhof and colleagues conducted interviews with 20 participants in a self-management programme. These patients considered the training and education as a social activity in itself and appeared to benefit from the social support by staff and other patients (Monninkhof *et al.*, 2004). This may be of particular importance as patients often feel they are not taken seriously by their own social network.

By increasing overall activity tolerance, rehabilitation may also reduce some physical barriers to sexual activity. However, Curgian and Gronkiewicz advise that when discussing sexuality with patients it is important to explain that sexual activity will be accompanied by dyspnoea. It is important to convince patients and their partners that dyspnoea during sex is no more dangerous than in other activities (Curgian and Gronkiewicz, 1988). Furthermore, an intervention that aims to help patients and their partners adapt to the disease and reduce interpersonal conflicts may be more effective than an intervention which focuses solely on sexual problems (Ibañez *et al.*, 2001).

Impact of rehabilitation on psychological well-being

Studies on effects of exercise on cognitive processes are rather scarce, but there is some evidence that the combination of exercise, education and stress management can improve cognitive performance (verbal fluency) (Emery *et al.*, 1998, 2001).

Self-efficacy also appears to be amenable to intervention. Scherer and Schmieder were able to demonstrate improvement in patients' sense of self-efficacy in an outpatient rehabilitation programme. In addition to physical exercise and education, specific interventions with regard to self-efficacy consisted of: realistic goal-setting, observational learning (seeing how others perform a comparable task), encouragement and praise when successfully performing a specific activity and stress management (relaxation training) (Scherer and Schmieder, 1997). Similar improvements in self-efficacy were obtained as a result of cognitive and behavioural interventions in the Atkins study (Atkins *et al.*, 1984).

Commentary on psychological assessment, formulation and intervention

Assessment of physical and psychosocial functioning

According to the British Thoracic Society (2001: 827), 'the outcomes of rehabilitation should be observed with the appropriate measures of impairment, disability and handicap'. It is important to note though, that the choice of measurement instruments may affect the results that are obtained. Generic health status instruments (such as the Medical Outcomes Study 36-item Short Form (MOS SF-36), Nottingham Health Profile and Sickness Impact Profile) allow for comparison between patient groups and yield a single summary score but may be less responsive (the ability to detect improvements after intervention) than specific measures (Guyatt *et al.*, 1999).

Most widely used specific measurement instruments are the St. George's Hospital Respiratory Questionnaire (SGRQ) and the Chronic Respiratory Questionnaire (CRQ). The SGRQ has three dimensions: respiratory symptoms; activities limited by, or causing, breathlessness; and psychosocial impact on daily life. The CRQ has four subscales: dyspnoea, fatigue, emotional functioning and mastery. The CRQ focuses on limitations in activities that are important to the individual patient, whereas these items are standardised in the SGRQ. However, data comparing the responsiveness of both instruments do not clearly favour one over the other (Jones, 2001).

Assessment of patients' emotional functioning is complicated for two reasons. First, epidemiologic studies use many different measurement instruments, making a comparison between these studies very complicated.

Second, symptoms of psychopathology (e.g. sleep problems, fatigue, loss of vitality or appetite) are common in patients with COPD, but they are not necessarily related to affective disorders. It is therefore important to use an instrument that does not refer to somatic complaints (e.g. HADS) or to control for these confounding variables in the analysis of psychological problems.

Assessment of the effectiveness of psychosocial interventions

The interventions aimed to reduce psychosocial burden often comprise multiple techniques (e.g. relaxation therapy, physical exercise, stress management, education and cognitive-behavioural therapy). This makes it difficult to determine the effectiveness of each separate component. Also, most intervention studies use small samples. This decreases the power to detect significant results (Brenes, 2003). Meta-analyses are used to compare the results of several studies. However, as many programmes use different approaches to treat psychological problems and different instruments to measure improvement, meta-analyses are often not possible (Rose *et al.*, 2002).

Long-term effects of rehabilitation

Rehabilitation programmes have been able to show improvement in many aspects of quality of life. However, the usefulness of the intervention is debatable when the effects are only observable immediately after the programme. Training effects are reversible, which means that they are maintained only so long as exercise is continued. The use of post-rehabilitation supervision programmes, designed to encourage patients to adhere to the training regimen after the formal rehabilitation programme, may result in a prolonged effect of rehabilitation, as was shown by Ries and co-workers (Ries *et al.*, 1995). However, these follow-up programmes themselves have a fixed duration so their long-lasting effects have not been unequivocally demonstrated yet (Wempe and Wijkstra, 2004). In order to obtain maintenance of effect, Troosters and colleagues advise weekly strenuous exercise sessions, preferably supervised by a physiotherapist, following pulmonary rehabilitation (Troosters *et al.*, 2005).

Strijbos and colleagues have suggested that home-based rehabilitation programmes may be superior to outpatient programmes in producing long-term effects. In their study the initial improvements of outpatient rehabilitation on exercise capacity and dyspnoea had returned to baseline levels after 12 months. However, the improvements of home-based rehabilitation were still significant at 18 months. One explanation for this difference is that as patients get accustomed to exercising at home, this would make it easier for them to continue the exercise regimen after the formal rehabilitation programme (Strijbos *et al.*, 1996).

Summary and suggestions for future interventions

In an attempt to integrate the results from previous research in the field of pulmonary rehabilitation, we will end this commentary with some recommendations for the content and organisation of pulmonary rehabilitation programmes.

It is believed that the physical symptoms of fatigue and dyspnoea lead to reduced exertion tolerance and consequently a reduction in (social) activities. In turn, refraining from physical activity is thought to be responsible for an additional deterioration of exercise tolerance. This may cause the patient to enter a downward spiral. An important goal of rehabilitation is to break this vicious circle.

Rehabilitation programmes with a comprehensive approach, in our view, will produce the greatest improvement. By comprehensive, we mean that rehabilitation programmes fare best with a holistic approach, acknowledging the interaction between physical, behavioural, emotional and cognitive processes. It appears that most interventions that combine physical exercise training with psychosocial interventions produce favourable results in psychological well-being (mostly anxiety and depression). However, interventions without a physical component are not able to show such improvement (cf. Blake *et al.*, 1990; Eiser *et al.*, 1997; Emery *et al.*, 1998). Exercise training is therefore a necessary, but not sufficient, element in the attempt to optimise patients' quality of life. Psychologists, as part of a multidisciplinary team, can play an important role in the treatment of several common problems (anxiety/depression, adjustment problems, non-compliance to treatment, neuropsychological problems, social/marital problems, end-of-life decisions and conflicts between patient and healthcare provider) (Labott, 1998).

Besides being comprehensive, a programme should be individually tailored. By tailored, we mean that the programme should incorporate patients' individual goals and motivation. The available resources in a rehabilitation programme should be incorporated, depending on the goals of the individual (Sivaraman Nair, 2003). Involving patients in goal-setting during rehabilitation and adjusting the programme to individual needs may enhance compliance to treatment regimen and the sustaining of gains made.

Behavioural change, and especially maintenance, is a key factor in long-term effects. It is important to discuss motivation and possibilities for continuation at the end of a rehabilitation programme (for example at a physiotherapy practice). The transition to everyday life without the supervision and reinforcement by staff members is a critical moment and continuation of exercises appears to be very difficult for patients (Cicutto *et al.*, 2004). In our opinion, the involvement of the social network (family members, friends, other patients) during and after rehabilitation is of particular importance in the prevention of relapse.

Service and organisational aspects

Organisation of pulmonary rehabilitation

Worldwide there appear to be differences in the organisation of pulmonary rehabilitation programmes. In 1998, Kida and colleagues studied content and organisation of these programmes in North America, Europe and Japan. Pulmonary rehabilitation programmes were available at 56 per cent of the hospitals in North America and 74 per cent of the hospitals in Europe, but at only 20 per cent of the hospitals in Japan. Most rehabilitation programmes were conducted in an outpatient setting in North America (98 per cent), whereas both outpatient (55 per cent) and inpatient programmes (65 per cent) were adopted in Europe. The high cost of inpatient programmes and different healthcare insurance systems in North America and Europe may be responsible for this difference. More than 80 per cent of the patients in European and North American pulmonary rehabilitation programmes suffered from COPD. In Japan this percentage was 34 per cent. Other frequent conditions are tuberculosis (28 per cent) and bronchial asthma (16 per cent). Finally, important differences were found in the components that were incorporated in North American, European and Japanese programmes. Family education, nutritional instruction, treadmill, walking training, and increasing the activities of daily living were elements that were more often used in North American rehabilitation programmes than in European or Japanese programmes (Kida *et al.*, 1998).

Recently, Yohannes and Connolly have investigated the pulmonary rehabilitation programmes in the UK. Approximately 40 per cent of the hospitals with a physiotherapy department in the UK run a pulmonary rehabilitation programme (Yohannes and Connolly, 2004). These programmes usually have an outpatient setting. Usually patients visit the outpatient centre twice a week for a period of eight weeks, though the range in programme duration varies considerably (5–24 weeks). Besides COPD patients, asthmatic patients are frequently (in 68 per cent of the centres) included. Exercise training and education are used in more than 90 per cent of the programmes. Other frequent components are nutritional support (87 per cent), relaxation training (84 per cent) and training in activities of daily living (81 per cent). Ninety per cent of the rehabilitation centres accept smoking patients, but only half offer smoking cessation support in their programme. Interestingly, patients who participate are relatively young. Only 10 per cent of the centres report a mean age of over 70. Lack of awareness about rehabilitation among geriatricians and morbidity among older patients may explain the low proportion of older patients in rehabilitation. Overall, it is estimated that less than 1.5 per cent of the COPD population in the UK has access to pulmonary rehabilitation.

Drop-out in rehabilitation

Although the effects of rehabilitation on several components of quality of life have now been demonstrated, a substantial proportion of the eligible patients fail to enter or complete rehabilitation programmes. Only limited research has been conducted on the psychosocial factors that may contribute to non-adherence in pulmonary rehabilitation programmes. Young and co-workers investigated possible factors that contribute to non-adherence during a four-week outpatient pulmonary rehabilitation programme for moderate-to-severe COPD patients. Of the 91 participants in the study, 30 (33 per cent) did not begin the programme and six (7 per cent) did not finish the programme. Factors that were related to non-adherence were: being divorced, living alone and living in a rented accommodation. Furthermore, smokers were more likely to be non-adherent. No differences were found in terms of physiological measures (body mass index, perceived dyspnoea, FEV_1, FVC and six-minute walking distance) or psychological variables (such as depression, anxiety or a tendency to experience hyperventilation). Those who were less satisfied with disease-specific social support were also characterised by non-adherence. Perceived general social support turned out to be unrelated to adherence (Young et al., 1999).

Shenkman (1985) conducted a study to identify factors that are associated with attrition in a pulmonary rehabilitation programme. Forty patients with COPD entered a nine-week rehabilitation programme, of whom 29 patients (73 per cent) did not complete the programme. Besides a lower education and lower income, patients who dropped out reported more irritability, anxiety, helplessness/hopelessness and alienation than patients who completed the programme (Shenkman, 1985). Although more research is needed in this area, it appears that psychosocial factors have an effect on attendance and drop-out during rehabilitation above and beyond the effect of pulmonary functioning (Fischer et al., 2007). Hence, apart from the aim of reducing psychological burden, behavioural scientists may positively influence drop-out rates by treating the underlying psychosocial factors.

Key areas for future research

This chapter has outlined some of the most important issues concerning COPD and pulmonary rehabilitation. Though many areas have been covered extensively in the literature, some areas within pulmonary rehabilitation deserve further study. First, in terms of efficiency, the optimal duration of the rehabilitation programme and the desired intensity of the exercise need to be further examined. Second, future research has to demonstrate the benefits of interventions aimed to maintain the gains from rehabilitation (after-care programmes). Third, adherence and drop-out during pulmonary rehabilitation programmes need to be further investigated, in order to optimise the use of available resources and reduce chances of biased results in effectiveness studies. Fourth, most firm conclusions about the effects of rehabilitation can be drawn from meta-analyses. However, these analyses can only compare clinical trials that have used identical measurement instruments. A standardisation in the outcomes measures is therefore needed to perform such analyses. Fifth, the effect of different psychological interventions alongside a rehabilitation programme deserves further attention. Thus far, randomised controlled interventions with adequate power, investigating the relative benefits of single and combined intervention techniques have been scarce. Finally, there is a need for research on the benefits of comprehensive rehabilitation programmes for psychological and social well-being of patients with COPD. Since social performance and participation in everyday life are the ultimate goals of pulmonary rehabilitation, it is surprising how little is known about the value of rehabilitation programmes in this domain.

References

Agustí, A. G. N., Noguera, A., Sauleda, J., Sala, E., Pons, J. and Busquets, X. (2003). Systemic effects of chronic obstructive pulmonary disease. *The European Respiratory Journal*, 21, 347–360.

American Thoracic Society (1999). Pulmonary rehabilitation – 1999. *American Journal of Respiratory Critical Care and Medicine*, 159, 1666–1682.

Antonelli Incalzi, R., Gemma, A., Marra, C., Capparella, O., Fuso, L. and Carbonin, P. (1997). Verbal memory impairment in COPD: Its mechanisms and clinical relevance. *Chest*, 112, 1506–1513.

Atkins, C. J., Kaplan, R. M., Timms, R. M., Reinsch, S. and Lofback, K. (1984). Behavioral exercise programs in the management of chronic obstructive pulmonary disease. *Journal of Consulting and Clinical Psychology*, 52, 591–603.

Blake, R. L., Vandiver, T. A., Braun, S., Bertuso, D. D. and Straub, V. (1990). A randomized controlled evaluation of a psychosocial intervention in adults with chronic lung disease. *Family Medicine*, 22, 365–370.

Bowen, J. B., Votto, J. J., Thrall, R. S., Haggerty, M. C., Stockdale-Woolley, R., Bandyopadhyay, T. and ZuWallack, R. L. (2000). Functional status and survival following pulmonary rehabilitation. *Chest*, 118, 697–703.

Brenes, G. A. (2003). Anxiety and chronic obstructive pulmonary disease: Prevalence, impact, and treatment. *Psychosomatic Medicine*, 65, 963–970.

British Thoracic Society (2001). Pulmonary rehabilitation. *Thorax*, 56, 827–834.

Cicutto, L., Brooks, D. and Henderson, K. (2004). Self-care issues from the perspective of individuals with chronic obstructive pulmonary disease. *Patient Education and Counselling*, 55, 168–176.

Curgian, L. M. and Gronkiewicz, C. A. (1988). Enhancing sexual performance in COPD. *Nurse Practitioner*, 13, 34–35.

de Godoy, D. V. and de Godoy, R. F. (2003). A randomized controlled trial of the effect of psychotherapy on anxiety and depression in chronic obstructive pulmonary disease. *Archives of Physical Medicine and Rehabilitation*, 84, 1154–1157.

Devine, E. C. and Pearcy, J. (1996). Meta-analysis of the effects of psycho-educational care in adults with chronic obstructive pulmonary disease. *Patient Education and Counselling*, 29, 167–178.

Donner, C. F. and Lusuardi, M. (2000). Selection of candidates and programmes. In C. F. Donner and M. Decramer (eds) *Pulmonary rehabilitation*. European Respiratory Monograph 13, 132–142.

Eiser, N., West, C., Evans, S., Jeffers, A. and Quirk, F. (1997). Effects of psycho-therapy in moderately severe COPD: A pilot study. *The European Respiratory Journal*, 10, 1581–1584.

Emery, C. F., Schein, R. L., Hauck, E. R. and MacIntyre, N. R. (1998). Psycho-logical and cognitive outcomes of a randomized trial of exercise among patients with chronic obstructive pulmonary disease. *Health Psychology*, 17, 232–240.

Emery, C. F., Honn, V. J., Frid, D. J., Lebowitz, K. R. and Diaz, P. T. (2001). Acute effects of exercise on cognition in patients with chronic obstructive pulmonary disease. *American Journal of Respiratory Critical Care and Medicine*, 164, 1624–1627.

Fischer, M. J., Scharloo, M., Abbink, J. J., Thijs-Van Nies, A., Rudolphus, A., Snoei, L., Weinman, J. A. and Kaptein, A. A. (2007). Participation and drop-out in pulmonary rehabilitation. A qualitative analysis of the participants' perspective. *Clinical Rehabilitation*, in press.

Fuchs-Climent, D., Le Gallais, D., Varray, A., Desplan, J., Cadopi, M. and Préfaut, C. (1999). Quality of life and exercise tolerance in chronic obstructive pulmonary disease: Effects of a short and intensive inpatient rehabilitation program. *American Journal of Physical Medicine and Rehabilitation*, 78, 330–335.

GOLD (Global Initiative for Chronic Obstructive Lung Disease) (2004). *Global strategy for the diagnosis, management, and prevention of chronic obstructive pulmonary disease, executive summary*. Available from http://www.goldcopd.com/

Guyatt, G. H., Stubbing, D., Goldstein, R. S., King, D. R. and Feeny, D. H. (1999). Generic and specific measurement of health-related quality of life in a clinical trial of respiratory rehabilitation. *Journal of Clinical Epidemiology*, 52, 187–192.

Halbert, R. J., Isonaka, S., George, D. and Iqbal, A. (2003). Interpreting COPD prevalence estimates: What is the true burden of disease? *Chest*, 123, 1684–1692.

Ibañez, M., Aguilar, J. J., Maderal, M. A., Prats, E., Fårrero, E., Font, A. and Escarrabill, J. (2001). Sexuality in chronic respiratory failure: Coincidences and divergences between patient and primary caregiver. *Respiratory Medicine*, 95, 975–979.

Ionescu, A. A. and Schoon, E. (2003). Osteoporosis in chronic obstructive pul-monary disease. *The European Respiratory Journal Supplement*, 46, 64s–75s.

Jaakkola, M. S. (2002). Environmental tobacco smoke and health in the elderly. *The European Respiratory Journal*, 19, 172–181.

Jones, P. W. (2001). Health status measurement in chronic obstructive pulmonary disease. *Thorax*, 56, 880–887.

Kaptein, A. A. and Dekker, F. W. (2000). Psychosocial support. *European Respiratory Monograph*, 13, 58–69.

Kida, K., Jinno, S., Nomura, K., Yamada, K., Katsura, H. and Kudoh, S. (1998). Pulmonary rehabilitation program survey in North America, Europe, and Tokyo. *Journal of Cardiopulmonary Rehabilitation*, 18, 301–308.

Kim, H. F., Kunik, M. E., Molinari, V. A., Hillman, S. L., Lalani, S., Orengo, Petersen, N. J., Nahas, Z. and Goodnight-White, S. (2000). Functional impairment in COPD patients: The impact of anxiety and depression. *Psychosomatics*, 41, 465–471.

Kunik, M. E., Braun, U., Stanley, M. A., Wristers, K., Molinari, V., Stoebner, D. and Orengo, C. A. (2001). One session cognitive behavioural therapy for elderly patients with chronic obstructive pulmonary disease. *Psychological Medicine*, 31, 717–723.

Kutty, K. (2004). Sleep and chronic obstructive pulmonary disease. *Current Opinion in Pulmonary Medicine*, 10, 104–112.

Labott, S. M. (1998). COPD and other respiratory diseases. In P. M. Camic and S. J. Knight (eds) *Clinical handbook of health psychology: A practical guide to effective interventions* (1st edition, pp. 99–122). Seattle, WA: Hogrefe and Huber Publishers.

Lacasse, Y., Brosseau, L., Milne, S., Martin, S., Wong, E., Guyatt, G. H., Goldstein, R. S. and White, J. (2001). Pulmonary rehabilitation for chronic obstructive pulmonary disease. *Cochrane Database of Systematic Reviews*, 4.

McCathie, H. C. F., Spence, S. H. and Tate, R. L. (2002). Adjustment to chronic obstructive pulmonary disease: The importance of psychological factors. *The European Respiratory Journal*, 19, 47–53.

Maillé, A. R., Kaptein, A. A., de Haes, J. C. J. M. and Everaerd, W. Th. A. M. (1996). Assessing quality of life in chronic non-specific lung disease – a review of empirical studies published between 1980 and 1994. *Quality of Life Research*, 5, 287–301.

Mannino, D. M., Homa, D. M., Akinbami, L. J., Ford, E. S. and Redd, S. C. (2002). Chronic obstructive pulmonary disease surveillance – United States, 1971–2000. *Respiratory Care*, 47, 1184–1199.

Meek, P. M. and Lareau, S. C. (2004). Critical outcomes in pulmonary rehabilitation: Assessment and evaluation of dyspnea and fatigue. *Journal of Rehabilitation Research and Development*, 40, 13–24.

Monninkhof, E., van der Aa, M., van der Valk, P., van der Palen, J., Zielhuis, G., Koning, K. and Pieterse, M. (2004). A qualitative evaluation of a comprehensive self-management programme for COPD patients: Effectiveness from the patients' perspective. *Patient Education and Counselling*, 55, 177–184.

Monninkhof, E. M., van der Valk, P. D. L. P., van der Palen, J., Herwaarden, C. L. A., Partridge, M. R., Walters, E. H. and Zielhuis, G. A. (2002). Self-management education for chronic obstructive pulmonary disease. *Cochrane Database of Systematic Reviews*, 4.

Murray, C. J. and Lopez, A. D. (1997). Alternative projections of mortality and disability by cause 1990–2020: Global Burden of Disease Study. *Lancet*, 349, 1498–1504.

National Institutes of Health, National Heart, Lung and Blood Institute (2003).

Chronic obstructive pulmonary disease: Data fact sheet. Available from: http://www.nhlbi.nih.gov/health/public/lung/other/copd_fact.pdf

National Institutes of Health, National Heart, Lung and Blood Institute (2004). Morbidity and mortality: 2004 chartbook on cardiovascular, lung and blood diseases. Available from: http://www.nhlbi.nih.gov/resources/docs/04_chtbk.pdf

Nicolson, P. and Anderson, P. (2003). Quality of life, distress and self-esteem: A focus group study of people with chronic bronchitis. *British Journal of Health Psychology*, 8, 251–270.

Oliver, S. M. (2001). Living with failing lungs: The doctor–patient relationship. *Family Practice*, 18, 430–439.

Pauwels, R. A. and Rabe, K. F. (2004). Burden and clinical features of chronic obstructive pulmonary disease (COPD). *Lancet*, 364, 613–620.

Petty, T. L. (1993). Pulmonary rehabilitation: A personal historical perspective. In R. Casaburi and T. L. Petty (eds) *Principles and practice of pulmonary rehabilitation* (1st edition, pp. 1–8). Philadelphia: W. B. Saunders Company.

Rennard, S., Decramer, M., Calverley, P. M. A., Pride, N. B., Soriano, J. B., Vermeire, P. A. and Vestbo, J. (2002). Impact of COPD in North America and Europe in 2000: Subjects' perspective of Confronting COPD International Survey. *The European Respiratory Journal*, 20, 799–805.

Ries, A. L., Kaplan, R. M., Limberg, T. M. and Prewitt, L. M. (1995). Effects of pulmonary rehabilitation on physiologic and psychosocial outcomes in patients with chronic obstructive pulmonary disease. *Annals of Internal Medicine*, 122, 823–832.

Rose, C., Wallace, L., Dickson, R., Ayres, J., Lehman, R., Searle, Y. and Burge, P. S. (2002). The most effective psychologically-based treatments to reduce anxiety and panic in patients with chronic obstructive pulmonary disease (COPD): A systematic review. *Patient Education and Counselling*, 47, 311–318.

Rossi, G., Florini, F., Romagnoli, M., Bellantone, T., Lucic, S., Lugli, D. and Clini, E. (2005). Length and clinical effectiveness of pulmonary rehabilitation in outpatients with chronic airway obstruction. *Chest*, 127, 105–109.

Scharloo, M., Kaptein, A. A., Weinman, J. A., Willems, L. N. A. and Rooijmans, H. G. M. (2000). Physical and psychological correlates of functioning in patients with chronic obstructive pulmonary disease. *Journal of Asthma*, 37, 17–29.

Scherer, Y. K. and Schmieder, L. E. (1997). The effect of a pulmonary rehabilitation program on self-efficacy, perception of dyspnea, and physical endurance. *Heart Lung*, 26, 15–22.

Shenkman, B. (1985). Factors contributing to attrition rates in a pulmonary rehabilitation program. *Heart Lung*, 14, 53–58.

Sivaraman Nair, K. P. (2003). Life goals: The concept and its relevance to rehabilitation. *Clinical Rehabilitation*, 17, 192–202.

Stratelis, G., Jakobsson, P., Molstad, S. and Zetterstrom, O. (2004). Early detection of COPD in primary care: Screening by invitation of smokers aged 40 to 55 years. *British Journal of General Practice*, 54, 201–206.

Strijbos, J. H., Postma, D. S., van Altena, R., Gimeno, F. and Koëter, G. H. (1996). A comparison between an outpatient hospital-based pulmonary rehabilitation program and a home-care pulmonary rehabilitation program in patients with COPD: A follow-up of 18 months. *Chest*, 109, 366–372.

Theander, K. and Unosson, M. (2004). Fatigue in patients with chronic obstructive pulmonary disease. *Journal of Advanced Nursing*, 45, 172–177.

Troosters, T., Casaburi, R., Gosselink, R. and Decramer, M. (2005). Pulmonary rehabilitation in chronic obstructive pulmonary disease. *American Journal of Respiratory Critical Care and Medicine*, 172, 19–38.

van Ede, L., Yzermans, C. J. and Brouwer, H. J. (1999). Prevalence of depression in patients with chronic obstructive pulmonary disease: A systematic review. *Thorax*, 54, 688–692.

van Manen, J. G., IJzermans, C. J., van der Zee, J. S., Bindels, P. J. E., Dekker, F. W. and Schadé, E. (2002). Risk of depression in patients with chronic obstructive pulmonary disease and its determinants. *Thorax*, 57, 412–416.

van Manen, J. G., van der Zee, J. S., Bottema, B. J., Bindels, P. J., IJzermans, C. J. and Schadé, E. (2001). Prevalence of comorbidity in patients with a chronic airway obstruction and controls over the age of 40. *Journal of Clinical Epidemiology*, 54, 287–293.

Varkey, A. B. (2004). Chronic obstructive pulmonary disease in women: Exploring gender differences. *Current Opinion in Pulmonary Medicine*, 10, 98–103.

Wempe, J. B. and Wijkstra, P. J. (2004). The influence of rehabilitation on behaviour modification in COPD. *Patient Education and Counselling*, 52, 237–241.

WHO (World Health Organization) (2004). *World Health Report 2004.* Available from: http://www.who.int/whr/2004/annex/topic/en/annex_2_en.pdf

Withers, N. J., Rudkin, S. T. and White, R. J. (1999). Anxiety and depression in severe chronic obstructive pulmonary disease: The effects of pulmonary rehabilitation. *Journal of Cardiopulmonary Rehabilitation*, 19, 362–365.

Yohannes, A. M. and Connolly, M. J. (2004). Pulmonary rehabilitation programmes in the UK: A national representative survey. *Clinical Rehabilitation*, 18, 444–449.

Young, P., Dewse, M., Fergusson, W. and Kolbe, J. (1999). Respiratory rehabilitation in chronic obstructive pulmonary disease: Predictors of nonadherence. *The European Respiratory Journal*, 13, 855–859.

Chapter 8

Cardiovascular rehabilitation

Paul Bennett

This chapter examines the psychological impact of a number of outcomes of coronary heart disease (CHD), particularly focusing on myocardial infarction (MI), and how psychologically based interventions may benefit patients who experience these conditions. Each of these health problems may require a variety of medical interventions, and people who develop them may attend a variety of different rehabilitation programmes. However, all these programmes have two main goals:

- changing risk behaviours, such as smoking and low levels of exercise;
- helping people adjust emotionally to their illness and any treatment they may have.

These goals may be achieved by a variety of means: participation in an exercise programme, for example, may both improve cardiovascular fitness and reduce depression or anxiety as the individual feels they are gaining control over their illness. Likewise, changes in depression or anxiety may improve adherence to medication regimens or exercise programmes. Nevertheless, any interventions can be divided roughly into those that address behavioural change, and those that address emotional issues. Accordingly, this chapter will introduce a number of intervention approaches targeted at each outcome. The interventions discussed are not specialist interventions to be used only with a minority of patients. Rather, they can usefully be incorporated into any rehabilitation programme – and many are. Before addressing these issues, however, the chapter begins by examining the prevalence of CHD, and briefly reviews the evidence of its psychological impact on the individual.

Epidemiology

About 117,000 people die of an MI in the UK each year – a figure that equates to about one in five deaths in men and one in six deaths in women (British Heart Foundation: http://www.heartstats.org). About half the people who have an MI die within 28 days. Of those who survive the immediate period after their MI, the risk of re-infarction diminishes, but remains elevated for up to 10 years. About 9 per cent of men and 5 per cent of women aged 55–64 years, and about 14 per cent of men and 8 per cent of women aged 65–74 years, have or have had angina in the UK (http://www.heartstats.org). Based on these figures, the British Heart Foundation estimates that there are over a million men and 920,000 women living in the UK who have at least one episode of angina (www.heartstats.org). Finally, an estimated 489,000 men and 403,000 women have heart failure (www.heartstats.org), a figure based on prevalence levels of around 1 per cent of men and women aged less than 65 years, rising to 7 per cent of those aged 75–84 years and 15 per cent of those aged 85 years or more.

Impact of disease

The onset of disease seems to trigger appropriate behaviour change such as changes in diet or exercise, although some changes may be relatively short term. Hajek *et al.* (2002), for example, found that six weeks following an MI, 60 per cent of those who had previously smoked no longer did so. One year after MI, the percentage of those remaining a non-smoker fell to 37 per cent. Diet may also change in the short term, although old habits may creep back over time. Leslie *et al.* (2004), for example, found that 65 per cent of participants in their nutritional programme were eating five portions of fruit or vegetables a day at its end: a figure that fell to 31 per cent over the next year. Levels in fitness may change markedly following participation in specific exercise programmes (see, for example, Hevey *et al.*, 2003). Again, however, these changes may not be maintained in the long term. Lear *et al.* (2003), for example, reported minimal changes from baseline on measures of leisure-time exercise and treadmill performance one year following MI despite participants taking part in a rehabilitation programme.

The emotional consequences of an MI may be profound and persistent. Dickens *et al.* (2004), for example, reported that 20 per cent of MI patients became depressed in the period immediately following the infarction. A further 21 per cent became depressed over the following year. Lane *et al.* (2002) found a 31 per cent prevalence rate of elevated depression scores during hospitalisation. The 4- and 12-month prevalence rates were 38 per cent and 37 per cent respectively. The same group reported the prevalence of elevated state anxiety to be 26 per cent in hospital, 42 per cent at four-month follow-up, and 40 per cent at the end of one year. Interest in the rates of post-traumatic stress disorder as a consequence of MI has recently increased, with prevalence rates typically being around 8–10 per cent up to one year following infarction (e.g. Bennett *et al.*, 2002).

Factors associated with distress may change over time. Dickens *et al.* (2004), for example, found that predictors of depression at the time of the

MI were being young, female, having a past psychiatric history, being socially isolated, experiencing other life problems, and lacking a close confidant. Onset over the year following infarction was associated with having frequent angina. Post-traumatic stress disorder may be predicted by a number of factors, including neuroticism, the level of intrusive thoughts about the event while in hospital, and lack of social support (Bennett et al. 2002).

Each of these emotional reactions can influence important outcomes following MI. Depressed and anxious individuals are less likely to attend cardiac rehabilitation classes than those with less distress (Lane et al., 2001). Paradoxically, they are more likely to contact doctors and make and attend outpatient appointments, as well as have more readmissions (Strik et al., 2004), in the year following infarction than their less anxious counterparts. Many of these appointments will be due to worry and health concerns rather than cardiac problems. The impact of mood on health behaviour change appears to be modest. Huijbrechts et al. (1996) reported that depressed and anxious patients were less likely to have stopped smoking five months after their MI than their less distressed counterparts. Bennett et al. (1999) reported a modest association between depression and levels of exercise, but no association between depression and levels of smoking, alcohol consumption, or diet. Finally, Shemesh et al. (2004) found that high levels of post-traumatic stress disorder symptoms, but not depression, were significant predictors of non-adherence to aspirin.

Depression has consistently been associated with delayed return or failure to return to previous work and low ratings of work or social satisfaction. Soderman et al. (2003), for example, found depression to predict low levels of resumption of full-time work and reduced working hours. Delay in returning to work was predicted by greater concerns about health and low social support. Resuming work at a lower activity level than previously was associated with older age, higher health concerns, and patients' expectations of lower working capacity (independently of actual capacity).

The mechanisms through which depression and other negative emotions influence disease have not been fully investigated (although it may well be linked to increased levels of platelet aggregation and low heart rate variability that may accompany depressive states: Carney et al., 2002). However, the likelihood is that cognitive processes mediate any impact on behaviour. Petrie et al. (1996) found that attendance at cardiac rehabilitation was significantly related to a stronger belief during admission that the illness could be cured or controlled. Return to work within six weeks was significantly predicted by the perception that the illness would last a short time and have less negative consequences for the patient. Patients' belief that their heart disease would have serious consequences was significantly related to later disability in work around the house, recreational activities, and social interaction. Although the authors did not investigate it, these negative attributions and expectations are likely to be associated with depression and/or anxiety.

Another individual risk factor may be based more on personality than on mood. The Type A personality comprises high levels of easily aroused anger or hostility, time urgency, and competitiveness. The impact of this personality or behavioural pattern has proven somewhat controversial. Early studies (e.g. Rosenman *et al.*, 1975) indicated that being Type A personality significantly increased risk of infarction in healthy middle-aged men. However, a number of methodologically questionable studies on individuals who had already experienced an infarction did not replicate these early findings. As a consequence, Type A behaviours are no longer considered relevant to CHD (see Bennett and Carroll, 1990). Instead, the one dimension of easily aroused hostility is now seen as the primary pathogenic factor. Matthews *et al.* (2004), for example, found high-hostility men were 60 per cent more likely than low-hostility men to develop CHD in their sample of over 500 men followed up for a period of 16 years. Despite this change in emphasis, there is significant evidence that changes in Type A behaviour can significantly reduce risk of re-infarction (see Friedman, 1989).

The partners of patients also experience high levels of distress, often greater than that reported by the patient. Stern and Pascale (1979) found that the women at greatest risk of depression or anxiety were those married to men who denied their infarction. In this situation, partners experienced high levels of anxiety when their partner engaged in what they considered to be unsafe behaviours, such as high levels of physical exertion or continued smoking, which they are unable to control. In addition, many wives appear to inhibit angry or sexual feelings, and become overprotective of their husbands (Stewart *et al.*, 2000). Bennett and Connell (1999) found two contrasting processes to influence anxiety and depression in patients' partners. The primary causes of partner anxiety were the physical health consequences of the MI, and in particular the perceived physical limitations imposed on their partner by their MI. By contrast, the strongest predictors of partner depression were the emotional state of their spouse, the quality of the marital relationship, and the wider social support available to them.

Ways of working with patients

This section considers a number of strategies for achieving the two primary goals of rehabilitation: facilitating behavioural change and emotional adjustment. The following three approaches may be of primary benefit in facilitating behavioural change:

motivational interviewing;
educational interventions;
problem-focused counselling.

Motivational interviewing

As the evidence reviewed above suggests, not everyone is motivated to change behaviours that increase risk of disease progression, even after acute events such as an MI. This group of individuals can be particularly challenging to health professionals. More so, because what evidence there is suggests that such people are unlikely to respond to exhortations to change their behaviour, nor are they likely to benefit from interventions designed to show them how to change their behaviour. The best approach to use with such individuals is one that increases their own *intrinsic* motivation to change.

The intervention generally considered most likely to be effective for people who lack apparent motivation to change is known as motivational interviewing (Miller and Rollnick, 2002). As its name suggests, its goal is to increase an individual's motivation to consider change – not to show them how to change. If the interview succeeds in motivating change, only then can any intervention proceed to considering ways of achieving that change. Motivational interviewing is designed to help people to explore and resolve any ambivalence they may have about changing their behaviour. The approach assumes that when an individual is facing the need to change, they may have beliefs and attitudes that both support and counter change. Prior to the interview, thoughts that counter change probably predominate – or else the person would be actively making change. Nevertheless, the goal of the interview is to elicit both sets of beliefs and attitudes, and to bring them into sharp focus, perhaps for the first time: 'I know smoking does damage my health', 'I enjoy smoking', and so on. This is thought to bring the individual to a decision point, which is resolved by rejecting one set of beliefs in favour of the other. These may (or may not) favour behavioural change. If an individual decides to change their behaviour, the intervention will then focus on consideration of how to achieve change. If the individual still rejects the possibility of change, they would typically not continue in any programme of behavioural change.

The motivational interview is deliberately non-confrontational. Miller and Rollnick consider the process of motivational interviewing to be a philosophy of supporting individual change and not attempting to persuade an individual to go against their own wishes. When the intervention was first developed, it was based on exploration of two key issues:

- 'What are the good things about your present behaviour?'
- 'What are the not so good things about your present behaviour?'

The first question is important as it acknowledges that the individual is gaining something from their present behaviour and should reduce the potential for resistance and argument. This process of exploration is not

Table 8.1 Four key strategies outlined by Miller and Rollnick to increase motivation to change behaviour

Express empathy by the use of reflective listening.	This means engaging with the individual and trying to see things from their perspective rather than that of a health professional trying to encourage change. This helps develop an alliance between patient and health professional rather than a potentially adversarial relationship.
Avoid arguments by assuming the individual is responsible for the decision to change.	This removes the onus of the health professional to actively persuade. In the end, it is up to the individual whether they change their behaviour, not the health professional.
'Roll' with resistance rather than confronting or opposing it.	Again, this means avoiding arguments and attempts at direct persuasion.
Support belief in the ability to change.	If the individual is unwilling to contemplate change because they are not sure they can achieve it, then part of the conversation could usefully focus on looking for evidence of the person's ability to change and feeding this back to them, to increase their confidence in achieving change.

Source: Miller and Rollnick (2002).

simply a one-question approach. Both the questions above are leads into a wider detailed exploration of these issues. However, once the individual has considered each issue (both for and against change), they are summarised by the health professional in a way that highlights the contradiction between the two sets of issues: 'So, smoking helps you cope with stress, but it causes trouble at home because your wife doesn't want you to smoke'. Once this has been fed back to the individual, they are invited to consider how this information makes them feel. Only if they express some interest in change should the interview then go on to consider how to change. More recently, Miller and Rollnick have suggested that patients may be encouraged to consider more actively the benefits of change, and how things may be different were change achieved. Other key strategies are outlined in Table 8.1.

The motivational approach can be extremely powerful, even where people show high levels of resistance. Take the example of Mr Jones, who had continued smoking despite having had two infarctions and being told that he may require two below-the-knee amputations due to ischaemia in his lower legs if he continued smoking:

Mr Jones: I know you want me to give up smoking. The doctors have told me that I have to give up, but I'm not going to. I know it's your job, but you can't persuade me! It's the one pleasure that I have, and I'm not giving it up.

Nurse: OK . . . I'm not going to try and persuade you to stop smoking. In the end it is your choice. However, I am interested in why you smoke and why you are so firmly against changing despite all the hassle you have had from the doctors. So, what do you get out of smoking?

Mr Jones: Oh! (*looks surprised and relieved and starts talking in a much more non-confrontational manner*). Well, I've smoked all my life, ever since I was a kid really. It's difficult to give up something you've done for so long. It's part of my life. In a way, that's the main thing really – it's just part of my life. I can't see life without smoking. It helps me keep calm, and most of my mates are smokers – so it's part of my social life.

Nurse: So, it's difficult to see how to give up and how life would be without smoking . . .

Mr Jones: That's about it, really. I've tried to give up in the past and it's been really difficult. I've been back to smoking pretty quickly, so it's difficult to see myself giving up, even if I wanted to . . .

Nurse: Oh, so you've tried in the past to quit. What led you to that?

Mr Jones: Well, I know it really does make my heart bad, and I get out of breath when I smoke. So, it really makes it obvious the harm I'm doing to myself. But it's one thing to say you want to quit and another to actually do it. And I know I can't quit, so what's the point of even trying?

Note at this point that, by not challenging or actively trying to persuade Mr Jones, the conversation has shifted from his not *wanting* to give up, to not *feeling able* to give up – although because of the confrontational way this had been discussed previously, this had not been clear. So, the nurse moves from highlighting the pros and cons of behavioural change, and takes this as a cue to look at how and why things have gone wrong before, in the hope that this may lead to consideration of behavioural change.

Nurse: You say you have tried to stop smoking in the past. How did you set about this?

Mr Jones: *Well, I just tried to do it . . . What do you call it? Will power?*

Nurse: How well did that work? Not too good from what you say . . .

Mr Jones: No, not very well. I started to feel awful, sweaty, shaky, and I had to have a cigarette. And once you give in, then it's back to smoking, isn't it.

Nurse: It sounds like you were having withdrawal symptoms from the nicotine. Did you take any nicotine replacements like Nicorette or something like that?

Mr Jones: No, just tried on my own.
Nurse: That may be why you had problems. It's possible that if you
              used something to help the withdrawal then it may have been
              easier to quit.
Mr Jones: Oh right, what does that involve then?

Note here that the nurse did not try to persuade Mr Jones that he could stop smoking, but rather began to search for evidence of why things went wrong in the past. False reassurance with no basis in fact will not encourage change. Here, however, there were some clues as to why things went wrong previously and how they could be changed to increase Mr Jones's chances of successfully quitting. This was fed back to him, and he is now beginning to think about stopping smoking, despite the nurse making no attempt at active persuasion through the conversation. In fact, Mr Jones did go on to state he wanted to quit smoking, and was successful in stopping smoking using nicotine replacement therapy.

Educational interventions

Assuming individuals want to change, the issue then becomes how best to help them achieve change. Education programmes often used to be based on the assumption that if you told people what to do, they would set about doing so. However, these proved less than optimal and good education programmes now inform people both about *what* to change and *how* to change. A good example of this transition can be found in leaflets on smoking cessation available in the UK, which have shifted from a major emphasis on disease and damaged lungs to consideration of planning and implementing strategies of change.

Perhaps the best example of this approach in the context of cardiac rehabilitation and angina management can be found in the work of Lewin and colleagues (e.g. Lewin *et al.*, 1992). Their Heart Manual, which is targeted at patients who have had an MI, focuses on guiding patients through a progressive change of risk factors, including diet, exercise, and teaching relaxation techniques. Patients follow the manual at home for a period of six weeks, each week working towards a progressively targeted goal for each behaviour. Over this time, they also receive telephone calls from expert nurses to discuss their progress and any problems they are experiencing. A key principle of the intervention is that change is gradual and progressive. The most important key to stepwise approaches to behavioural change is that each stage is both 'doable' and sufficiently large to give the user a feeling that they are successfully achieving meaningful change. This increases both the user's confidence in their ability to achieve change and their motivation to keep working with a programme.

One new and potentially important educational intervention has been developed by Petrie and colleagues (Petrie *et al.*, 2002). They interviewed patients during the in-patient phase following an MI to find out their core beliefs about their illness: the factors they thought caused it, its potential consequences to their life, how curable they considered it to be, how much control they thought they had over the condition, and its likely time-line. They then corrected any misunderstandings that became evident during the interview. The benefit of this relatively novel approach is that it allows health professions to have a focused approach to assessing and addressing any inappropriate beliefs we know to affect outcome (see Petrie *et al.*, 1996).

The internet also provides a key source of information for many patients This provides both formal 'official' sites and 'unofficial' sites. One of many web-based health information sites is now provided by the American Heart Association (Yancy, 2002). Heart Profilers (http://www.americanheart.org/profilers) provides a web-based interactive tool through which patients can obtain a personalised report of 'scientifically accurate' treatment options, a list of questions to ask their doctor on their next visit (which has been shown to improve doctor–patient communication and patient satisfaction), and key information they need to participate in their treatment. Within the site, menus lead to information related to heart failure and CHD, hypertension, high cholesterol, and atrial fibrillation. How effective this type of intervention is, is difficult to assess. However, people who access health- and illness-related websites are generally more knowledgeable than those who do not. Of course, this may be the result of better-informed people being more likely to access internet sites relevant to their illness. Nevertheless, these data suggest that the Internet, and other self-help resources, may prove a valuable tool in achieving behavioural change.

Problem-focused counselling

Changing behaviours such as smoking or food choices can be difficult within the context of our complex lives. We frequently know what we should be doing, but still fail to put these intentions into action. One way to increase the chances of intentions actually leading to actions involves planning and thinking through how any desired changes can be made. One of the most frequently used approaches to this process was developed by Egan (1998). His problem-focused counselling approach involves three phases, through which the identification and change of any factors that are inhibiting behavioural change can be achieved:

- problem exploration and clarification;
- goal setting;
- facilitating action.

PROBLEM EXPLORATION AND CLARIFICATION

The goal of the first stage is to help an individual identify the problems he or she is facing that may be contributing to their problems or interfering with attempts at behavioural change. The goal of this stage is to clarify *exactly* what problems the individual is facing, and in some detail: only then can appropriate problem-solving strategies be applied. The most obvious way of eliciting this type of information is to ask direct questions. Egan also suggests the use of prompts and probes requesting information. A further method of encouraging problem exploration is through the use of what Egan termed 'empathic feedback': 'So, you are telling me that you felt very lonely when your partner refused to talk about . . .'

GOAL SETTING

Once particular problems have been identified, some people may feel they are able to deal with them and need no further help in making appropriate changes. Others may need further support in determining what they want to change and how to change it. The first stage in this process is to help them to decide the goals they wish to achieve, and to frame their goals in specific rather than general terms (e.g. 'I will try to relax more' versus 'I will take 20 minutes out each day to practise some yoga'). If the final goal seems too difficult to achieve in one step, the identification of sub-goals working towards the final goal should be encouraged.

Some goals may be apparent following the problem exploration phase. However, should this not be the case, Egan identified a series of strategies designed to help the patient identify and set goals. One of the most important is to encourage them to explore new perspectives – to think about new ways of doing things. At this stage, direct challenges or advice giving ('Well, why don't you take some time out each day to relax?') may result in resistance or feelings of defeat. The individual should be encouraged to explore their own solutions rather than them being provided by the health professional.

FACILITATING ACTION

Once goals have been established, some people may need no further support in achieving them. However, some people may not be able to plan how they could achieve any goals they wish to achieve. Accordingly, the final stage is to plan ways of achieving the identified goals. It can be helpful to work towards relatively easy goals at the beginning of any attempt at change, before working towards more difficult-to-change goals as the individual gains skills or confidence in their ability to change.

The following vignette provides an example of problem-focused counselling and how the appropriate assessment of a problem can ensure that any attempts at change are successful.

Case vignette 8.1

Following an infarction at a relatively early age, Mrs T was found to be obese and to have a raised serum cholesterol level. After seeing a dietician, she agreed to lose 2 lbs a week over the following months. She was given a leaflet providing information about the fat and calorific content of a variety of foods and a leaflet describing a number of 'healthy' recipes.

On her follow-up visits, her cholesterol level and weight remained unchanged. So, the dietician changed her tactics and began to explore why Mrs T had not made use of the advice she had been given. Mrs T explained that she already knew which were 'healthy' and 'unhealthy' foods. Indeed, she had been on many diets before – without much success. They then began to explore why this was the case. At this point, the key problem became apparent.

Mrs T's husband supported her attempts to lose weight, and was prepared to change his diet to help her. However, her sons often demanded meals late at night when they got back from the pub, often the worse for drink. As a consequence, Mrs T often started to cook late at night at the end of what may have been a successful day of dieting. She then nibbled high-calorie food while cooking. This had two outcomes. First, she increased her calorie input. Second, she sometimes catastrophised ('I've eaten so much, I may as well abandon my diet for today') and ate a full meal at this time. It also reduced her motivation to follow her diet the following day.

Once this specific problem had been identified, Mrs T set a goal of not cooking late-night fry-ups for her sons. She decided that if her sons wanted a fry-up they could cook it themselves. Once the goal was established, Mrs T felt a little concerned about how her sons would react to her no longer cooking for them. So, she and the counsellor explored ways in which she could set about telling them – and sticking to her resolution. She finally decided she would tell them in the coming week, explaining why she felt she could no longer cook for them at that time of night. She even rehearsed how she would say it. This she did, with some effect, as she did start to lose weight.

If nothing else, this vignette shows the danger of making implicit assumptions about what is preventing change (in this case, the dietician assumed it was lack of knowledge about healthy foodstuffs). Time spent assessing the precise cause of any problems an individual is experiencing is time well spent, and ensures that the rest of any intervention is focusing on appropriate issues.

Emotional adjustment

While any negative emotional outcome following the onset of disease is worthy of treatment in itself, the adverse impact that emotional distress can have on rehabilitation or even the prognosis of CHD should make the treatment of such problems key to any rehabilitation programme. This section introduces one well-known approach to reducing emotional distress, and one that is perhaps less well-known:

- cognitive-behavioural interventions;
- written emotional expression.

Cognitive-behavioural interventions

Cognitive-behavioural interventions assume that emotional distress results not just from the things that happen to us, but how we interpret them. They consider distress often to involve misinterpretations of events or exaggerations of the negative elements within them, and a loss of focus on any positive aspects of the situation. The most basic cognitive intervention is to identify such distorted thinking, and to help the individual look at the situation from a different perspective. See, for example, in the dialogue below, how Tom exaggerates the negative consequences of his MI and how the nurse encourages him to consider other ways of looking at the situation:

Tom: Well, that's it . . . I've had a heart attack . . . and I know I'll lose my job now. . . and what's going to happen about money. I can see we're going to have to sell the house, or at least the cars . . .

Nurse: That's a lot of things to be worrying about . . . Tell me, why do you think you'll lose your job?

Tom: Well, heart attacks are bad news, aren't they. Most people have to stop work when they have one, don't they?

Nurse: Some people do – but most people can go back to work. Having a heart attack doesn't have to disable you and stop you working . . . Most people get back to the same or a similar lifestyle to the one they had before their heart attack . . . What sort of job do you have?

Tom: I'm a manager in a large marketing company.

Nurse: So, your job is not very physically demanding . . . it doesn't put a lot of strain on the heart. So, going back to work isn't going to be difficult from a physical point of view.

Tom: No, I guess not . . .

Nurse: I wonder . . . you must have known a number of people who have had a serious illness in your line of work. How does the company treat them? Do they have to leave?

Tom: In some ways that would be crazy, if they are a good worker and can still work, the company would keep them on.

Nurse: So as far as you know, the company tries to keep people on even if they are ill.

Tom: So there's no real need for the company to have a problem with me?

Nurse: Perhaps not . . .

Tom: So, things might not be that bad after all . . . wow, I feel better after thinking that through . . .

Here, Tom is encouraged to rethink some of the assumptions he has made about the company's response to his illness and not simply to accept them as true. Note that the nurse did not try to reassure him directly, but gave him some relevant information and then encouraged him to look for evidence to challenge his own assumptions – a much more powerful procedure. In a more formal cognitive-behavioural programme, the health professional may talk through any inappropriate assumptions that the individual may make and teach them to challenge them as they occur in real life. The educational approach of Petrie and colleagues (2002) described above also adopts this type of approach in a formal and systematic manner, identifying the types of beliefs that are likely to affect how engaged an individual is in any rehabilitation programme and providing evidence to challenge them.

RELAXATION TRAINING

A second approach – usually used in stress management programmes – involves teaching relaxation skills. The goal of teaching relaxation skills is to enable the individual to relax as much as is possible and appropriate, both throughout the day and at times of particular stress. This contrasts with procedures such as meditation, which provide a period of deep relaxation and 'time out', as sufficient in themselves. Relaxation skills are best learned through three phases:

- learning basic relaxation skills;
- monitoring tension in daily life;
- using relaxation at times of stress.

The first stage of learning relaxation skills is to practise them under optimal conditions where there are no distractions and it is relatively easy to relax. Ideally, an experienced practitioner should lead the patient through the relaxation process. This can then be added to by continued practice at home, typically using taped instructions. The relaxation process most commonly taught is based on Jacobson's deep muscle relaxation technique. This involves alternately tensing and relaxing muscle groups throughout the body in an ordered sequence. Over time, the emphasis of practice shifts towards relaxation without prior tension, or relaxing specific muscle groups while using others, to mimic use of relaxation in the 'real world'.

At the same time as practising relaxation skills, individuals can begin to monitor their levels of physical tension throughout the day. Initially, this serves as a learning process, helping them to identify how tense they are at particular times of the day and the triggers of any excessive tension. Such monitoring may also help identify future triggers to stress, and provide clues as to when the use of relaxation procedures may be particularly useful. After a period of learning relaxation techniques and monitoring tension, individuals can begin to integrate relaxation into their daily lives. At this stage, relaxation involves reducing tension to appropriate levels while engaging in everyday activities. Initially this may involve trying to keep as relaxed as possible and appropriate at times of relatively low stress and then, as the individual becomes more skilled, using relaxation at times of increasing stress. The goal of relaxation at these times is not to escape from the cause of stress, but to remain as relaxed as possible while dealing with the particular stressor. An alternative strategy involves relaxing at regular intervals (such as coffee breaks) throughout the day.

Written emotional expression

Perhaps the most unexpected therapeutic approach now being developed for people with physical health problems is variously termed narrative or written emotional expression. The work stems from findings of Pennebaker in the 1980s (see Esterling et al., 1999) of the beneficial psychological effects of a writing task in which participants wrote about an event or issue from the past that had caused them upset or distress in a way that explored their emotional reaction to that event. Participants would typically write about the event for about 15–20 minutes on three or four consecutive days. Typical instructions for this exercise were:

1   Find a place where you will not be disturbed. If you don't want to write, you can talk into a tape recorder.
2   Plan on your writing for a minimum of three days and a minimum of 15 minutes a day. The only rule is that you write continuously. If you run out of things to say, simply repeat what you have already written.

3   Really let go and write about your very deepest thoughts and feelings
      about X. How does X relate to other parts of your life? For example,
      how does it tie into issues associated with your childhood, your
      relationship with your family and friends, and the life you have now.
      How might it be related to your future, your past, or who you are now?
      Why are you feeling the way you are and what other issues are being
      brought up by this?

4   You can write about the same general topic every day or a different one
      each day. Don't worry about spelling or grammar. Your writing is for
      you and you alone. Many people throw away their writing samples as
      soon as they are finished. Others keep them and even edit them.

5   Be your own experimenter. Try writing in different ways. If you find
      that you are getting too upset in your writing, then back off and change
      directions. Your goal here is to better understand your thoughts and
      feelings associated with X. See which approach to writing works best
      for you.

Alternative instructions may ask users to write about a particular issue,
such as their emotional response to specific traumas such as an MI. The
outcome of this type of intervention, although very simple, appears to be
very powerful, with a number of papers reporting both emotional and
physical benefits following its use.

Future research

Many of the approaches discussed in this chapter have been used in a variety
of settings, and shown to be of benefit in a variety of patient populations
(see, for example, Bennett, 2004). Some have been shown to be of specific
benefit to cardiac patients. Black *et al.* (1998), for example, have shown a
cognitive-behavioural approach to be of benefit to depressed cardiac
patients. Oldenburg *et al.* (1989) reported a programme in which cardiac
rehabilitation patients were encouraged to problem-solve and think through
how they could implement relevant behavioural change within their life
context. This proved superior to a programme that provided educational
materials only. The Heart Manual has been shown to reduce distress among
patient groups (e.g. Lacey *et al.*, 2004) – although its impact on behaviour is
less well documented. Motivational interviewing techniques have been
shown to be effective in diet and exercise programmes, although not so
effective among smokers (Burke *et al.*, 2003). However, there is surprisingly
little evidence of the effectiveness of many of the interventions in cardiac
populations, and no real evidence of which is the best approach to follow,
nor do we know what sort of person will benefit most from the different
intervention approaches. While their use is supported from research in other

patient populations, much remains to be researched in the context of cardiac rehabilitation programmes.

References

Bennett, P. (2004). Psychological interventions in secondary care. In A. Kaptein and J. Weinman (eds) *Introduction to health psychology*. Oxford: Blackwell.

Bennett, P. and Carroll, D. (1990). Type A behaviours and heart disease: Epidemiological and experimental foundations. *Behavioural Neurology*, 3, 261–277.

Bennett, P. and Connell, H. (1999). Dyadic responses to myocardial infarction. *Psychology, Health & Medicine*, 4, 45–55.

Bennett, P., Owen, R., Koutsakis, S. and Bisson, J. (2002). Personality, social context, and cognitive predictors of post-traumatic stress disorder in myocardial infarction patients. *Psychology and Health*, 17, 489–500.

Bennett, P., Mayfield, T., Norman, P., Lowe, R. and Morgan, M. (1999). Affective and social cognitive predictors of behavioural change following myocardial infarction. *British Journal of Health Psychology*, 4, 247–256.

Black, J. L., Allison, T. G., Williams, D. E., Rummans, T. A. and Gau, G. T. (1998). Effect of intervention for psychological distress on rehospitalization rates in cardiac rehabilitation patients. *Psychosomatics*, 39, 134–143.

Burke, B. L., Arkowitz, H. and Menchola, M. (2003). The efficacy of motivational interviewing: A meta-analysis of controlled clinical trials. *Journal of Consulting and Clinical Psychology*, 71, 843–861.

Carney, R. M., Freedland, K. E., Miller, G. E. and Jaffe, A. S. (2002). Depression as a risk factor for cardiac mortality and morbidity: A review of potential mechanisms. *Journal of Psychosomatic Research*, 53, 897–902.

Dickens, C. M., Percival, C., McGowan, L., Douglas, J., Tomenson, B., Cotter, L., Heagerty, A. and Creed, F. H. (2004). The risk factors for depression in first myocardial infarction patients. *Psychological Medicine*, 34, 1083–1092.

Egan, G. (1998). *The skilled helper: Models, skills, and methods for effective helping*. Monterey, CA: Brooks Cole.

Esterling, B. A., L'Abate, L., Murray, E. J. and Pennebaker, J. (1999). Empirical foundations for writing in prevention and psychotherapy: Mental and physical health outcomes. *Clinical Psychology Review*, 19, 79–96.

Friedman, M. (1989). Type A behavior: Its diagnosis, cardiovascular relation and the effect of its modification on recurrence of coronary artery disease. *American Journal of Cardiology*, 64, 12C–19C.

Hajek, P., Taylor, T. Z. and Mills, P. (2002). Brief intervention during hospital admission to help patients to give up smoking after myocardial infarction and bypass surgery: Randomised controlled trial. *British Medical Journal*, 324, 87–89.

Hevey, D., Brown, A., Cahill, A., Newton, H., Kierns, M. and Horgan, J. H. (2003). Four-week multidisciplinary cardiac rehabilitation produces similar improvements in exercise capacity and quality of life to a 10-week program. *Journal of Cardiopulmonary Rehabilitation*, 23, 17–21.

Huijbrechts, I. P., Duivenvoorden, H. J. and Deckers, J. W. (1996). Modification of smoking habits five months after myocardial infarction: Relationship with personality characteristics. *Journal of Psychosomatic Research*, 40, 369–378.

Lacey, E. A., Musgrave, R. J., Freeman, J. V., Tod, A. M. and Scott, P. (2004). Psychological morbidity after myocardial infarction in an area of deprivation in the UK: Evaluation of a self-help package. *European Journal of Cardiovascular Nursing*, 3, 219–224.

Lane, D., Carroll, D., Ring, C., Beevers, D. G. and Lip, G. Y. (2001). Predictors of attendance at cardiac rehabilitation after myocardial infarction. *Journal of Psychosomatic Research*, 51, 497–501.

Lane, D., Carroll, D., Ring, C., Beevers, D. G. and Lip, G. Y. (2002). The prevalence and persistence of depression and anxiety following myocardial infarction. *British Journal Health Psychology*, 7, 11–21.

Lear, S. A., Ignaszewski, A., Linden, W., Brozic, A., Kiess, M., Spinelli, J. J., Pritchard, P. H. and Frohlich, J. J. (2003). The Extensive Lifestyle Management Intervention (ELMI) following cardiac rehabilitation trial. *European Heart Journal*, 24, 1920–1927.

Leslie, W. S., Hankey, C. R., Matthews, D., Currall, J. E., and Lean, M. E. (2004). A transferable programme of nutritional counselling for rehabilitation following myocardial infarction: A randomised controlled study. *European Journal of Clinical Nutrition*, 58, 778–786.

Lewin, B., Robertson, I. H., Irving, J. B. and Campbell, M. (1992). Effects of self-help post-myocardial-infarction rehabilitation on psychological adjustment and use of health services. *Lancet*, 339, 1036–1040.

Matthews, K. A., Gump, B. B., Harris, K. F., Haney, T. L. and Barefoot, J. C. (2004). Hostile behaviors predict cardiovascular mortality among men enrolled in the Multiple Risk Factor Intervention Trial. *Circulation*, 109, 66–70.

Miller, W. and Rollnick, S. (2002). *Motivational interviewing: Preparing people to change addictive behaviour.* New York: Guilford Press.

Oldenburg, B., Allam, R. and Fastier, G. (1989). The role of behavioral and educational interventions in the secondary prevention of heart disease. *Clinical and Abnormal Psychology*, 27, 429–438.

Petrie, K. J., Weinman, J., Sharpe, N. and Buckley, J. (1996). Role of patients' view of their illness in predicting return to work and functioning after myocardial infarction: Longitudinal study. *British Medical Journal*, 312, 1191–1194.

Petrie, K. J., Cameron, L. D., Ellis, C. J., Buick, D. and Weinman, J. (2002). Changing illness perceptions after myocardial infarction: An early intervention randomized controlled trial. *Psychosomatic Medicine*, 64, 580–586.

Rosenman, R. H., Brand, R. J., Jenkins, D., Friedman, M., Straus, R. and Wurm, M. (1975). Coronary heart disease in Western Collaborative Group Study: Final follow-up experience of 8 1/2 years. *Journal of the American Medical Association*, 233, 872–877.

Shemesh, E., Yehuda, R., Milo, O., Dinur, I., Rudnick, A., Vered, Z. and Cotter, G. (2004). Posttraumatic stress, nonadherence, and adverse outcome in survivors of a myocardial infarction. *Psychosomatic Medicine*, 66, 521–526.

Soderman, E., Lisspers, J. and Sundin, O. (2003). Depression as a predictor of return to work in patients with coronary artery disease. *Social Science and Medicine*, 56, 193–202.

Stern, M. J. and Pascale, L. (1979). Psychosocial adaption postmyocardial infarction: the spouses' dilemma. *Journal of Psychosomatic Research*, 23, 83–87.

Stewart, M., Davidson, K., Meade, D., Hirth, A. and Makrides, L. (2000).

Myocardial infarction: Survivors' and spouses' stress, coping, and support. *Journal of Advanced Nursing*, 31, 1351–1360.

Strik, J. J., Lousberg, R., Cheriex, E. C. and Honig, A. (2004). One year cumulative incidence of depression following myocardial infarction and impact on cardiac outcome. *Journal of Psychosomatic Research*, 56, 59–66.

Yancy, C. (2002). Online program aids heart patients and their doctors. *Circulation*, 106, 2299.

Chapter 9

Primary care and rehabilitation

Robert G. Frank and Andrea M. Lee

Overview

Primary care is gaining currency internationally as the most effective treatment delivery system. There are parallels between the complex care needs of individuals with chronic or disabling conditions and treatment systems providing primary care including the need for comprehensive, continuous care. This chapter examines the intersections between primary care and rehabilitation and the opportunities for psychologists in these systems. Specifically, we examine if rehabilitation can be considered a version of primary care. Primary care is viewed as less expensive than specialty care systems such as the myriad of services involved in rehabilitation. A challenge for rehabilitation primary care models that do not reduce levels of care, is justifying costs. Most often, higher levels of care are justified by arguing that the higher cost is offset by better outcomes. In other words, improved quality of care or avoiding unnecessary treatment reduces secondary problems (such as depression associated with illness). Psychologists have a long history of invoking cost offsets to justify psychological care. In this chapter, rehabilitation primary care systems are considered as potential cost offset targets. Cost offsets are examined to understand if that model can be applied to rehabilitation primary care models and the implications for psychologists.

Primary care

Primary care has been defined by the Institute of Medicine as the 'provision of integrated, accessible health care services by clinicians who are accountable for addressing a large majority of personal health needs, developing a sustainable partnership with patients, and practicing in the context of the family and community' (Donaldson *et al.*, 1994: 15).

Primary care serves as the entry point for the provision of health services to patients. Termed 'first contact care', this function is thought to reduce morbidity and mortality (Frank *et al.*, 2004a). Effective primary care leads participants to have fewer hospital days and lessens excessive use of emergency care services and specialty care (Hurley *et al.*, 1989; Moore, 1979).

Primary care emphasizes continuous care in which the primary care provider (PCP) routinely follows the patient for prevention and acute care. Continuous care allows integration of prevention into routine care. Individuals receiving continuous care have fewer hospitalizations and fewer operations (Rakel, 2002). Children receiving continuous care are more likely to receive routine immunizations, more likely to keep clinic appointments, and are more likely to take prescribed antibiotics (Becker *et al.*, 1974).

Effective primary care is comprehensive, integrating multiple disciplines. Health care systems delivering primary care are able to manage a broad array of conditions without referral to specialties outside the primary care system. Primary care providers are willing to admit, and manage, a broad array of patients in hospital settings, nursing homes, and at home. Referrals are inversely related to the comprehensiveness of a primary care setting (IOM, 2001; Bray *et al.*, 2004).

Other characteristics of comprehensive primary care are the provision of preventive care and the assessment of lifestyle issues upon health outcomes. Primary care is characterized by personalized care, coordinated by the PCP. The PCP is viewed by the patient as the manager of their health care and this expectation is appropriate. Three medical disciplines – family medicine, internal medicine, and general pediatrics – are routinely recognized as primary care specialties. Increasingly, obstetrician-gynecologists and nurse practitioners are also viewed as primary care practitioners.

Primary care providers are the first contact provider in the health care system. As the entry point for health care, PCPs encounter undifferentiated symptoms, such as chest pain, fatigue, dizziness, headache, back pain, insomnia or abdominal pain, most of which do not reflect underlying disorders (Kroenke and Mangelsdorff, 1989; Blount, 2003). Only 25 per cent of presenting symptoms reflect underlying biological causes.

Effective integration in primary care is distinguished by coordinated services, despite different physical locations, or the integration of services provided at the same location. Integrated care emphasizes treatment outcomes including medical and behavioral elements. Especially important is the integration of psychological or mental health treatment. Indeed, Blount (2003) argued that the integration of behavioral health services into medical settings characterizes primary care. Increased efficacy has been found in integrated practices. Practices that are integrated through co-location or coordinated care demonstrate improved access to mental health services, increased patient satisfaction with medical services, improved medical provider satisfaction, improved compliance, and clinical outcomes (Blount, 2003).

Psychology and primary care

Bray and colleagues (2004) have argued that although psychologists are not prepared to assess blood pressure or treat many other physical symptoms, they are prepared to assess and treat common behavioral problems and to provide behavioral interventions for psychological aspects of illness. Psychologists are critical to the assessment, prevention, and treatment of behavioral aspects of many chronic illnesses such as diabetes, hypertension, and chronic pain syndromes (see Bray *et al.*, 2004, for more detailed description).

Bray and colleagues (2004: 8) stated that 'psychologists are able to provide primary care behavioral health services and to diagnose or manage a number of health problems seen in primary care settings'. They went on to define primary care psychology as:

> the provision of health and mental health services that includes the prevention of disease and the promotion of healthy behaviors in individuals, families and communities . . . Primary care psychologists are experts in: (a) assessment and evaluation of common psychosocial symptoms, signs and problems that are seen in primary care patients; (b) psychosocial management of acute and chronic health and illness conditions with which primary care patients often present; (c) collaboration with other PCPs and primary care teams; and (d) identifying appropriate experts for referral and collaboration. Primary care psychologists have a basic understanding of common biomedical conditions seen within primary care, the medical and pharmacological treatments of those conditions, and how they interact and affect the psychosocial functioning of patients and their families and communities.
>
> (Bray *et al.*, 2004: 8)

The evolution of primary care

Since the 1960s, the number of generalist physicians has declined. Between 1960 and 1992, the number of generalist physicians declined from approximately half of all physicians to only one-third of all physicians (Phelps and Reed, 2004). As concerns regarding escalating costs in health care rose in the 1990s (Bingaman *et al.*, 1993), primary care systems were increasingly viewed as an alternative to higher cost specialty care (Frank, 1997a; Starfield, 1997). Health care delivered by individuals trained in highly specialized disciplines tends to utilize high technology, episode-based care provided by many specialists, each representing a different organ system (IOM, 1994). The combination of specialized care focusing on narrower problems and the higher utilization of technology in specialty practice creates higher costs in that model of health services delivery. Primary care, emphasizing first-contact, continuous care has been viewed as an alternative to specialty care that divides patients by organ systems. In addition to providing more coordinated care, primary care is less expensive than specialty care (Starfield, 1997).

The movement to utilize primary care providers as 'gatekeepers' for the health care system did not go unnoticed by specialty groups. In *Physical Medicine and Rehabilitation* (PM&R), several physician leaders encouraged examination of the discipline as a primary care provider for individuals with disability. As early as 1973, Justus Lehmann noted that physiatrists should prepare to assume full responsibility as primary care physicians for individuals with disabling conditions (Lehmann, 1974). This call was reiterated by Martin Grabois in 1996. Grabois called for the reorganization of PM&R as a 'primary care or principal care specialty for individuals with disability' (Grabois, 1996: 218).

Several rehabilitation programs heeded the urgings to create models of rehabilitation primary care. Each of these efforts utilized variations of traditional rehabilitation practices to provide coordinated, continuous, first-contact care for individuals with disabling conditions. In Boston, USA, the Urban Medical Group developed a program serving home-bound individuals with disability using support from a physician located in a central office (Buschbacher et al., 1996). Medicare and Medicaid created a capitated model of reimbursement for the frail elderly at An Loc in San Francisco. Rancho Los Amigos offers a primary care outpatient clinic. In Northwest Wisconsin, the Quick Program was developed to offer a variation of primary care in the form of a transdisciplinary outpatient program. This program provides outpatient services to individuals with two or more functional impairments. The program did not offer true primary care, but did demonstrate the effectiveness of a physiatrist-led team approach to integrated care (Buschbacher et al., 1996).

During the 1990s the Rehabilitation Institute of Michigan (RIM) offered primary care for individuals with disability in conjunction with the state of Michigan. The RIM Program recognized that individuals with disability have limited access to primary care because of limited opportunities for transportation, limited accessibility, and limited knowledge of disabling conditions among providers. The program also recognized that effective preventive services can prevent the exacerbation of many existing conditions in individuals with disability (Gans et al., 1993). The RIM program utilized a collaborative team approach to provide primary care services to individuals with disability. Each patient was seen by a physiatrist and internist upon entry into the program. Ongoing care was provided by either physician alone, or together. Team case management was provided by the physiatrist. The internist managed most medical care. Twenty-four-hour call and specialty consultation were available. Weekly conferences were held to review patient progress. Treatment protocols for common disorders such as seizures in brain injury were developed (Buschbacher et al., 1996).

Buschbacher *et al.* (1996) note that a variety of factors suggest the need for a unique form of primary care serving individuals with disability. First, primary care practitioners trained in traditional programs cannot meet the complex needs of individuals with disabling conditions or multiple co-morbities. It is unlikely that traditional primary care training programs will increase their emphasis upon complex disabling conditions, as the number of individuals afflicted are relatively small. The demand for traditional primary care, combined with the fact that individuals with disability have more difficulty accessing care, means traditional primary care programs are not likely to see more individuals with disability. Transportation opportunities for individuals with disability are limited; and once the individual arrives for care, many treatment facilities have poor egress. Individuals with disability often present higher risk of greater impairment and poorer outcomes; the margin of health and illness is narrower. Because rehabilitation teams often provide the vast majority of care for individuals with conditions such as brain injury, spinal cord injury or spinal bifida, it is reasonable to assume that primary care rehabilitation models, or variations on that theme, can be developed to serve the primary care needs of individuals with other chronic or disabling conditions.

Chronic illness

Chronic health conditions and disabling conditions account for the majority of health care spending in the United States and other countries. Chronic health conditions include chronic diseases and impairments (Hoffman *et al.*, 1996; Frank *et al.*, 2004b). In the United States, almost one-third of the population, 100 million individuals, are affected by chronic health conditions (Hoffman *et al.*, 1996). Chronic health conditions create increasing disability through recurrent episodes incurring high cost, lost work days and risk of long-term disability.

Management of chronic health conditions requires unique systems that are rarely created in today's health care delivery systems. As in rehabilitation settings, the effective management of chronic health conditions requires a paradigm of health care services that emphasizes the shift from patient to consumer of health services. Effective consumers require knowledge of the market and mechanisms allowing them to effectively select and utilize services. This new model of services must focus on knowledge and partnership with the consumer as a way of increasing access to health services.

Chronic conditions in children have been treated differently to chronic conditions in adults. Children with special health care needs are defined as 'those who have chronic physical, developmental, behavioral, or emotional problems and who require health and related services beyond that required by children generally' (McPherson *et al.*, 1998: 138). Children with special health care needs require a continuum of health care services, including pediatric rehabilitation services combined with other acute services and interdisciplinary treatment of these children (Farmer *et al.*, 2003). In the United States, children with special health needs disproportionately utilize health services. Approximately 10 per cent of all children account for 70 per cent of health care expenditures (Newacheck, 1990).

Traditional models of health care for children with special health care needs have relied, as in the case of adults, upon the biomedical model. These programs have been anchored by systems focusing upon acute care issues using hospital care. Since the 1990s, services for children with special health care needs have expanded to emphasize community-based services that are family centered, designed to meet the medical, educational, social, and emotional needs (Farmer *et al.*, 2003) of the child. This paradigm emphasizes wellness instead of illness. The child and family utilizing services transition from being 'patients' to educated consumers/partners in the treatment regime.

In most health care systems, the most common form of health care delivery systems for children is fragmented, uncoordinated care provided by various state and local agencies. These services can be broadly categorized as personal medical services, community health services, and health-related support services (Shi and Singh, 2001). The personal medical services sector includes primary and secondary health services delivered to the individual child in clinics or hospitals. In the United States, these services tend to be funded by a private or public medical insurance fund or paid for by the individual directly (out-of-pocket). The community health sector provides population-wide services such as immunization or routine screenings. These programs are typically funded by state or federal agencies. The last sector, health-related services, includes family education programs, foster care, and respite care (see Farmer *et al.*, 2003).

Although this network of care appears comprehensive, in the United States it is often fragmented with little coordination. Because individuals, even within families, may be covered by differing payment systems, there is often significant fragmentation and discontinuity of services. Families find it difficult to navigate the care system and frequently experience frustration. Fragmentation is enhanced by the training models preparing PCPs. Although there is frequent discussion of coordinated systems of care, the most common emphasis of primary care delivery systems is upon the predominant model emphasizing short-term acute health problems (Frank *et al.*, 2004b).

Integrated primary care

Alternative models, emphasizing the role of psychologists, have been proposed. Recognizing that psychologists on rehabilitation teams often play central roles in the management of chronic and disabling conditions, Frank (1997a, 1997b, 1999) proposed the 'Cardinal Symptom' model of care. The Cardinal Symptom model recognizes that individuals with chronic conditions tend to view their care in the context of their most concerning symptoms. For example, an individual with a spinal cord injury often views his physiatrist as his primary physician. Similarly, an individual with advanced heart disease may view their cardiologist as their most critical provider. In the Cardinal Symptom model, a patient with spinal cord injury designates his physiatrist as his primary provider of care. Routine and complex care services are provided by the physiatrist with input from the rehabilitation team. The physiatrist can seek consultation from PCPs or other tertiary specialists. The coordination and integration of care is provided by the physiatrist and rehabilitation team because the patient views spinal cord injury as their central symptom.

The Cardinal Symptom model recognizes the importance of incorporating the consumer's perceptions and needs into the delivery of health services. The model recognizes the changing nature of the consumer's evaluation of health services. As consumers become more knowledgeable about their conditions, the role of critical health providers will become more consultative. The Cardinal Symptom model suggests that care must be comprehensive, provided by a coordinated group of providers. Care is organized around the patient's perceptions of who should comprise the treatment team.

Frank (1999) suggested that the rehabilitation team served as a good model of the Cardinal Symptom approach. Rehabilitation teams already provide comprehensive care for many individuals with acquired disability. Frequently, individuals with brain injury, stroke, or spinal cord injury receive the majority of their care through their rehabilitation providers. Frank et al. (2004b) noted that possible variations of the Cardinal Symptom model include the integration of a PCP who provides general care augmented by the rehabilitation team. In rural areas, the treating team could provide the majority of care aided by a local primary care provider for more immediate needs. A last variation has a primary care specialist with members of the rehabilitation team, such as the psychologist and physical and occupational therapist.

The Cardinal Symptom model suggests that psychologists can lead the treating team, serving as the clinician manager. Psychologists are ready for such leadership roles given their understanding of interpersonal processes. Because many aspects of care are psychological, psychologists are well prepared to coordinate care. Psychologists have a keen understanding of contextual barriers that affect health status. Health promotion and prevention behaviors, often dependent upon psychological factors, must be recognized for effective interventions. Service delivery systems that consider the individual, family-centered care, interdisciplinary team interactions, and the organization of health systems, as proposed by the Cardinal Symptom model, will greatly enhance outcomes.

Psychologists have emerged as organizers and leaders of comprehensive teams designed to treat chronic illness. Janet Farmer, a psychologist at the University of Missouri, and her colleagues in Missouri, developed a research demonstration project designed to better model critical aspects of care for children with special health needs. The Missouri Partnership for Enhanced Delivery of Services (MO-PEDS), a three-year research demonstration project, is the only known project of this type led by a psychologist. MO-PEDS was a research project designed to modify the primary care system and improve services for children with chronic health conditions, especially in rural areas (Farmer et al., 2003). The MO-PEDS project enhanced environmental support for children and their families by improving the ability of primary care physicians to provide chronic care and by integrating enhanced practice into a publicly funded system (Medicaid). MO-PEDS included a team of primary and specialty physicians and nurse practitioners, with a care coordinator to integrate the health benefits with available community services (Farmer et al., 2003). The MO-PEDS project had an advisory council, composed of national, regional, and local collaborators. This group enhanced local community and state links. Through the advisory council, the project emphasis upon family-centered and community-oriented care was monitored and enhanced. The advisory council facilitated the adoption of the American Academy of Pediatrics' medical home model (Sia, 1992). The medical home model called for each child to have a primary care provider in their home community who knows the child and the family and views the parents as partners in care, and provides coordinated, continuous care (Farmer et al., 2003).

The objective of MO-PEDS was to develop a family- and community-centered program. In the process, the role of providers was moderated to focus more on the needs of consumers than status or convenience of providers. This leveling reflects changes likely in evolving 'information societies' (Frank et al., 2004b).

The MO-PEDS project demonstrates many of the attributes espoused by the Cardinal Symptom model. Led by a psychologist, the MO-PEDS project provided family-centered care anchored to community services integrating primary care and specialty care. As in models suggested within physiatry, the model of care in MO-PEDS or the Cardinal Symptom model requires extensive physician involvement. As physicians are typically the highest-cost personnel in the health care system, the viability of these approaches for routine care is questionable. While the enhanced coordination and integration of care is clearly beneficial, the additional cost implied in these models may prove prohibitive. To date, no program has implemented a version of the Cardinal Symptom model while evaluating cost.

Analyzing cost in an integrated system

Most often, in the absence of cost data, additional health care services are justified on the basis of 'cost offsets'. Cost offsets, sometimes referred to as medical cost offsets, consist of potential cost savings in medical care resulting, or correlated with, the effective delivery of mental health, psychological care, or services such as rehabilitation. Cost offsets differ from cost effectiveness studies which balance net costs (including cost offsets) against potential benefits including reduced mortality, improved morbidity, or improved quality of life (Simon and Katzelnick, 1997). Cost offsets and cost effectiveness can be independent in that the absence of a cost offset does not imply a treatment is not cost effective. Medical cost offset analyses typically examine direct medical expenditures (Simon and Katzelnick, 1997).

Rehabilitation primary care models can be viewed as a cost offset paradigm. Cost offsets occur when health care costs for a service are offset by avoided services in another health sector. In the rehabilitation primary care models discussed earlier, including the Cardinal Symptom model and RIM primary care programs, chronic and disabling conditions are treated by a rehabilitation team. These models likely utilize more resources than a single provider, or even a small primary care clinic, might use. If additional health costs are avoided by these more comprehensive services, it is an example of a cost offset.

Cost offsets have been frequently examined from the perspective of psychological services. Medical cost offsets have been cited by psychologists as evidence of the value of psychological treatment (Rae, 2004). One of the first studies of medical cost offset was performed by Follette and Cummings (1968). Follette and Cummings examined the medical records of 152 randomly selected adults seeking medical care through the Kaiser Foundation Health Plan. Utilization of services during the year prior to receiving psychological services was recorded. Utilization for the five-year period following treatment was also assessed. The majority of patients (80) were seen for only a single session, while 41 were seen for between two and eight sessions, and 31 were seen for nine or more sessions. A comparison group, who had not received psychological treatment, matched for age, gender, and medical utilization rates, was created. Follette and Cummings found medical utilization increased for the comparison group, but decreased for the group receiving psychological treatment. The greatest increases occurred more than a year after treatment (Follette and Cummings, 1968; Hunsley, 2003). The patients receiving more treatment also evidenced declines in utilization, particularly in-patient days. Schlesinger *et al.* (1983) assessed the adjustment and utilization of health services of 700 patients who received psychological interventions and 1,300 patients who did not receive care. Those receiving psychological care were found to have 40 per cent lower annual medical costs. These differences proved greater than the cost of treatment, yielding a 5 per cent net saving for the treatment group after psychological treatment costs were included (Hunsley, 2003).

Schlesinger *et al.* (1983) conducted two meta-analyses of the literature. One analysis was based on Blue Cross Blue Shield Federal Employee Plan claims for 1974 to 1978, and the other was based on 58 published studies. They concluded that cost offsets were found in approximately 85 per cent of the studies. The clearest offsets occurred in reduction of inpatient days.

Chiles *et al.* (1999) performed a meta-analysis using 91 studies published between 1967 and 1997. Included in their sample were studies using patient groups undergoing surgery, histories of high utilization, and individuals referred specifically for psychological disorders. Chiles and colleagues examined the extent to which an offset was moderated by a type of psychological intervention. They found overall cost savings in the range of 20–30 per cent across all studies with 90 per cent of the studies reporting a cost offset (Hunsley, 2003). Only 7 per cent of the studies examining estimated cost savings reported that the costs of psychological treatment exceeded cost savings from the intervention (Hunsley, 2003). Hunsley (2003) re-analyzed Chiles *et al.*'s (1999) data to correct for the 'file drawer effect' (lack of publication of non-significant findings). Using the reported weighted effect size of 0.34, he found it would take 2,594 negative (no difference between treatment groups) studies to conclude that Chiles *et al.*'s results were due to sampling bias.

Hunsley (2003) noted that cost offset studies must be routinely updated to reflect current pricing in pharmacological costs and treatment. He also noted that cost offset studies might generalize at the theoretical level, yet have little specific application across national health care systems. Differences in national health systems mitigate interpretation of cost offsets (Hunsley, 2003).

Psychologists, facing increasing reductions in payment for clinical services, have shown great interest in the medical cost offsets. Arguing that psychological services net additional benefit by reducing overall health costs, psychologists have argued that reductions in coverage for psychological services are short-sighted. Although many have argued the importance of cost offsets to the field of psychology (Follette and Cummings, 1968; Simon and Katzelnick, 1997; Schlesinger *et al.*, 1983, Hunsley, 2003), critics have suggested that cost offsets are a methodological artifact, and even if they do exist, the benefit to the field of psychology is minimal.

Coyne and Thompson (2003) attacked the cost offset theory. They suggested that the Follette and Cummings (1968) study was

> an utter failure in terms of an ambitious effort to engage PC (primary care) patients in psychotherapy, and its results should be viewed with caution. Over 100,000 PC patients received automated screening, and

PCPs (primary care providers) were advised to consider mental health referral for half (422) of the patients screening positive for emotional distress. This resulted in only five referrals being completed, a result attributed to resistance by both PCPs and patients.

(Coyne and Thompson, 2003: 105)

Simon and Katzelnick (1997) note that the target of most cost offset studies are the so-called 'high utilizers' of care, individuals who have higher medical claims. One group of high utilizers, frequently treated by psychologists, are individuals with depression. Simon and Katzelnick note that individuals with depression have medical costs 1.5–2 times greater than non-depressed comparison samples. They describe similar high utilization patterns for individuals with anxiety disorders.

Simon and Katzelnick (1997) also note the methodological problems associated with cost offset research. The majority of studies have utilized cross-sectional designs. A study examining high utilization of health care among individuals with depression is subject to confounding. Any individual characteristic associated with both utilization and depression is a potential confounder, as long as this third factor does not lie in the causal pathway between depression and utilization (Simon and Katnelnick, 1997). Medical morbidity is such a confounding variable. Medical morbidity may mediate between depression and utilization or may be an independent, confounding factor. When Manning and Wells (1992) controlled for self-reported health (perceptions of health and physical limitations), in an analysis of Health Insurance Experiment data, they found less apparent impact of psychological distress on overall medical utilization.

Sturm (2001) argued that the strongest form of experimental design is the randomized clinical trial. He noted that several studies have found cost offsets using this design. For example, Von Korff et al. (1998) found a modest cost offset when primary care patients were provided with enhanced treatment for depression, including psychiatric care with drug management and education.

Sturm (2001) notes that although clinical trials provide the best evidence for cost offsets in specific situations they do not constitute the most appropriate basis for determining public policy. Clinical trials assess interventions with specific populations, which is different from determining broad public policy affecting many diverse individuals. Only clinical trials at the population level, randomizing treatments by communities or health plans, can provide the level of information needed.

Several large trials have utilized randomized trials to examine cost offsets. The Rand Health Insurance Experiment (Newhouse, 1993), a randomized trial, tested the effects of insurance benefit expansion by assigning families to differing levels of coverage of fee-for-service insurance. Participants with free mental health care were found to be twice as likely to use mental health services and to have almost twice the mental health costs of individuals in plans requiring a 95 per cent co-payment (Sturm, 2001).

The Medical Outcomes Study (Wells *et al.*, 1996), a large observational study, screened 22,000 outpatients with chronic disease, including depression, and followed a panel over time. No evidence of cost offsets was found in outpatient or inpatient utilization outcomes. Cost shifting *was* found where patients using mental health services were found to have fewer visits to general medical care. When patients discriminated the purpose of visits to either sector, the difference disappeared.

The Fort Bragg study (Bickman, 1996) compared traditional care to enhanced care in which access to an exemplary system of comprehensive mental health care was provided to children and adolescents. The study examined high utilizers of care and had a one year follow-up. Mental health expenditures were found to be much higher in the treatment group; there was no evidence of cost offsets.

Overall, the evidence for cost offsets for mental health treatment, despite widespread support among practitioners, is mixed. Review of the literature reveals conflicting evidence. The preponderance of evidence seems to suggest that cost offsets disappear when examined by the most rigorous methodological methods. It is reasonable to argue that treatment of psychological and mental health disorders is similar to other maladies in that more treatment costs more money. Similar arguments undoubtedly apply to rehabilitation models.

Summary

As currently conceived, rehabilitation and primary care occupy distinct niches in the health care system. Many writers have argued that the current practice in rehabilitation provides 'de facto' primary care for individuals with disability. Indeed, Frank and colleagues (Frank, 1997a; Frank *et al.*, 2004b) argued that the rehabilitation care model should be adapted to chronic health conditions. Many models of rehabilitation primary care are possible, but each approach faces the burden of justifying additional cost created by more practitioners for the complex care provided. Among psychologists, complex care, including the addition of psychological services to traditional health interventions, has been justified by presumed cost offsets in which the additional care is justified by avoided future health costs. Such a model seems applicable to primary rehabilitation care. Examination of the studies of cost offsets in psychology in the literature yields conflicting results. Additional studies using current cost data and more comprehensive sampling may help clarify the picture. While such studies are pursued, justification for psychological care and primary rehabilitation care should recognize possible cost offsets while more critically evaluating other implications of psychological care to individuals with chronic conditions and disability. Specific examination of the quality-of-life years created by effective psychological treatment for chronic and disabling conditions will greatly augment the field.

References

Becker, M. H., Drachman, D. H. and Kircht, J. P. (1974). Continuity of the pediatrician: New support for an old shibboleth. *Medical Care*, 84, 599–605.

Bickman, L. (1996). The evaluation of a children's mental health managed care demonstration. *Journal of the Mental Health Administration*, 23, 7–15.

Bingaman, J., Frank, R. G. and Billy, C. L. (1993). Combining a global budget with a market driven system: Can it be done? *American Psychologist*, 48, 270–276.

Blount, A. (2003). Integrated primary care: Organizing the evidence. *Families, Systems, & Health*, 21(2), 121–133.

Bray, J. H., Frank, R. G., McDaniel, S. H. and Heldring, M. (2004). Education, practice and opportunities for psychologists in primary care. In R. G. Frank, S. H. McDaniel, J. H. Bray and M. Heldring (eds) *Primary care psychology*. Washington, DC: American Psychological Association.

Buschbacher, R. M., Delisa, J. and Kevorkian, G. C. (1996). The physiatrist as a primary care physician for the disabled: A commentary. *American Journal of Physical Medicine & Rehabilitation*, 76(2), 149–153.

Chiles, J. A., Lambert, M. J. and Hatch, A. L. (1999). The impact of psychological interventions on medical cost offset: A meta-analytical review. *Clinical Psychology: Science and Practice*, 6(2), 204–220.

Coyne, J. C. and Thompson, R. (2003). Psychologists entering primary care: Manhattan cannot be bought for $24 worth of beads. *Clinical Psychology: Science and Practice*, 10(1), 102–108.

Donaldson, M., Yordy, K. and Vanselow, N. (eds) (1994). *Defining primary care: An interim report. Committee on the Future of Primary Care, Division of Health Care Services, Institute of Medicine* (Part 3, pp. 15–33). Washington, DC: National Academy Press.

Farmer, J. E., Clark, M. J. and Marien, W. E. (2003). Building systems of care for children with chronic health conditions. *Rehabilitation Psychology*, 48(2), 242–249.

Follette, W. T. and Cummings, N. A. (1968). Psychiatric services and medical utilization in a prepaid health plan setting. *Medical Care*, 5, 25–35.

Frank, R. G. (1997a). Lessons from the Great Battle: Health care reform, 1992–1994. John Stanley Coulter Lecture. *Archives of Physical Medicine and Rehabilitation*, 78(2), 120–124.

Frank, R. G. (1997b). A view from behavioral health. In *Proceedings of the 4th Congress of Health Professions Educators* (pp. 101–105). Washington, DC: Association of Academic Health Centers.

Frank, R. G. (1999). Rehabilitation psychology: We zigged when we should have zagged. *Rehabilitation Psychology*, 44(1), 36–51.

Frank, R. G., Hagglund, K. J. and Farmer, J. E. (2004b). Chronic illness management in primary care: The cardinal symptom model. In R. G. Frank, S. H.

McDaniel, J. H. Bray and M. Heldring (eds) *Primary care psychology.* Washington, DC: American Psychological Association.

Frank, R. G., McDaniel, S. H., Bray, J. H. and Heldring, M. (2004a). *Primary care psychology.* Washington, DC: American Psychological Association.

Gans, G. M., Mann, N. R. and Becker, B. E. (1993). Delivery of primary care to the physically challenged. *Archives of Physical Medicine and Rehabilitation,* 74, S15–S19.

Grabois, M. (1996). Facing new realities: Strategies for change. *Archives of Physical Medicine and Rehabilitation,* 77, 215–218.

Hoffman, C., Rice, R. and Sung, H. (1996). Persons with chronic conditions: Their prevalence and cost. *Journal of the American Medical Association,* 276, 1473–1479.

Hunsley, J. (2003). Cost-effectiveness and medical cost offset considerations in psychological service provision. *Canadian Psychology,* 44(1), 61–75.

Hurley, R. E., Freund, D. A. and Taylor, D. E. (1989). Emergency room use and primary care case management: Evidence from four Medicaid demonstration projects. *American Journal of Public Health,* 79, 843–846.

IOM (Institute of Medicine) (1994). *Defining primary care: An interim report.* Washington, DC: National Academy Press.

IOM (2001). *Crossing the quality chasm: A new health system for the 21st century.* Washington, DC: The National Academies Press.

Kroenke, K. and Mangelsdorff, A. D. (1989). Common symptoms in ambulatory care: Incidence, evaluation, therapy and outcome. *American Journal of Medicine,* 86, 262–266.

Lehmann, J. L. (1974). Physical medicine: Reflections and predictions. *Archives of Physical Medicine Rehabilitation,* 55, 2–3.

McPherson, M., Arango, P., Fox, H., Lauver, C., McManus, N., Newacheck, P. W., Perrin, J., Shonkoff, J. and Strickland, B. (1998). A new definition of children with special health care needs. *Pediatrics,* 102, 137–140.

Manning, W. and Wells, K. B. (1992). The effects of psychological distress and psychological well being on use of medical services. *Medical Care,* 30, 541–553.

Moore, S. (1979). Cost containment through risk sharing by primary care physicians. *New England Journal of Medicine,* 300, 1359–1362.

Newacheck, P. W. (1990). Financing the health care of children with chronic illnesses. *Pediatric Annals,* 19, 60–63.

Newhouse, J. P. and the Health Insurance Experiment Group (1993). *Free for all? Lessons from the Rand Health Insurance Experiment.* Cambridge, MA: Harvard University Press.

Phelps, R. and Reed, G. M. (2004). *Primary care psychology.* Washington, DC: American Psychological Association.

Rae, W. A. (2004). Financing pediatric psychology services: Buddy, can you spare a dime? *Journal of Pediatric Psychology,* 29(1), 47–52

Rakel, R. E. (2002). The family physician. In R. E. Rakel (ed.) *Textbook family practice* (6th edition, pp. 1513–1522). Philadelphia: W. B. Saunders.

Schlesinger, H. J., Mumford, E., Glass, G. V., Patrick, C. and Sharfstein, S. (1983). Mental health treatment and medical utilization in a fee-for-service system: Outpatient mental health treatment following the onset of a chronic disease. *American Journal of Public Health,* 73, 422–429.

Shi, L. and Singh, D. A. (2001). *Delivering health care in America: A systems approach* (2nd edition). Gaithersburg, MD: Aspen.

Sia, C. (1992). The medical home: Pediatric practice and child advocacy in the 1990s. *Pediatrics*, 90, 419–423.

Simon, G. E. and Katzelnick, D. J. (1997). Depression, use of medical services and cost-offset effects. *Journal of Psychosomatic Research*, 42, 333–344.

Starfield, B. (1997). The future of primary care in a managed care era. *International Journal of Health Services*, 27, 687–696.

Sturm, R. (2001). Economic grand rounds: The myth of the medical cost offset. *Psychiatric Services*, 52, 739–740.

Von Korff, M., Katon, W., Bush, T., Lin, E. H., Simon, G. E., Saunders, K., Ludman, E., Walker, E. and Unutzer, J. (1998). Treatment costs, cost offset, and cost effectiveness of collaborative management of depression. *Psychosomatic Medicine*, 60(2), 143–149.

Wells, K. B., Sturm, R., Sherbourne, C. D., Meredith, L. S. (1996). *Caring for depression*. Cambridge, MA: Harvard University Press.

Chapter 10

Sexual aspects of physical disability

Philip Clarke Henshaw

Media representations of sexuality exhibit a bias towards the fantasy model of sex (Zilbergeld, 1999); active and boundless sexual appetites, sexual athleticism and simultaneous and multiple orgasms. It is unsurprising in this context that non-disabled people develop problems with body image and sexual expression. Even within normal ageing, people may abandon sexual expression or seek plastic surgery for minor blemishes. Consider then the difficulties of developing or maintaining sexual identity with a chronic illness or disability, having been non-disabled before. Sexual problems and disability are two of the greatest social taboos. When combined, there are tremendous barriers to constructive sexual adjustment that can be compounded by insufficient knowledge and attitudes of healthcare staff, and the lack of comprehensive sexual health and dysfunction services.

It is only recently that health and rehabilitation professionals have considered seriously aspects of sexuality in enabling disabled people to enjoy and experience those elements of life which have previously been denied them through ignorance, distaste, prejudice and disempowerment (Williams, 1993). Physical health problems should rarely preclude the enjoyment of sex and intimacy. Even if a sexual problem has an untreatable cause, people can still enjoy the sensuality of physical contact and fantasy. Sexuality is woven densely into the fabric of human existence (Bancroft, 1989). Sex is an important contributor to quality of life and can provide a powerful sense of affirmation when life itself is threatened. The form and content of sexual expression may have to change, but this is no different to finding a new way to do the hoovering in a wheelchair. Health professionals often fail to see that people with chronic illness retain their sexual desire and need help expressing it in altered circumstances. Failure to address sexuality may be a consequence of sexual attitudes, embarrassment, inadequate training, patient–professional dynamics, wrongly gauged priorities or limitations of a healthcare setting. A comprehensive framework to ensure that patients and healthcare staff are able to address sexual problems, the PLISSIT model (Annon, 1974), was proposed over thirty years ago. Unfortunately, many services still fail to apply its principles. Its basic premise is that all staff should be trained how to give patients permission to address sexual problems and know the limits of their expertise so that they know when to refer to specialist services.

There have been great changes in knowledge and attitudes about sex in Western culture since the 1960s. Feminism and the human rights movement have been particularly important in changing attitudes about marriage, gender-power issues, same-sex relationships, disability and birth control. This has permitted the development of sexual therapy for single people, unmarried couples, same-sex relationships and people with disabilities. Polarised attitudes to these changes remain evident with many, often those with faith-based values, advocating a return to traditional values. The balance of attitudes can determine practice, e.g. what young people are taught about sex. The HIV pandemic can particularly polarise societies, but has resulted in better multidisciplinary sexual health services and research in endemic areas. More is known about the interplay of social factors with physical, mental and sexual health. Services have had to learn how to engage ostracised sub-populations, resulting in more affirmative approaches to sexuality and ethnic diversity.

Clinicians now have access to greater theoretical and therapeutic knowledge concerning sexuality. Sexual health is no longer just defined by physiology or infections; definitions encompass social, psychological and emotional dimensions. Consequently, service commissioners must place greater emphasis on funding multidisciplinary sexual health and dysfunction services. The development of oral treatments for erectile dysfunction (ED) has increased the sexual possibilities for many people with illness and disability, but has also been associated with a medicalisation of sexual problems, despite well-established biopsychosocial models. Their prescription for sexual performance anxiety, for example, will only serve to maintain an anxiety-based problem unless medication is used as an adjunct to psychological therapy.

Epidemiology and physical impact

Patient and professional knowledge about sex is generally poor. Sex and Relationship Education (SRE) in schools remains inadequate or non-existent, and healthcare practitioners do not receive sufficient training on sexuality. Myths are perpetuated in a climate of ignorance, so it is important to gain awareness of how physical conditions impact on sexuality. Gender disparities in knowledge should be recognised. The physiology of erections has been empirically studied since the mid-nineteenth century while the female genitals were more likely to be subjected to the mythical physiology of psychoanalysis (Murphy, 1998).

The sexual response depends on integrated hormonal, neural and vascular systems with peripheral genital physiology. Sexual perceptions or

Table 10.1 Categories of sexual dysfunction in men and women

Phase of response cycle affected	Men	Women
Desire	Hypoactive sexual desire disorder	Hypoactive sexual desire disorder
	Sexual aversion disorder	Sexual aversion disorder
Arousal	Erectile disorder	Female sexual arousal disorder
Orgasm	Male orgasmic disorder Premature ejaculation	Female orgasmic disorder
Pain	Dyspareunia	Dyspareunia Vaginismus

Source: Wincze and Carey (2001).

thoughts may be associated with particular cortical regions which remain unknown, but basal structures of the brain (e.g. hypothalamus) are involved (Murphy, 1998). The action of steroidal hormones such as testosterone and oestrogen are complex in humans and impact mostly at central and affective levels. During sexual activity, neuroendocrine mechanisms interact with spinal cord reflexes controlling vascular, secretory and neuromuscular events characteristic of genital arousal responses (Murphy, 1998). At a peripheral level, more is known about neuroendocrine mechanisms that regulate erections than genital changes in women. Essentially, an erection occurs when the three sponge-like smooth muscle tubes in the penis fill up with blood via increased inflow (vasodilation process) and decreased outflow (veno-occlusive mechanism). Three neural mechanisms regulate this process. Sildenafil (e.g. Viagra) acts at this peripheral level by increasing the tendency to vasodilation. Similar mechanisms are thought to control genital engorgement in women.

Masters and Johnson (1966) first observed the physiological changes occurring in humans engaged in sex and masturbation, resulting in a four-stage model of the sexual response. Discrete physiological changes occur in the excitement, plateau, orgasm and resolution phases. This underpins the dominant classification system for sexual problems in the *Diagnostic and statistical manual of mental disorders: Fourth edition – Revised* (DSM IV-R; APA, 2000), with the addition of a desire phase (necessary for excitement to occur) and sexual pain categories (see Table 10.1).

Sexual aversion is differentiated from hypoactive sexual desire when low or absent desire is accompanied by intense negative emotions about sex. Female sexual arousal disorder features lack of responsiveness in the excitement/plateau phases with low or absent engorgement and lubrication. Orgasmic disorders refer to persistently delayed or absent orgasm, while premature ejaculation concerns limited ability in males to control ejaculation. Dyspareunia is the experience of pain during intercourse, while in vaginismus the lower vaginal musculature is too contracted for penetration to occur. Symptoms must be accompanied by significant distress and require differentiation as lifelong or acquired, generalised or situational and due to psychological, medical or combined factors (Wincze and Carey, 2001). Some dysfunctions are more common in chronic illness. Schrover and Jensen (1988) noted that ED is especially prevalent in chronically ill men since the erectile mechanisms are easily impaired, while arousal problems in women are typical too. Orgasm is the most robust aspect of sexual response in chronic illness except for those with impairment of the spinal cord.

Many are highly critical of this classification system, as it fails to describe the kinds of problems that women experience. It emphasises a false equivalency between men and women, erases the relational context of sexuality and ignores differences between women. A different female classification system has been proposed based on a woman-centred definition of sexual problems: discontent or dissatisfaction with any emotional, physical or relational aspect of sexual experience (Kaschak and Tiefer, 2001). Causes can be socio-cultural, political, economic relational, psychological or medical. Similar criticisms and revisions are applicable to the classification of male sexual problems.

Neuroendocrine causes

The impact of neurological damage will depend on whether it occurs at higher cortical, basal or peripheral levels. The mind is the most important sexual organ. Brain injuries can alter subtle aspects of sexual expression, perception and identity. Basal damage can disturb the integration of neural and endocrine systems, causing an array of problems, while peripheral damage impacts in a more focused way on genital responses.

Damage to higher cortical functioning is characteristic of head injury. Personality changes, associated with frontal lobe damage, often lead to social difficulties in the expression of sexuality. Sexual disinhibition is common and may be accompanied by irritability, creating difficulties for the person in their social context (Williams, 1993). Similar patterns can occur in dementias too. Memory and attention impairments can alter the quality and frequency of sex. People may not recall that they have just had sex and so request it more frequently. Impairments of autobiographical or facial memory may make lovers appear unfamiliar. Impairments over a range of cognitive functions can render people less attractive. Temporal lobe involvement also appears to impact on sex and may be associated with precocious puberty.

Damage to the hypothalamus tends to result in sexual dysfunction because it has a central role in the integration of neuroendocrine mechanisms of the sexual response. Most women with hypothalamo-pituitary disease experience significant sexual dysfunction, including absent sexual appetite, problems with lubrication and orgasmic difficulties. Demyelination of basal brain and spinal cord structures might account for high rates of sexual impairment in multiple sclerosis. In women, symptoms include decreased sensation, reduced appetite and frequency of sex, orgasmic and arousal difficulties. Men report ED, decreased sensation and appetite and orgasmic dysfunction. Fatigue, weakness and reduced mobility may also affect sexual performance.

The sexual impact of spinal cord injury will depend on the injury, but those with complete upper motor neuron lesions are likely to have sexual impairment. Sipski and Alexander (1992) found 70–93 per cent of men retained reflex erections, despite the absence of penile sensation, but could not sustain erections arising from sexual thoughts (psychogenic). Ejaculation and orgasm are also likely to be absent. If the sacral cord is damaged then reflex erections are lost, but it is claimed that psychogenic erections can still occur. Psychogenic erections have been reported in men with complete lesions of the cord as high as the lowest vertebra of the thoracic spine (T12), associated with paraplegia, but the reasons why are not understood yet.

Surgery can damage peripheral nerve mechanisms. Pelvic plexus nerve damage causes ED as its fibres supply the corpora cavernosa. Radical surgeries for prostate and bladder cancers and those focused on the rectum, urethra, bladder, gall bladder and prostate can cause impairment. More precise knowledge of the cavernosal nerves have resulted in improvements in surgical techniques. Hysterectomies tend not to be associated with much sexual dysfunction, but removal of uterus and cervix changes the relationship between bladder, bowel, ovaries and vaginal vault and extensive disruption can disturb the autonomic nervous system of the pelvic plexus.

There are numerous misunderstandings about the effects of hormones on sexual functioning. Testosterone injections in men, even with low testosterone, rarely impact on sexual appetite. The interplay of hormone levels is much more subtle in humans than animals, e.g. after castration, erection may continue for years. Testosterone also influences female sexual desire. In men, hypogonadism can result in loss of sexual interest, ED and even ejaculatory failure, which may be reversed by testosterone administration. Oophorectomy reduces oestrogen and androgen levels by 50 per cent but has little effect on desire and arousal in most women. Adrenal insufficiency reduces sexual interest in both men and women (Hawton, 1985), while adrenal overactivity produces mixed effects in sexual interest. Hyperthyroidism can increase desire, while hypothyroidism impairs sexual interest in most women and some men. Hyperprolactinaemia is associated with ED and reduced sexual appetite, while women report orgasmic difficulties too. In renal failure, electrolyte and hormonal abnormalities may be partially responsible for ED and impaired sexual interest in both genders.

Vascular causes

Vascular damage is particularly bad news for men, and accounts for 50 per cent of ED cases with physical causes. History of peripheral vascular disease, ischaemic heart disease, cerebrovascular accident, hypertension, smoking, obesity and diabetes may indicate vascular damage. ED after myocardial infarction may be related to hypertension, arteriosclerosis or drug treatment. Erections may function when not accompanied by the muscular exertions of sex, which can divert blood away from the penis to muscles. While diabetes is an endocrine disorder, it primarily causes sexual dysfunction by impairing vascular mechanisms. In insulin-dependent diabetes, prevalence of ED increases greatly with age. Fifty per cent of men over 50 report ED. Sexual appetite and ejaculation appear unaffected. Arterial insufficiency and neuropathy are implicated. Sexual functioning in diabetic women has not been well studied, but women can experience reduced engorgement and vaginal dryness.

Musculo-skeletal causes

Muscular and skeletal impairments can impact on the physical expression of sex, via pain, fatigue and manoeuvrability. Patients with arthritis often fear that sex will exacerbate symptoms of pain, fatigue and joint limitation, but also have concerns about body image and attractiveness. Majerovitz and Revenson (1994) found that couples with rheumatoid arthritis did not experience significantly more sexual dissatisfaction than matched controls. The strongest predictor of sexual satisfaction in rheumatoid arthritis was severity of disease. Greater physical disability was related to lower sexual satisfaction in couples, and spouses reported lower sexual satisfaction when partners reported more arthritic pain. Loss of limb function and amputation can impact on the physical dynamics of sex too, but social and psychological factors are more important.

Pharmacological causes

A range of medications can impair sexual functioning, but effects can be different from one person to another and exist in association with other sexual impairments. Problematic medications include antidepressants (e.g. serotonin reuptake inhibitors), cancer medications and cardiovascular drugs (e.g. antihypertensives). The impact of all medications on sexual functioning should be considered by professionals. It may not be possible to change medications without increasing risks to general health, but some can be reduced before sex (e.g. those for pain control). Substance use can interplay with sex in various ways. Opiates can make it difficult to orgasm and desire may then decrease. At low doses, alcohol may enhance sex by reducing inhibitions, but at high levels it reduces sexual appetite and ability. People often use substances like cocaine and ketamine to enhance the experience of sex but this can increase vulnerability to sexually transmitted infections.

Review of key social, psychological and emotional impact

Social impact

Dominant social constructions (popular representations) of disability may be complex and contradictory, but have established a deviant and relatively powerless status for people with disabilities. They are seen as distinct and apart from the supposedly normal and natural majority (Williams, 1993), resulting in stigma and shame. Myths about sexuality and disability abound. Kaufman *et al.* (2003) note that people with disabilities are stereotypically seen as asexual, lacking in sexual desire, unattractive or pathetic choices as partners and incapable of 'proper sex'. These are also associated with people who choose disabled partners. The denial of the sexual attractiveness of people with disabilities has served to increase vulnerability to sexual abuse and assault, especially given their history of institutionalisation.

Disability and disfigurement can impact differently on men and women, by their interactions with body image, gender roles and gender traits (masculinity and femininity). There are greater social pressures on women to appear attractive and they are more vulnerable to body image problems than men. Their sense of femininity and social value can be undermined when disability makes it difficult to fulfil previous roles (e.g. motherhood). In men, disability can challenge masculine concepts of independence and assertive. Men may also have greater difficulty adjusting to disability in partners as they tend to be more negative in their attitudes to sexuality and disability, particularly towards women.

Between 2 and 22 per cent of the population engages in sexual activity with the same or both genders, and of the gay male and lesbian populations, 11 per cent have disabilities (Saad, 1997). Different kinds of sexual problems are evident. Low sexual desire is more common in lesbians, while delayed ejaculation is more prevalent in gay men. Relationship styles can be different to traditional marriage, with open rather than monogamous arrangements being common in gay men. Same-sex behaviour remains stigmatised and patients do not always disclose sexuality due to perceived or actual prejudice of staff. Some remain secretive and will not have 'come out', passing as heterosexuals to avoid stigma. Negative societal attitudes can be internalised (internalised homophobia) and associated with poor self-esteem and covert sexual lifestyles. In some cultures it is extremely difficult to be open about sexuality. Inequalities in legal partnership rights can impact on aspects of healthcare. Partners might not be recognised as next of kin or be consulted in decision-making. Dying without a Will can mean the primary family automatically inherits an estate. Homosexuality remains illegal in many Caribbean, Islamic and African nations, and migrant communities maintain strongly negative attitudes.

HIV may be an additional problem for gay men and those from minority ethnic communities. It can also cause disability and sexual dysfunction directly. Staff need to be aware of social factors associated with elevated HIV risk and the difficulties associated with living with HIV and disability. HIV remains highly stigmatised because of its association with controversial lifestyles such as homosexuality, intravenous drug use and multiple sexual partners. Young gay men are unlikely to receive teaching about gay sex and those with disabilities may be so concerned about adequacy that they fail to assert condom use. Young people with lower educational abilities are also more vulnerable to infection. People living with HIV and disability have to live with two highly stigmatised problems. Sexual dysfunction adds another and it may be difficult to address sexual difficulties associated with an increased risk of transmission of HIV/sexually transmitted infection. Men with ED often have greater difficulties using condoms, while women may fail in attempts to assert condom use due to men's preferences for sex without condoms and gender-power relationships.

The age at which people acquire illnesses affects their impact. Growing up with disabilities presents particular challenges to identity, body image and sexuality. Illnesses causing early mortality can leave young people confused about their ability to function socially and sexually. Young people with disabilities, especially learning disabilities, are still less likely than their non-disabled peers to receive adequate sex education (Burns, 1993). There are different challenges for those who are single compared to those in relationships. In established couples, illness may impact on many finely balanced aspects of relationship dynamics. Research suggests that separation and divorce is no more common in cancer patients than the general population, but that break-ups principally occur in couples with premorbid marital conflicts (Schrover and Jensen, 1988). When single, the challenge is to meet partners. If there is a visible indication of illness then there will be no control over disclosure and disfigurement may disturb the smooth flow of social interaction (Kent, 2003). If there are no visible signs of disability then the timing and style of disclosure must be negotiated and anticipatory anxiety may disturb interaction.

Case vignette 10.1: Ed, 22-year-old male with hydrocephalus

Ed was referred by his general practitioner as he was distressed by his sexual urges and wanted medication to reduce sexual feelings. He was born with hydrocephalus and had recently read that it could result in precocious puberty and high sexual appetite. Assessment revealed normal sexual development and appetite. Difficulties were better explained by psychological reaction to multiple health problems. Hydrocephalus had caused a subtle range of cognitive difficulties, including poor short-term memory. He had had a shunt inserted as a child to drain excess cerebral fluid, which created a scar down his neck, across his chest to his stomach. He also had asthma, eczema and irritable bowel syndrome.

While he appeared to function normally, with a job and circle of male friends, he never had girlfriends. He tended to play the fool when socialising and never seriously flirted with women for fears of sexual inadequacy and rejection. He thought that he had too many health problems to be a good catch and feared exposing his scar. Ed found it very difficult to talk openly about his sexual feelings. He tried to ignore his sexuality, even remaining abstinent from masturbation, but he could not stop wet dreams and erections.

Intervention worked to persuade him of the normality of his sexual appetite and the psychological causes of his distress. He was encouraged to express his sexual desires initially via self-exploration exercises and given written information on masturbation techniques, sex and women's bodies. Cognitive behavioural therapy addressed body image and self-esteem problems and he experimented with new ways in which to act in social situations, as opposed to playing the fool. He began to discuss his problems with close friends, who helped him to eventually start dating.

In older people, a resolvable problem with sex may be dismissed as part of normal ageing or be due to the stigma about sexuality in later life. Residential care, in which the sexuality of inhabitants is so often denied, may rule out the joy of partnership and sexuality when it is needed most. In acute care, single beds, open wards, lockless doors and routine observation make it difficult to cuddle, have sex or sleep together. Lovemaking and fantasy can become more vigorous in the final stages of life contrary to stereotypical beliefs. In home-based care, couples can better assert their territory and privacy.

Case vignette 10.2: Companionship in old age

Psychologists were asked to resolve staff conflict about the appropriateness of a sexual relationship in a residential home. Assessment revealed a caring pattern of companionship between the couple, despite difficulties of verbal assessment. Both were single and had Alzheimer's. Staff were embarrassed about sexual behaviour, feared that allowing sex was a failure in duties (because of the woman's poor communication abilities) and expressed prejudice and stigma about sex in old age. A series of meetings encouraged staff to discuss their difficulties and educate them about sex and old age. They were advised how to gently discourage sexual behaviour in public areas, by encouraging them to move to their private rooms rather than trying to stop sex.

Culture and ethnicity colour adjustment to illness and sexuality in many ways. In comparison to contemporary Western society, many cultures do not hold the individual as the most important social unit, and the concerns of the extended family hold priority over the individual when decisions are being made about sex and relationships. People may look to spiritual leaders and traditional healers for sexual expertise, and different gender-power dynamics may complicate sex (Davidson, 2000). Barriers to help-seeking include suspicion of health services and language difficulties. Mixed gender conversations about sex may be viewed negatively and compound assessment and therapy. Different attitudes about sex outside marriage, homosexuality, masturbation and foreplay may limit work too.

Psychological and emotional factors

Psychological and emotional factors can impact on every part of the sexual arousal cycle resulting in psychosexual difficulties. These may complicate sexual problems with physical aetiologies, or exist independently. They result from the interplay of cognitive, behavioural and physiological processes. Dysfunctional assumptions about sex can trigger emotional states that have physiological correlates that interfere with sexual arousal. In anxious states of mind, worries about sexual adequacy can trigger the adrenalin response, which may inhibit the genital blood flow necessary for engorgement and erections. Problems may become persistent if perceived sexual failure serves to reinforce dysfunctional assumptions about sexual adequacy, and is associated with avoidance of sex.

Psychosexual difficulties may have their origins prior to illness onset. Certain factors predispose people to develop sexual problems such as restrictive upbringing, disturbed family relationships, inadequate sexual information or sexual trauma (e.g. sexual assault). People develop schemas about sex, love, bodies and relationships, which may also reflect societal stigma about illness and disability. A schema is a mental representation of the self in the world, which serves to process and organise the information we receive from our senses. In the cognitive-behavioural model of sexual problems (Baker, 1993), distorted schemas can produce the dysfunctional assumptions, which then interfere with sex. Schemas indicative of a disturbed self-image can develop as a result of an interaction between cultural expectations, personality attributes and physical characteristics (Cash, 1996). These schemas may include dysfunctional beliefs that echo criticisms and insults from childhood about disability, illness, fatness, fitness, attractiveness, independence, athleticism, intelligence and other eugenic qualities:

- 'Only freaks fancy cripples.'
- 'I'm worth nothing if I can't stand on my own two feet.'
- 'I'm so dependent on others for help that I can never be a real man in bed.'
- 'Nobody wants a diseased partner.'
- 'You can't be sexy if everybody sees you as a deformed fool.'

Schemas may be unproblematic or balanced by compensatory behaviours such as going to the gym, fastidious skin care, weight control or adequate sexual relationships, until illness or disability changes appearance or physical agility, and challenges perceptions of sexual adequacy. Sexual difficulties often result after cancer treatment, due to both the iatrogenic effects of treatment and the psychological concerns of the couple about altered body image and sexual functioning. Women treated for breast and gynaecological cancers commonly report difficulties accepting their appearance and feel less attractive or feminine. Around 50 per cent report problems in sexual functioning and 30 per cent report sexual dysfunction developing in partners. Men often experience psychosexual difficulties associated with stigmatisation and shame after prostate cancer treatment. This is because of the association with the cancer's bodily location in lower or 'dirtier' parts of the body and associated loss of control over urination and defecation (Lodnert, 2002). It is relatively easy to learn about the mechanical ways that lovemaking can be adapted to accommodate a disabled body, but much harder to deal with the feelings and emotions of an individual who may have sexual urges and desires inside a body that is seen by them and the outside world as deformed and ugly (Denman, 2001).

A good sexual self-image is a blend of feeling physically attractive, skilled as a lover, and able to satisfy a partner's emotional needs for warmth, tenderness, passion or playfulness (Schrover and Jensen, 1988). Problematic schemas may reflect societal myths about sex and undermine self-image. Idealist notions of sex may become difficult to fulfil in the face of illness and disability:

- Penises are always strongly erect throughout sex.
- Both partners should always have orgasms.
- Good sex shouldn't be painful.
- You need to keep sex vigorous and varied to keep your man.

- Real sex involves penetration.
- Masturbation is wrong.

Not all men with diabetes gain benefits from oral medications like Viagra and have to find ways to enjoy sex with little or no erection. In spinal cord injury, some people have to adapt to the reality of sex without orgasm. For those without partners, solo sex may take on a more important role and be enhanced with sex toys. If sexual ideas and standards cannot be adjusted then anxious, detached or irritated states of mind will distract from sensual and sexual possibilities.

The behavioural response to sexual difficulties will determine whether problems are eased or maintained. Avoidance is the strongest behavioural factor. Avoidance of sex may be associated with avoidance of flirtation and cuddling because they will lead to sex. Some people adopt a detached state of mind in sex, acting only to pleasure their partners. People may only engage in transient relationships to avoid fears of failure and rejection. The monitoring of sexual performance also maintains difficulties. In ED, men monitor for loss of erection and often frantically attempt to regain it by manual stimulation. In delayed ejaculation or orgasmic difficulties, people focus too much on the timing of orgasm and similarly make overworked attempts to achieve it. The couple's reactions to sexual difficulties are crucial. Negative reactions that maintain difficulties include arguments, criticism, blaming and reduced intimacy (e.g. no physical contact after experiencing sexual difficulties). An explorative and relaxed approach, in which an individual or couple experiments with different acts, positions and methods of stimulation, is more likely to result in enhanced pleasure.

People with chronic illness such as HIV and cancer are more vulnerable to psychological problems than the general population, and these may impact on sexual expression. In depression, sexual appetite may decrease or increase, just as some depressed people go off their food, others comfort-eat. Sex can relieve stress. Emotions associated with adjustment reactions such as anger, anxiety and withdrawal may not be compatible with sex. Sexual patterns in the adjustment period are not indicative of long-term patterns. It is common for people with HIV to go off sex after diagnosis. Sex can remind people of how they contracted HIV and be associated with worries about transmission and thoughts of being dirty, infected and undesirable. Previous patterns normally re-establish as people come to terms with infection.

Commentary on psychological assessment and formulation

Accurate and comprehensive assessment is crucial for formulation, but clinical insight is necessary too. The atmosphere and dynamics of patient–therapist relationships reveal much more than standard questions. Patients are normally not used to talking to strangers about sex. Some are relieved and excited to talk openly, while others are shy and reticent. Wincze and Carey (2001) advise us to assume:

- Patients will be embarrassed and have difficulty discussing sex.
- They will not understand medical terminology.
- They will be misinformed about sexual functioning.
- They may be in crisis.
- Couples will not have been open with each other or freely discussed sexual matters.

The psychologist needs to identify and manage the barriers to engagement, such as shame and embarrassment, fears of judgement and patient–therapist mismatches. Erotic attractions and repulsions must be managed too (Denman, 2004). Clinicians may find certain problems difficult due to moral beliefs or embarrassment, e.g. anal sex or use of sex workers. Patients observe fine detail of non-verbal communication for signs of judgement and discomfort. Some test the limits, e.g. gay men may elaborate the fine details of sex with multiple partners. This may seem aggressive but the patient often needs reassurance that a therapist is comfortable with gay lifestyles. It is inadvisable for a homophobic practitioner to work with gay and lesbian clients. If there is a mismatch, then the difficulties must be addressed. Frank discussion of the difficulties may ease the situation so that work can proceed. Alternatively, onward referral may be arranged amicably. Failure to address difficulties can result in tense and unproductive sessions. Scepticism of the psychological model can also be a barrier as medication may be easier than psychological therapy.

Psychological assessment is best accompanied by a medical assessment of sexual function, so that findings can be compared, uncertainties in cause clarified and treatment coordinated. It begins with collection of demographic information as an opportunity to gain information on lifestyle and context. Detailed information about sexual problems and abilities in different situations is required, so that factors that make things easier and more difficult can be identified. In erectile difficulties, exact information is required about nocturnal, morning, pre-penetrative, penetrative and solo erections. Variations provide clues to the influences of anxiety. Emotional, behavioural and cognitive reactions to successful and unsuccessful sex are elicited in the patient and their partner. Thoughts, emotions and dialogues of the couple about disability and sex must be noted. Mythical beliefs and fears, such as the possibility of having a heart attack during sex, must be elicited. These undermine sexual confidence and may be associated with avoidance of certain types of sexual activity.

The therapist needs to have an understanding of how sex and relationship problems interplay with physical and mental health, social identity and life ambitions. A full history, including sexual history, is collected. This includes information on sexual development (first sex, number of partners, sexual experimentation, sexual abuse and assault, attitudes to masturbation, pre-morbid sexual functioning, patterns of difficulty since illness onset), psychological and psychiatric history, patterns of difficulty through the lifespan, early family experiences and parental relationships. It is wrong to assume that problems started after illness. Professionals must enquire about sexual difficulties at key points within the lifespan. Psychologists always try to collect outcome measures so that the effectiveness of therapy can be evaluated. This will include the very specific measures of sexual functioning already described, and may be aided by the use of standardised questionnaires for factors such as mood and anxiety, body image, sexual risk cognitions and sexual and relationship satisfaction.

Case vignette 10.3: Premature ejaculation and ED in a man with diabetes

A 46-year-old Bangladeshi man with type II diabetes was referred to a sexual dysfunction service by his general practitioner. He had developed ED and premature ejaculation (PE) over the previous year. He could achieve partial erection (40 per cent) for three to five minutes and tended to ejaculate within two minutes of penetration. Assessment concluded that diabetes-related changes impaired his erections. While peripheral neuropathy might have impaired his ability to control ejaculation, careful questioning revealed that he could tell when orgasm was about to happen, but had lost his ability to hold back. This was associated with the onset of erection problems, reduced libido and decreased frequency of sex. He never masturbated (a risk factor for PE) as he thought it damaged health and was religiously forbidden. Initial intervention involved prescribing oral medication for ED and teaching him how to regain control over ejaculation using the start-stop technique. Negative beliefs about masturbation were corrected. A local imam explained that the start/stop technique was permissible as he had a medical problem and a duty to satisfy his wife.

Despite several changes in type and amount of medication, he continued to experience intermittent ED. A performance anxiety model of ED, similar to Figure 10.1, was used to explain the problem. Intervention aimed to teach him skills to decrease anxiety about ED, maximise ability to regain erections and continue with sex if he could not regain the erection. This involved reappraising the impact of diabetes on his sense of masculinity and sexual confidence. Perfectionist beliefs that he should maintain a solid erection throughout sex were challenged. He believed that he could not regain erections, so had to

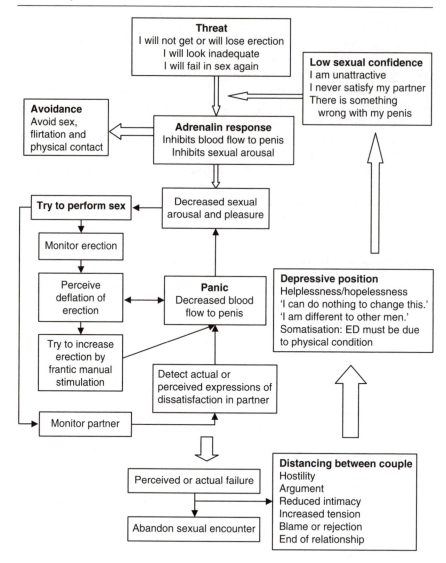

Figure 10.1 Schematic formulation of ED caused by performance anxiety

Case vignette 10.3: *continued*

practise gaining and intentionally losing erections by himself and with his wife (wax-wane technique). Alternative ways to satisfy his wife via oral and manual stimulation were also emphasised.

Elements of the intervention in psychological therapy for sexual problems will depend partly on whether the person is single or in a relationship. If they are in a relationship the couple may not be willing to attend together, due to cultural factors, embarrassment or perceived cause being in one partner only. The development of cognitive-behavioural interventions for a variety of psychosexual presentations has made it much easier to work constructively with individuals. When working with couples and people in relationships, dual skills in sex and relationship therapies are required. Problems may reside more in the relationship dynamics than sex. If the practitioner is unskilled in relationship therapy, referral to another service may be necessary.

In individual therapy a range of elements of intervention are considered and matched with the formulation. This may include basic sex education, masturbation or self-exploration training, sexual myth challenging and behavioural experiments (e.g. practising gaining and losing an erection in front of a partner). Essentially the cognitive-behavioural therapy approach is to build understanding of the cognitive and behavioural factors that inhibit the sexual response. It requires work on underlying dysfunctional schemas about body, sexual identity and relationships. Interventions for self-esteem are often blended. Basic education about the physiological characteristics of states of mind and compatibility/incompatibility with the sexual response is important. Work with couples may include similar elements and effectively demonstrate how each individual's thoughts and reactions interact. Work may also involve the sensate focus approach of sex therapy (Hawton, 1985). This therapeutic model teaches couples how to relax physically together and build up their sexual relationship from non-genital sensual touch and massage to penetrative intercourse.

Service and organisational aspects

Rehabilitation services are under pressure to provide maximal physical and functional improvement in minimal time and at minimal cost, and many units put off providing sexuality education and counselling (Dunn, 1997). This is contrary to the well-respected principles of the multilevel PLISSIT model (Annon, 1974). PLISSIT stands for *p*ermission, *l*imited *i*nformation, *s*pecific *s*uggestions, and *i*ntensive *t*herapy. This approach incorporates all healthcare staff working with patients. All should be able to work with the first two levels of the model. They should feel comfortable enough to give permission for the patient to address sexual concerns and have enough knowledge about the interactions of specific disabilities and illnesses with sexuality to provide limited information (Sipski and Alexander, 1997). They should know the limits of their ability and knowledge so that they can refer patients to a specialist service for more specific suggestions or intensive therapy.

At a specialist service level, the assessment and treatment of sexual problems in people with illness and disability require a coordinated medical and psychological approach to deal with a range and mixture of aetiologies and treatments. A complement of male and female professionals helps to accommodate cultural and individual preferences for therapist gender. Unfortunately, coordinated clinics with a truly multidisciplinary team remain rare. Many health districts will have inadequate or absent specialist services for sexual problems. In this case, audits of sexual concerns and problems within clinical populations, together with political lobbying within higher management, may alert fundholders to the need for establishing services, which are too often characterised as a luxury that cannot be afforded.

Key areas for future research

Funding to conduct large-scale research can be extremely difficult to obtain, but most health services are compelled to undertake smaller-scale service-related research, such as audits. Audit projects might focus on whether organisations are meeting the standards of the PLISSIT model and small-scale projects could examine the barriers to sexual healthcare within their specialities.

There are many areas where more research is needed, but it can be difficult to conduct research in sex and disability for similar organisational reasons. Sexual issues often cause concern to ethics committees; for example, consider reactions to a project seeking to ask detailed questions about sex in terminal illness. More qualitative studies are required that capture the experience of sexual adjustment to a range of illnesses and disabilities – across a range of genders, sexualities and age groups. Partners' experiences of adjustment are commonly overlooked. Researchers might use semi-structured interviews with couples to capture some of the dynamics of couple communication about sex. Such work is likely to produce ideas for further quantitative research.

References

Annon, J. (1974). *The behavioural treatment of sexual problems: Volume one.* Honolulu: Enabling Systems, Inc.

APA (American Psychiatric Association) (2000). *Diagnostic and statistical manual of mental disorders: Fourth edition – Revised.* Washington, DC: APA.

Baker, C. D. (1993). A cognitive-behavioural model for the formulation and treatment of sexual dysfunction. In J. M. Ussher and C. D. Baker (eds) *Psychological perspectives on sexual problems: New directions in theory and practice.* London and New York: Routledge.

Bancroft, J. (1989). *Human sexuality and its problems*. Edinburgh, London, Melbourne and New York: Churchill Livingstone.

Burns, J. (1993). Sexuality, sexual problems, and people with learning difficulties. In J. M. Ussher and C. D. Baker (eds) *Psychological perspectives on sexual problems: New directions in theory and practice*. London and New York: Routledge.

Cash, T. F. (1996). The treatment of body image disturbances. In K. Thompson (ed.) *Body image, eating disorders and obesity*. Washington, DC: American Psychological Association.

Davidson, O. (2000). HIV/GU medicine/sexual health. In N. Patel, E. Bennett, M. Dennis, N. Dosanjh, A. Mahtani, A. Miller and Z. Naditshaw (eds) *Clinical psychology, 'race' and culture: A training manual*. Leicester: BPS Books (The British Psychological Society).

Denman, C. (2004). *Sexuality: A biopsychosocial approach*. Basingstoke, UK and New York: Palgrave Macmillan.

Denman, M. (2001). Problems with life events. In R. Skrine and H. Montford (eds) *Psychosexual medicine: An introduction*. London, New York and New Delhi: Arnold.

Dunn, K. L. (1997). Sexuality education and the team approach. In M. L. Sipski and C. J. Alexander (eds) *Sexual function in people with disability and chronic illness: A health professional's guide*. Gaithersburg, MD: Aspen Publishers, Inc.

Hawton, K. (1985). *Sex therapy: A practical guide*. Oxford: Oxford University Press.

Kaschak, E. and Tiefer, L. (2001). *A new view of women's sexual problems*. New York: The Haworth Press.

Kaufman, M., Silverberg, C. and Odette, F. (2003). *The ultimate guide to sex and disability: For all of us who live with disabilities, chronic pain and illness*. San Francisco: Cleis Press, Inc.

Kent, G. (2003). Appearance anxiety. In S. Llewelyn and P. Kennedy (eds) *Handbook of clinical health psychology*. Chichester: John Wiley & Sons.

Lodnert, G. (2002). Prostate cancer and body shame with special regard to sexual functioning. In P. Gilbert and J. Miles (eds) *Body shame: Conceptualisation, research and treatment*. Hove and New York: Brunner-Routledge.

Majerovitz, S. D. and Revenson, T. A. (1994). Sexuality and rheumatic disease: The significance of gender. *Arthritis Care & Research*, 7, 29–34.

Masters, W. H. and Johnson, V. E. (1966). *The human sexual response*. Boston, MA: Little, Brown.

Murphy, M. (1998). The neuroendocrine basis of sexuality and organic dysfunction. In H. Freeman, I. Pullen, G. Stein and G. Wilkinson (eds) *Seminars in psychosexual disorders*. London: Gaskell/Royal College of Psychiatrists.

Saad, S. C. (1997). Disability and the lesbian, gay man, or bisexual individual. In M. L. Sipski and C. J. Alexander (eds) *Sexual function in people with disability and chronic illness: A health professional's guide*. Gaithersburg, MD: Aspen Publishers, Inc.

Schrover, L. R. and Jensen, S. B. (1988). *Sexuality and chronic illness: A comprehensive approach*. New York: The Guilford Press.

Sipski, M. L. and Alexander, C. J. (1992). Sexual function and dysfunction after spinal cord injuries. *Physical Medicine and Rehabilitation Clinics of North America*, 3, 811–828.

Sipski, M. L. and Alexander, C. J. (1997). *Sexual function in people with disability and chronic illness: A health professional's guide.* Gaithersburg, MD: Aspen Publishers, Inc.

Williams, D. (1993). Sexuality and disability. In J. M. Ussher and C. D. Baker (eds) *Psychological perspectives on sexual problems: New directions in theory and practice.* London and New York: Routledge.

Wincze, J. P. and Carey, M. P. (2001). *Sexual dysfunction: A guide for assessment and treatment.* New York and London: The Guilford Press.

Zilbergeld, B. (1999). *The new male sexuality.* New York: Bantam.

Part 3

General organisational challenges and developments

Chapter 11

Adherence to medical regimens

Judith A. Erlen and Donna Caruthers

Introduction

Adherence to prescribed medical regimens continues to be a challenge for both patients and their healthcare providers. On average, patient adherence is 50 per cent for uncomplicated treatment regimens, such as taking one medication. Unfortunately, the more typical patient seen in the healthcare setting has multiple disorders resulting in a more complex treatment regimen and greater expectations of the patient. From the patient's perspective, these treatments often require self-management or home caregiver management, as in the case of patients with physical disabilities or a diagnosis of Alzheimer's disease. Within complex healthcare systems, patients are confronted with issues related to self-management, such as the constraints imposed by limited resources (e.g. financial, time, support) and inadequate information. Providers find that the complex system and the limited time that they spend with patients tax their ability to adequately assess patient treatment adherence and implement corresponding intervention strategies. The World Health Organization (2003) defined treatment adherence as the level of correspondence between the patient's behavior to implement a treatment plan (e.g. medications, diet, and/or lifestyle changes) and the regimen offered by the healthcare provider. This definition requires an active patient–provider partnership and good communication between the partners to identify and enact the treatment plan.

Globally, developing and impoverished countries/locations have even lower than the average 50 per cent regimen adherence rates. Poverty adds an economic barrier to adherence since the lack of resources places treatment adherence in competition for basic necessities (World Health Organization, 2003). In some cases, healthcare providers and their patients must face daunting struggles in these developing areas of the world to obtain necessary treatments before adherence can be addressed. Once therapies are available, dispelling myths and increasing patients' understanding of the available treatment(s) is necessary to assist patients to move forward in the self-management of their healthcare, including treatment adherence.

The significance of improving poor treatment adherence lies in its impact on patient clinical outcomes, quality of life, morbidity, and mortality. Poor treatment adherence increases wasteful spending within medical care and contributes to nearly $300 billion in costs in the United States (DiMatteo, 2004a). In addition, quality of life suffers and patients experience additional disruptions in their lives with respect to the complications of poor adherence. On the other hand, when patients can be assisted to improve their treatment adherence, disrupting symptoms subside and quality of life may improve.

Influencing factors of treatment adherence

When patients present for treatment in rehabilitative settings, a full assessment is often completed before a multidisciplinary treatment regimen is forged and ultimately discussed with the patient. Many issues and variables are considered in the process of selecting the best treatment option(s). Since treatment adherence impacts clinical outcomes, healthcare providers need to incorporate within their assessments and planning the identification and consideration of factors that influence treatment adherence. Adherence to a treatment regimen requires cognitive processing in order to follow a prescribed course of therapy; however, the combination of adherence-influencing factors and the complexity of the treatment regimen make adherence a complicated behavior to examine and improve. These influencing factors include characteristics relative to the patient, healthcare system, and therapy. For patients with physical disabilities, these factors can facilitate adherence, as in the case of social support, or can act as barriers to adherence, as in the case of stigma. Table 11.1 illustrates that the presence of these different factors can enhance or diminish adherence behavior.

Psychosocial factors

Personal characteristics considered to influence adherence include emotional, social, and psychological factors. Negative emotional or affective factors have long been associated with poor adherence to treatment, as well as relapse in maintaining a change in behavior. This category includes negative reactions to stress, depressive symptoms, and feelings of anxiety. Specifically, the presence of depressive symptoms places patients at greatest risk for poor adherence (DiMatteo et al., 2000). Although a few studies have found a relationship between increases in depression and adherence in chronic disorders (e.g. hypertension and asthma), others have shown that the increase in symptoms more directly impacted adherence rather than the increase in depressive symptomatology (Ford et al., 1989). Patients have also identified the negative feelings of stress and anxiety leading to a relapse from a treatment regimen, such as smoking cessation (Gwaltney et al.,

Table 11.1 The impact of influencing factors on
              treatment adherence

Influencing factor	Impact upon treatment adherence
Psychosocial	
Depressive symptoms	Diminish
Negative affect	Diminish
Motivation	Enhance
Self-efficacy	Enhance
Quality of life	Enhance
Loss of cognitive function (memory)	Diminish
Social and economic	
Social support	Enhance
Stigma/social attitudes	Diminish
Lack of access to care	Diminish
Healthcare disparity	Diminish
Health system and therapy-related	
Patient–provider relationships	Enhance
Personal control	Enhance
Presence of symptoms/side effects	Diminish
Regimen complexity	Diminish

2001). However, other studies have identified situational factors as more predictive for relapse from treatment than negative emotions (Shiffman *et al.*, 1996). Clearly, this area of affective states, in particular depressive symptoms, requires clinical appraisal in the rehabilitative setting, as well as further study with respect to promotion and intervention of treatment adherence. The experience of these negative feelings may be static through the course of rehabilitative treatment and beyond. Therefore, the rehabilitative patient is at particular risk for adherence problems if alterations in emotions occur when clinical and/or personal setbacks arise or progress does not match the patient's expectations.

In addition to affective states, other psychological characteristics have been examined for their impact upon treatment adherence. These include a patient's perception of personal motivation or readiness, self-efficacy, quality of life, and cognitive function (e.g. memory and attention). Motivation, self-efficacy, and quality of life pertain to patients' perceptions of themselves, the treatment plan, and health. Cognitive factors not only include the patients' actual ability to perform, but also their perceptions of their cognitive abilities. Motivation and self-efficacy positively influence treatment adherence. Older patients who had received anterior cruciate ligament reconstruction were found to be more adherent to rehabilitative therapy if they were self-motivated to complete their therapy sessions (Brewer *et al.*, 2003). A study of multiple sclerosis patients found baseline self-efficacy to be a predictor of adherence to daily self-administered injections of glatiramer acetate therapy, a medication that reduces the frequency of relapses when patients have relapsing-remitting multiple sclerosis (Fraser *et al.*, 2003).

Treatment adherence has long been associated with improvements in quality of life and medical outcomes. Spinal cord patients benefit from adherence from long-term exercise training with respect to their perceptions of their quality of life and clinical outcomes (Ditor *et al.*, 2003; Hicks *et al.*, 2003). Furthermore, one study suggests quality of life may diminish during the transition between the rehabilitation environment and home (Lucke *et al.*, 2004). More research is needed to examine the impact of this relationship upon treatment adherence.

Forgetfulness is the leading reason why patients do not adhere to prescribed therapy and attendance at clinic appointments (Dunbar-Jacob *et al.*, 2000). In particular, decrements in working memory and attention diminish treatment adherence. Age-related cognitive changes can alter whether a patient remembers to take medication, complete an exercise session, and attend scheduled clinic appointments. However, other factors may also impact working memory and attention. Treatment side effects, pain, increase in symptoms, insomnia, and fatigue are all examples of additional factors that can impact memory. For the rehabilitative patient experiencing pain, adequate pain management and adherence to that pain therapy may be necessary to ensure adherence to the other components of their therapy, like exercise.

Social and economic factors

Social factors that influence treatment adherence include social support, stigma or attitudes of others, health disparities, and access to care. The influence of social support on adherence varies. For some patients, social support has a limited effect on adherence rates, while other patients find social support very helpful in maintaining adherence. When adherence is critical to thwarting rapid progression of a disease, such as with HIV, social support may become more of a positive influence and need of the patient.

The type of social support available also needs to be examined. The term 'social support' includes a wide spectrum that is dependent upon how it is defined. The continuum of social support types can range from simple encouragement and reminders, to actual treatment dispensing by a family member. This latter type of hands-on assistance includes caregiving activities and has other implications with respect to the adherence of the caregiver to the treatment regimen. Therefore, social support is also needed for the caregiver, as in the case of caregivers for patients who have a stroke, Alzheimer's disease, and high spinal cord injuries. Thus, the presence of social support is considered to enhance treatment adherence (DiMatteo, 2004b).

Social support is not limited to just the patient side of the treatment spectrum. Healthcare providers also require support within their medical care system. For example, healthcare providers can be more effective with their patients when new or updated treatment guidelines are readily available from the medical system (Cherry *et al.*, 2004). Communication between all parties is essential to establish adequate social support for patients, caregivers, and healthcare providers.

Stigma and the attitudes of others act as barriers to adherence. The presence of stigma is not limited to disorders or situations associated with alterations in body image, such as physical disabilities, obesity, and skin disorders. Stigma and the attitudes of others can also arise when patients have disorders such as HIV/AIDS, cancer, addictions, and mental health problems. In addition to diminishing the potential for adherence to treatment, stigma may also impact other factors that relate to treatment adherence, including access to healthcare, social interaction, and social support. For example, the impact of stigma on women with HIV/AIDS, particularly African American women, impacts their quality of life and mortality more than males (Carr and Gramling, 2004). Interventions need to specifically target vulnerable populations to decrease the impact of stigma in order that these individuals reach a higher level of wellness and overall functioning including employment, decrease in mortality, and ultimately improvement in their quality of life. Studies suggest that the presence of stigma is a predictor of poor self-efficacy and treatment management in long-term chronic conditions, such as epilepsy and pulmonary disease (DiIorio *et al.*, 2003). Finally, stigma or negative societal attitudes have an impact across the developmental or age continuum, gender, and race (Sirey *et al.*, 2001). Healthcare providers need to address stigma with assessment and intervention throughout the care of their patients.

At the heart of most health-related disparity issues is the lack of adequate economic resources; limited financial resources have implications for adherence across ethnicity, gender, and age. Furthermore, health disparities and financial constraints impact patient access to care. There is a distinct relationship between low adherence rates and poor outcomes for individuals living in impoverished areas. When the lack of adequate resources requires competition in seeking food, shelter, and/or medical assistance/treatment, treatment adherence becomes a lesser concern of patients and their families. As with stigma, these disparities in access and economics can alter other factors besides adherence, such as increasing negative affective responses and decreasing self-efficacy. Poor responses to this multidimensional process ultimately result in detriments to treatment adherence and clinical outcomes. Thus, there is a need for more research regarding health disparities and improving access to care across medical systems delivering care for both acute and chronic conditions.

Health system and therapy-related factors

Although the dispensing of prescriptions for medication and treatment is part of the therapy process, the therapeutic relationship between the patient and provider can impact the success of therapy, particularly the patient's treatment adherence. Patients not only should, but also must be a part of the decision-making process regarding their medical management. When the decision making is one-sided with all decisions made by the provider, treatment adherence will potentially suffer since the patient's perspective and beliefs about the therapy have not been heard or considered. If there are negative beliefs regarding the treatment offered, the outcome expectancy of that treatment may be low and therefore lead to poor adherence. More often than not, patients perceive a lack of personal control in medical care settings, which may diminish the patient's motivation, self-efficacy, and affect. By enabling patients to be well informed and part of the decision-making process, providers can more readily assess and manage the previously mentioned factors influencing treatment adherence. This process helps to promote communication between the provider and patient, the patient's sense of personal control, and patient motivation to participate in physical, occupational, medication, or dietary therapies (Berg et al., 2002).

The presence of side effects or symptoms due to the disorder or treatment can also impact patient adherence. Although symptoms may drive some patients to be adherent to their treatment regimen, as is the case with asthma, symptoms can interfere with functioning by increasing fatigue, diminishing attentiveness and memory, and altering a patient's daily routines. In addition, symptoms may raise doubts in patients' minds about their treatment and ability to handle their treatment regimen. Unfortunately, the likely outcome is poor treatment adherence. Healthcare providers need to be proactive and anticipate the experience of potential side effects and symptoms. Early planning with the patient and offering guidelines for such events may assist in maintaining the patient's motivation to adhere to their treatment plan.

In order to support patient treatment adherence, healthcare providers need to assess the complexity of the treatment regimen. Simple treatment regimens are associated with better treatment adherence, such as single daily doses of medication and exercise. When treatments become more complex with multiple daily dose administrations, extensive exercise plans, time-consuming regimens, or difficult meal preparations, treatment adherence is more likely to diminish (Berg et al., 2002). Frequent daily dosing of the therapy (e.g. medications, exercise) can tax working memory and lead to 'forgetting' and decreased adherence. The feeling that one has had enough of the treatment may also become a problem and lead to a decrease in motivation to be adherent. Innovative strategies, such as combining music with exercise, can increase adherence to an exercise regimen as observed with patients participating in pulmonary rehabilitation activities (Bauldoff et al., 2002, 2005).

Overlap of influencing factors

These factors influencing treatment adherence may present in isolation; however, healthcare providers are more likely to encounter patients with multiple factors that present differently over time in the patient's course of therapy (Dunbar-Jacob et al., 2002). Due to this overlap of factors, ongoing assessment is needed to identify changes in these factors. Healthcare providers need to assist patients to capitalize on the benefit of enhancing factors while intervening with strategies to counter the effects of barriers to adherence. For example, patients participating in a complex treatment regimen that includes physical, pharmaceutical, and diet therapy have the potential for diminishing adherence over time. Therefore, strategies are needed to maintain or improve motivation, self-efficacy, and symptom management in order to enhance adherence. In addition, interventions may be necessary to offset barriers to adherence, such as depressive symptoms and economic problems. These factors need to be included as part of the ongoing assessment of patients in rehabilitative settings. Many of these factors may be anticipated due to the nature of the patient's problem or reason for rehabilitative therapy. When the presence and effect of these factors with respect to treatment adherence are considered, patients are more likely to achieve desired clinical outcomes and quality of life.

Adherence: a continuing problem

Despite knowing that adherence to treatment regimens is necessary for successful management of their health problems, many patients are poor adherers. Even adhering to short-term regimens can be problematic. Lifestyle changes may be required so that patients with physical disabilities can implement the therapeutic regimen. For example, the patient who needs to implement a prescribed exercise regimen several times each day may need to alter work schedules or need assistance with transportation to get to the gymnasium. Adherence for patients with chronic disorders decreases over time; the longer one continues with a therapy, the more likely the person is to become nonadherent (Deschamps et al., 2004). Quite possibly, people with physical disabilities will also have difficulty sustaining adherence because of the long-term nature of their health condition.

Early adherence researchers focused on describing the phenomenon and attempted to identify predictors of poor adherence. Currently, investigators are designing and testing interventions to improve adherence. These studies are demonstrating mixed results and may not be replicable. There is no common definition or measure of adherence across studies.

Treatment adherence research: current findings

Treatment adherence research has focused on medication behavior, weight loss and dietary regimens, exercise, smoking cessation regimens, and appointment keeping or attendance. Researchers are recognizing that they must also address confounding variables such as comorbidities, age, and sex when measuring and developing interventions to improve adherence. Obtaining statistically significant results is not the only goal; investigators must also consider whether the findings are clinically meaningful. Hence, conducting adherence research presents numerous challenges.

Because adherence to a treatment regimen is associated with better clinical outcomes, researchers are designing and testing interventions to improve adherence. Healthcare providers and patients are often consulted so that realistic and practical interventions are designed: one goal of these studies is to have findings that allow for the translation of the experimental condition to the clinical setting. The theoretical bases for these intervention studies include social cognitive theory, self-management theory, the theory of planned behavior, the transtheoretical model, and the health belief model, among others. There is often an educational and behavioral component in the intervention. Individual face-to-face or telephone sessions, group sessions, videotapes, educational booklets, and web-based tutorials are some of the techniques used to deliver the intervention.

Research on adherence to medication regimens continues to show variable rates of adherence; persons with life-threatening disorders such as HIV/AIDS or cancer often have better adherence rates (DiMatteo, 2004a). New drugs often present new challenges for patients when the regimens are introduced. For example, when protease inhibitors were first used to treat HIV/AIDS, side effects and regimen complexity affected adherence (Deeks et al., 1997). A study of patients with hypertension following renal artery stenting showed that physical symptoms related to side effects of the medications, such as loss of appetite and dizziness, negatively affected adherence, whereas the multi-drug regimen did not (Reddy et al., 2003).

Case vignette 11.1: Successful intervention to increase medication adherence

Mr S was a 36-year-old African American male diagnosed with HIV. Several of his prescribed antiretroviral medications required twice a day dosing. Mr S participated in an individualized telephone intervention with a nurse as part of

an adherence intervention study for patients diagnosed with HIV and prescribed antiretroviral medications (NIH/NINR R01 NR04749). The nurse
noted that Mr S was intelligent, highly motivated, used community resources,
and verbalized having a supportive network. He stated that he was typically
adherent to taking his medication twice a day; however, he indicated that the
times between taking the doses varied, which was verified by electronic event
data from his medication monitoring cap. He admitted that he did not have a
set plan for taking his twice-daily medication, but thought he was taking it
correctly. The nurse educated him about the importance of taking his
medication at the same time each day for both doses. She also helped him to
design a plan that used daily events in his life to cue his medication administration to approximately the same time each day. Mr S was usually successful
with this plan, although there were rare occasions of unplanned events
impacting his schedule. Further intervention by the nurse focused on
providing additional information and developing a plan to accommodate
unplanned events. This intervention was based on the needs of Mr S and
designed specifically for him. As a result, he was able to increase his
adherence to the medication regimen.

Since studies show that physical activity decreases mortality, researchers
are designing and testing interventions to promote exercise adherence.
Results from these studies suggest that there are both long-term and short-
term benefits. Exercise adherence leads to increased physical performance at
six months and 18 months and decreased disability at six months as
measured by attendance in a study of obese or overweight patients with
osteoarthritis of the knee (van Gool *et al.*, 2005). Morey *et al.* (2002)
showed that exercise programs in older adults with chronic disorders had a
protective effect against mortality.

**Case vignette 11.2: Successful intervention to increase exercise
adherence**

Mrs P, a 69-year-old female with severe chronic obstructive pulmonary
disease (COPD; FEV_1/FVC ratio = 42 per cent), completed a formal pulmonary rehabilitation program consisting of eight weeks of exercise training
and multidisciplinary educational programming. Adherence to a formal
pulmonary rehabilitation program enabled Mrs P to complete a distance of
1,250 feet for a six-minute walk. Two months later, upon visiting her

pulmonologist, Mrs P complained of increasing dyspnea, which she stated was impacting her ability to exercise. She admitted to abandoning her maintenance exercise program. A follow-up six-minute walk was completed at the pulmonologist's office with a 25 per cent reduction in walking distance to 950 feet. This finding was clinically significant. At this point, Mrs P enrolled in an eight-week study testing distractive auditory stimuli in the form of music to reduce perceptions of dyspnea during exercise (NIH/NINR F31 NR07599). Upon study completion, Mrs P reported that listening to music during exercise reduced her dyspnea; she was exercising longer at a higher intensity. Adherence to the use of music as a distracter resulted in Mrs P's six-minute walk distance improving by 21 per cent to 1,150 feet.

Research in the area of self-management suggests that patients with different physical disabilities or multiple co-morbid disorders have similar self-management issues or problems (Lorig et al., 2001). To enable patients to self-manage, health providers need to use problem-solving strategies to increase self-care confidence, knowledge, and appropriate healthcare utilization. Tasks which are common across chronic disorders (e.g. arthritis, stroke, heart disease, and lung disease) include symptom monitoring and response, pharmacological management, nutritional support, exercise maintenance, and lifestyle adaptation, among others (Lorig et al., 1996). Problem-solving educational strategies have been found to be more beneficial than 'information-only' programming (Bodenheimer et al., 2002). For example, the use of a tailored self-management program for arthritis delivered by mail resulted in decreasing disability within the first year and improving role function and self-efficacy (Lorig et al., 2004).

Dietary adherence varies in patients with type 1 and type 2 diabetes mellitus. Adherence to regular planned meals or diets to promote weight loss or fat reduction is poor (World Health Organization, 2003). Results from a qualitative study of 92 women participating in the Women's Health Initiative showed that adherence to a dietary regimen to promote weight loss requires a long-term personal commitment (Kearney et al., 2002). The women in this study supported the findings of Shannon et al. (1997) in relation to the importance of self-efficacy in believing that one can implement the regimen.

Studies addressing smoking cessation have found that adherence to the intervention protocol has a greater likelihood of increasing quitting (Cooper et al., 2005). Likewise, Borrelli and colleagues (2004) reported that relapse is higher among those who do not adhere to the protocol; women relapse more than men. Even though there has been considerable effort placed on smoking cessation, researchers continue to show a high rate of relapse.

Other work has focused on appointment keeping and program attendance. Often these outcomes are embedded within a larger study of interventions to improve regimen adherence and are used as corroborating measures of adherence. For example, van Gool and colleagues (2005), Cooper and his collaborators (2005), and Morey and her research team (2002) measured program attendance and found that those who had greater attendance had better adherence. These researchers concluded that attending the sessions is necessary in order to obtain the information on strategies designed to promote adherence.

Summary

The current research on evidence-based intervention strategies to promote adherence continues to show that the definition of good adherence varies. Although the evidence suggests that the interventions improve adherence, they are usually expensive, complex, and lengthy and therefore cannot easily be translated into practice. There continues to be a gap in the understanding regarding the interaction of pharmacologic and behavioral therapies to improve outcomes (Hitsman *et al.*, 2001). Researchers are unable to generalize beyond their study population because those who participate self-select; this potentially introduces a selection bias into the study that may be difficult to control. In addition, results from those studies aimed at identifying predictors of good adherence may not be transferable to other patient groups.

The studies also demonstrate the methodological issues when conducting adherence research. Measurement continues to be problematic. Researchers question whether to use one or multiple measures of adherence. Some investigators rely on patient self-report of adherence which is considered by many to be an unreliable means of assessing adherence. There continues to be a need for consistent, feasible, and accurate measures of adherence behavior.

Service and organizational strategies

The goal of those who work on the service side of healthcare is to help the patient overcome the barriers to adherence and facilitate good adherence. In order to assist their patients, providers first must be able to diagnose poor adherence. Then they need to develop strategies that address complex regimens, side effects, forgetting, knowledge deficits, social support, depression, self-efficacy, drug abuse, and the patient–provider relationship. Table 11.2 displays examples of strategies that healthcare providers, family and friends, and community resources can offer to promote adherence.

Table 11.2 Resources and strategies to promote improved adherence

Resource	Strategy
Healthcare providers	Establish supportive relationships
	Maintain open communication
	Develop trust
	Be available
	Develop partnership
	Individualize the regimen
	Use a team approach
	Collaborate with other providers
Family and friends	Offer social support
	Establish a schedule
	Simplify the regimen
	Work within the patient's daily routine
	Provide direct care
Community resources	Develop drop-in centers
	Institute bilingual support services
	Offer support groups
	Establish community-based case managers
	Provider peer counselors

Healthcare providers

The patient–provider relationship is critical; trust is essential. There is a need to establish effective ongoing communication. Patients need to believe they can discuss issues that they are having with maintaining adherence with the healthcare provider. Patients also need to feel that they will be supported as they learn to self-manage their physical disability. The patient has to be satisfied that the provider has the patient's best interests uppermost. Often more than one healthcare provider is involved in the patient's care, requiring that there be close collaboration among all those who are involved in assisting the patient. A collaborative approach between physicians and nurses has been found to be successful in promoting health in persons with type 2 diabetes mellitus (Taylor *et al.*, 2005).

Creating a partnership is crucial for patients with disabilities because they will have long-term healthcare needs. Each patient's situation is different; therefore, rules and procedures must not be imposed on the patient by the healthcare provider. Rather, the partners need to negotiate the plan and work together to establish the regimen. They can discuss strategies that others have found useful and then consider how they might be useful for a particular patient. In other words, strategies to facilitate adherence must be tailored to the patient's situation rather than being required. Individualizing the treatment regimen and involving the patient will help the patient to have more personal control over their health situation.

Even before strategies are identified and discussed, there is a need to assess the patient's readiness and motivation to begin the treatment regimen. Questions that need to be asked include: Are systems in place to enable the patient to be successful? Does the patient understand the treatment regimen? Has the patient had an opportunity to practice the regimen and to ask questions? Does the plan fit the patient's situation? What is the patient's level of self-efficacy? Does the patient believe that they can carry out the plan? Together, the patient and the provider need to do this assessment so that they have a similar basis for developing the treatment regimen. Other options will need to be considered when the patient is not ready to begin the treatment regimen even though it needs to be initiated. For example, home health aides or family members may need to take on this responsibility initially.

Integrating the adherence strategies requires tailoring the treatment plan to the patient's situation. Given that the mutually established goal is adherence, patients and providers need to simplify and tailor the regimen as much as possible. The more complicated the regimen is, the less likely that the patient will adhere to it. Healthcare providers need to break the regimen into its various parts and identify those aspects that are absolutely essential. Ascertaining the patient's daily routine is also necessary. Together, the provider and patient can then tailor the regimen and the steps that are necessary to fully implement the plan. Developing an adherence strategy that gradually builds the patient's skill in executing the regimen helps to build self-confidence and ensure that the regimen is integrated into the patient's daily routine.

Other patients may need some type of assistive device to be able to adhere to the treatment regimen. While this may be a prosthetic device such as an artificial leg, it may also be a cane or a walker. Having to use such assistive devices can add burden and thus limit adherence to the treatment regimen.

Family and friends

Family and friends can provide both social support and actual caretaking regarding the treatment regimen. Having social support has the potential to increase adherence; patients feel encouraged. Their family and friends are interested in their well-being.

If family members or friends need to be involved in the patient's treatment regimen because there may be times when the patient is unable to self-manage the regimen, then they will need to learn how to provide the required treatment. When possible, patients need to negotiate their care with these family members or friends so that the patient retains some element of personal control. Patients who have physical disabilities because of a cerebro-vascular accident, a motor vehicle accident, multiple sclerosis, or chronic pain may require that others regularly provide their care so that adherence is maintained.

Community resources

Community resources also need to be available to provide support to promote treatment regimen adherence. Drop-in centers can offer health services that do not require that patients have an appointment. Telephone hotlines can provide emergency assistance when patients need help adhering to their regimen. Service providers need to be bilingual or have interpreters available so that a patient's questions can be answered. Establishing peer support groups for patients with physical disabilities provides a means where patients can come together and tell their stories of what it is like to live with such disabilities and also what they do to maintain their health. This storytelling enables patients to ventilate their feelings and also provides strategies that others have used to promote regimen adherence. Peer support offered by caring individuals is one way that patients may be able to reintegrate the self and get their life back together.

Rather than provide peer support through a group mechanism, peer counselors offer support on an individual basis. These individuals are often based in a community service organization that focuses on individuals with specific conditions. Thus, if patients access other services through the organization, they can also access the counselors. These individuals may have the same physical disability as the patient who is seeking help. These counselors have usually had some training in counseling techniques. They are able to use these techniques to actively listen and to help the patient regain or maintain personal control.

Providing community-based case managers may be another type of support for patients with physical disabilities who are trying to implement adherence strategies. These individuals are healthcare professionals who manage a group of patients. Because of their expertise, they can assist patients to access other services or to find additional resources.

Key areas for future research

There is an increasing amount of research describing adherence and examining potential strategies to improve adherence; however, other areas also need to be studied. The strategies that have been developed and tested on one group of individuals cannot automatically be applied to other populations. The evidence to date on adherence clearly shows that 'one size does not fit all'.

Researchers need to continue to conduct randomized controlled clinical trials on interventions to improve adherence to treatment regimen with patients who have various physical disabilities. There is also the need to examine questions related to healthcare costs, quality of life, and health outcomes when patients do or do not adhere. Interventions to sustain adherence are needed since those with physical disabilities may live with the condition for the remainder of their lives. Researchers also need to pay particular attention to the design and methods of their studies because of the many confounding variables and the measurement issues surrounding adherence.

There is a growing interest in the role of culture and adherence. Culture can affect a person's perception of and response to their health problem or disabling condition. Many studies do not have samples that are ethnically and racially diverse. Researchers have focused primarily on whether differences exist between Caucasians and African American populations; however, limited attention has been given to Hispanic and Asian populations.

Likewise, there is also the need to examine health disparities as they relate to adherence. What is the role of socioeconomic status in relation to adherence? Patients with disabilities may have limited access to transportation services. They may be unable to access the resources that are needed to adhere to their regimen.

Another growing area with potential impact on adherence is the role of functional health literacy. Researchers usually assess the educational level of their subjects; however, completion of high school or college is not an indicator of health literacy. As researchers develop adherence interventions and evaluate them, there is a need to consider that patients have different levels of health literacy. Thus, any material that is produced needs to consider those with low, moderate, or high health literacy. Alternate versions of the intervention need to be designed and tested with individuals who have lower functional health literacy.

A related area of interest is that of cognitive function and adherence. Adherence is a cognitively demanding task. However, to date there has been limited research examining cognitive ability and adherence. In those studies that *have* attempted to address this question, there has been a limited cognitive assessment of the participants or the measures that were selected were not sensitive enough to detect the cognitive problems related to adherence. Designing and testing strategies to improve adherence should consider the various cognitive tasks that are involved with remembering to implement and actually implementing the treatment regimen. Additionally, there is a need to examine forgetfulness and everyday memory loss as they relate to adherence; habit training and developing routines become important components of an intervention for patients with these problems.

Personality characteristics also merit attention. Given the limited work that has been done, descriptive studies that examine the influence of these characteristics on adherence are needed. If a link can be established between personality characteristics and adherence, then interventions to promote adherence may need to be designed and tested that are specific to the various personality characteristics.

The increasing development of new technologies for self-monitoring clearly shows promise for at least some populations; these technologies may be very helpful to patients with physical disabilities. Automated telephone and web-based applications have the potential to assist patients with treatment adherence issues without demanding more time from providers. Tele-health strategies expand the geographical scope of monitoring and treatment facilitation for both providers and patients. Web-based strategies are becoming more common as people look to the internet for help with managing their health condition. Web-based programming has been successful with smoking cessation by collecting information that is then used to individualize interventions (Strecher *et al.*, 2005). Current research is testing the feasibility and effectiveness of using robots with older populations while personal digital assistants (PDAs) are being tested for use as monitoring tools and autonomous treatment delivery devices. Future treatment adherence trends may include greater use of electronic timers, digital pedometers, and/or pill bottles with built-in alarms as useful reminders for patients to maintain adherence to various treatment protocols for medication taking and rehabilitative exercise.

The thrust of research is moving toward developing and evaluating multidisciplinary interventions. The evidence is mounting that adherence to a therapeutic regimen requires changes in lifestyle and may be affected by factors such as culture, health literacy, personality, patient–provider communication, and cognitive function. Therefore, researchers must include multiple perspectives in order to gain a more comprehensive understanding of this very complex health issue for people with disabilities.

Acknowledgements

The authors want to acknowledge partial support of this chapter from the following grants from the National Institutes of Health/National Institute of Nursing Research: R01 NR04749, P30 NR03924, F31 NR07599, and F31 NR07343. The authors also want to thank Ms Jenny Hull, BS, RN for her contribution in writing Case vignette 11.1: Successful intervention to increase medication adherence, and Gerene Bauldoff, PhD, RN for her contribution in writing Case vignette 11.2: Successful intervention to increase exercise adherence.

References

Bauldoff, G. S., Hoffman, L. A., Zullo, T. G. and Sciurba, F. C. (2002). Exercise maintenance following pulmonary rehabilitation: Effect of distractive stimuli. *Chest*, 122(3), 948–954.

Bauldoff, G. S., Rittinger, M., Nelson, T., Doehrel, J. and Diaz, P. T. (2005). Feasibility of distractive auditory stimuli on upper extremity training in persons with chronic obstructive pulmonary disease. *Journal of Cardiopulmonary Rehabilitation*, 25(1), 50–55.

Berg, J., Evangelista, L. S. and Dunbar-Jacob, J. (2002). Compliance. In I. M. Lukin and P. Larsen (eds) *Chronic illness: Impact and interventions* (5th edition, pp. 203–232). Boston, MA: Jones and Bartlett Publishers.

Bodenheimer, T., Lorig, K., Holman, H. and Grumbach, K. (2002). Patient self-management of chronic disease in primary care. *Journal of the American Medical Association*, 288(19), 2469–2475.

Borelli, B., Papandonatos, G., Spring, B., Hitsman, B. and Niaura, R. (2004). Experimenter-defined quit dates for smoking cessation: Adherence improves outcomes for women but not for men. *Addiction*, 99, 378–385.

Brewer, B. W., Cornelius, A. E., Van Raalte, J. L., Petitpas, A. J., Sklar, J. H., Pohlman, M. H., Krushell, R. J. and Ditmar, T. D. (2003). Age-related differences in predictors of adherence to rehabilitation after anterior cruciate ligament reconstruction. *Journal of Athletic Training*, 38(2), 158–162.

Carr, R. L. and Gramling, L. F. (2004). Stigma: A health barrier for women with HIV/AIDS. *Journal of the Association of Nurses in AIDS Care*, 15(5), 30–39.

Cherry, D. L., Vickrey, B. G., Schwankovsky, L., Heck, E., Plauchm, M. and Yep, R. (2004). Interventions to improve quality of care: The Kaiser Permanente-Alzheimer's Association Dementia Care Project. *American Journal of Managing Care*, 10(8), 553–560.

Cooper, T. V., Klesges, R. C., DeBon, M. W., Zbikowski, S. M., Johnson, K. C. and Clemens, L. H. (2005). A placebo controlled randomized trial of the effects of phenylpropanolamine and nicotine gum on cessation rates and postcessation weight gain in women. *Addictive Behaviors*, 30, 61–75.

Deeks, S. G., Smith, M., Holodniy, M. and Kahn, J. (1997). HIV-1 protease inhibitors: A review for clinicians. *Journal of the American Medical Association*, 277, 145–153.

Deschamps, A. E., DeGraeve, V., van Wijngaerden, E., DeSaar, V., Vandamme, A. M., van Vaerenbergh, K., Ceunen, H., Bobbaers, H., Peetermans, W. E., De Vleeschouwer, P. J. and DeGeest, S. (2004). Prevalence and correlates of non-adherence to antiretroviral therapy in a population of HIV patients using medication event monitoring system. *AIDS Patient Care and STDs*, 18, 644–657.

DiIorio, C., Osborne Shafer, P., Letz, R., Henry, T., Schomer, D. L. and Yeager, K. (2003). The association of stigma with self-management and perceptions of health care among adults with epilepsy. *Epilepsy Behavior*, 4(3), 259–267.

DiMatteo, M. R. (2004a). Variations in patients' adherence to medical recommendations: A quantitative review of 50 years of research. *Medical Care*, 42(3), 200–209.

DiMatteo, M. R. (2004b). Social support and patient adherence to medical treatment: A meta-analysis. *Health Psychology*, 23(2), 207–218.

DiMatteo, M. R., Lepper, H. S. and Croghan, T. W. (2000). Depression is a risk factor for noncompliance with medical treatment: Meta-analysis of the effects of anxiety and depression on patient adherence. *Archives of Internal Medicine*, 160(14), 2101–2107.

Ditor, D. S., Latimer, A. E., Ginis, K. A., Arbour, K. P., McCartney, N. and Hicks,

A. L. (2003). Maintenance of exercise participation in individuals with spinal cord injury: Effects on quality of life, stress and pain. *Spinal Cord*, 41(8), 446–450.

Dunbar-Jacob, J., Schlenk, E. A. and Caruthers, D. (2002). Adherence in the management of chronic disorders. In A. J. Christiansen and M. H. Antoni (eds) *Chronic medical disorders: Behavioral medicine's perspective* (pp. 69–82). Oxford: Blackwell Publishers Ltd.

Dunbar-Jacob, J., Erlen, J. A., Schlenk, E. A., Ryan, C. M., Serieka, S. M. and Doswell, W. M. (2000). Adherence in chronic disease. In J. J. Fitzpatrick and J. Goeppinger (eds) *Annual review of nursing research* (Vol. 18). New York: Springer Publishing Company.

Ford, F. M., Hunter, M., Hensley, M. J., Gillies, A., Carney, S., Smith, A. J., Bamford, J., Lenzer, M., Lister, G., Ravazdy, S. and Steyn, M. (1989). Hypertension and asthma: Psychological aspects. *Social Science Medicine*, 29(1), 79–84.

Fraser, C., Hadjimichael, O. and Vollmer, T. (2003). Predictors of adherence to glatiramer acetate therapy in individuals with self-reported progressive forms of multiple sclerosis. *Journal of Neuroscience Nursing*, 35(3), 163–170.

Gwaltney, C. J., Shiffman, S., Norman, G. J., Paty, J. A., Kassel, J. D., Gnys, M., Hickcox, M., Waters, A. and Balabanis, M. (2001). Does smoking abstinence self-efficacy vary across situations? Identifying context-specificity within the Relapse Situation Efficacy Questionnaire. *Journal of Consulting Clinical Psychology*, 69(3), 516–527.

Hicks, A. L., Martin, K. A., Ditor, D. S., Latimer, A. E., Craven, C., Bugaresti, J. and McCartney, N. (2003). Long-term exercise training in persons with spinal cord injury: Effects on strength, arm ergometry performance and psychological well-being. *Spinal Cord*, 41(1), 34–43.

Hitsman, B., Spring, B., Borelli, B., Niaura, R. and Papandonatos, G. D. (2001). Influence of antidepressant pharmacotherapy on behavioral treatment adherence and smoking cessation outcome in a combined treatment involving fluoxetine. *Experimental and Clinical Psychopharmacology*, 9, 355–362.

Kearney, M. H., Rosal, M. C., Ockene, J. K. and Churchill, L. C. (2002). Influences on older women's adherence to a low-fat diet in the Women's Health Initiative. *Psychosomatic Medicine*, 64, 450–457.

Lorig, K. R., Ritter, P. L., Laurent, D. D. and Fries, J. F. (2004). Long-term randomized controlled trials of tailored-print and small-group arthritis self-management interventions. *Medical Care*, 42(4), 346–354.

Lorig, K., Stewart, A., Ritter, P., Gonzalez, V., Laurent, D. and Lynch, J. (1996). *Outcome measures for health education and other health care interventions.* Thousand Oaks, CA: Sage Publications, Inc.

Lorig, K. R., Ritter, P., Stewart, A. L., Sobel, D., Brown, B. W., Bandura, A., Gonazalez, V., Laurent, D. D. and Holman, H. R. (2001). Chronic disease self-management program: 2-year health status and health care utilization outcomes. *Medical Care*, 39(11), 1217–1223.

Lucke, K. T., Coccia, H., Goode, J. S. and Lucke, J. F. (2004). Quality of life in spinal cord injured individuals and their caregivers during the initial 6 months following rehabilitation. *Quality of Life Research*, 13(1), 97–110.

Morey, M. C., Pieper, C. F., Crowley, G. M., Sullivan, R. J. and Puglisi, C. M. (2002). Exercise adherence and 10-year mortality in chronically ill older adults. *Journal of the American Geriatrics Society*, 50, 1929–1933.

Reddy, B. K., Kennedy, D. J., Colyer, W. R., Burket, M. W., Thomas, W. J., Khuder, S. A., Shapiro, J. I., Topp, R. V. and Cooper, C. J. (2003). Compliance with antihypertensive therapy after renal artery stenting. *Biological Research for Nursing*, 5, 37–46.

Shannon, J., Kirkley, B., Ammerman, A., Keyserling, T., Kelsey, K., DeVellis, R. and Simpson, R. J., Jr. (1997). Self-efficacy as a predictor of dietary change in a low socio-economic status Southern adult population. *Health Education and Behavior*, 24, 357–368.

Shiffman, S., Gnys, M., Richards, T. J., Paty, J. A., Hickcox, M. and Kassel, J. D. (1996). Temptations to smoke after quitting: A comparison of lapsers and maintainers. *Health Psychology*, 15(6), 455–461.

Sirey, J. A., Bruce, M. L., Alexopoulos, G. S., Perlick, D. A., Raue, P., Friedman, S. J. and Meyers, B. S. (2001). Perceived stigma as a predictor of treatment discontinuation in young and older outpatients with depression. *American Journal of Psychiatry*, 158(3), 479–481.

Strecher, V. J., Shiffman, S. and West, R. (2005). Randomized controlled trial of a web-based computer-tailored smoking cessation program as a supplement to nicotine patch therapy. *Addiction*, 100(5), 682–688.

Taylor, K. I., Oberle, K. M., Crutcher, R. A. and Norton, P. G. (2005). Promoting health in type 2 diabetes: Nurse-physician collaboration in primary care. *Biological Research for Nursing*, 6, 207–215.

van Gool, C. H., Penninx, B. W., Kempen, G. I., Rejeski, W. J., Miller, G. D., van Eijk, J. T., Pahor, M. and Messier, S. P. (2005). Effects of exercise adherence on physical function among overweight older adults with knee osteoarthritis. *Arthritis and Rheumatism*, 53(1), 24–32.

World Health Organization (2003). *Adherence to long-term therapies: Evidence for action*. Geneva, Switzerland: World Health Organization.

Chapter 12

Rehabilitation planning

Jane Duff

Background and introduction

Acquired physical disability impacts upon all aspects of an individual's life: physical, emotional, social and vocational. Rehabilitation involves either regaining old skills or learning new and compensatory skills to cope with a changed life circumstance and fundamentally involves behaviour change. Rehabilitation has been defined as 'a reiterative, active, educational and problem solving process focused on a patient's behaviour (disability)' (Wade and de Jong, 2000: 1386, parenthesis in original). It is a team effort involving the knowledge and skills of an interdisciplinary team in partnership with the patient. Rehabilitation can only be effective with the individual's proactive involvement in the process and they need to be provided with a framework to understand the new skills that need to be acquired in order to manage the consequences of their changed physical state. Active client involvement in rehabilitation has been found to facilitate long-term physical and psychological adjustment (Norris-Baker *et al.*, 1981) and helps to translate and maintain skills in the person's everyday life. Goal orientated rehabilitation planning is critical for people with acquired disability. It enables the individual to develop a sense of control over their new life circumstance and to be taught and to learn the skills essential for resuming an independent and satisfying life. Implicit within a goal planning system are many of the key aspects of The Expert Patient approach (Department of Health, 2001) which aims to increase a patient's sense of control, the individual becoming an active participant in their own health care, and to develop skills to effectively manage their health condition, which in turn promotes the individual's adjustment and accommodation to their changed circumstance. Such approaches have also been found to reduce morbidity, mortality and secondary complications (Department of Health, 2001). This chapter outlines the history and development of goal setting theory and the central issues of this theory within rehabilitation services. The role of the interdisciplinary team, the quality of communication and the need to ensure patient involvement are highlighted as key processes which impact on the effectiveness of rehabilitation planning and provision.

Goal setting history and theory

Goal planning theory was formulated from the basic premise that goals affect action (Ryan, 1970, in Locke and Latham, 2002). 'A goal is the object or aim of an action, for example, to attain a specific standard of proficiency, usually within a specified time limit' (Locke and Latham, 2002: 705). Locke and Latham (1990), in their history of goal setting theory, consider there to be two influences: experimental psychology (concerning intention and motivation) and management theory. However, goal setting theory has developed from a number of routes since its inception and acknowledges the role of behavioural principles and implementation strategies, social learning and more recently, cognitive factors and self-efficacy (Locke *et al.*, 1984; Locke and Latham, 2002), in the regulation of action. The theoretical principles of goal setting assume that all action and behaviour is goal directed either through unconscious (e.g. digestion or blood circulation) or conscious (e.g. hunting for food or work production) means (Locke and Latham, 1990). Goal directedness is influenced by the value and significance of the goals and the individual's intention in achieving the goal. However, Locke and Latham (1990) comment that specifying a person's goal does not provide a full explanation of that action. They suggest that this is only the first level of explanation and that there are two further levels which influence goal generation and achievement: the situational context, e.g. peer pressure and cultural standards; and the individual's values, motivation and personality.

Locke and Latham (1990) acknowledge the importance and contribution of Bandura's (1986) social-cognitive theory in the application of goal setting theory. They consider role modelling to have a social influence on action which significantly affects goal choice and commitment. Self-efficacy is recognised to have an even wider role; Locke and Latham (1990) comment that it not only has an impact on goal choice and commitment, but also has a direct effect on performance. Self-efficacy refers to the individual's belief in their own ability to manage situations and when this is high, individuals are more likely to work effectively. Evidence indicates a clear interrelationship between self-efficacy, goal setting and performance (Locke and Latham, 1990). Goal achievement is highest when specific goals of moderate difficulty, rather than very easy or very hard goals, are set in the context of high levels of expectancy and self-efficacy (Locke and Latham, 2002). Other factors which moderate goal achievement are the individual's commitment to the goal and the feedback received about attainment. Attention, effort and persistence mediate this attainment.

Goal planning (or individual programme planning) was also implicit within the deinstitutionalisation and normalisation approaches of the 1970s and early 1980s (Houts and Scott, 1975; De Kock et al., 1988) which aimed to support learning and physically disabled clients as they moved from residential to community settings and to provide the users with 'an individual, comprehensive review of their needs and to generate specific service objectives to meet them' (De Kock et al., 1988: 152).

Treatment theory

Treatment theory (Keith and Lipsey, 1993) has provided an account of how goal implementation takes place within physical rehabilitation. The theory provides a model of the relationships between determinants of treatment: patient characteristics, internal factors (including resources) of the service/organisation and external or environmental factors. All of these factors impact on the treatment approach and provision, namely goal planning, for the patient. The theory also identifies possible outcomes by which to measure rehabilitation provision.

Goal setting is a frequently utilized approach within rehabilitation planning and delivery. Its pre-eminence has developed through two factors: behavioural studies examining the rehabilitation process; and its practical utility. Behavioural research in a variety of rehabilitation settings suggests that there is a discrepancy between what actually occurs and what rehabilitation staff believe occurs during rehabilitation. Active treatment has been found to account for only a small proportion of patient time, and that passive disengaged behaviour occupies at least as frequent a proportion of the rehabilitation day (Keith and Lipsey, 1993; Kennedy et al., 1988). Kennedy et al. (1988) studied patient involvement and participation in rehabilitation within a spinal cord injury rehabilitation service. They found that patients were engaged in a high level of solitary behaviour throughout the day and suggested that there is an under-utilization of therapeutic potential and thus rehabilitation quality. They also found that patients were not involved in decision making or formal rehabilitation planning meetings. In contrast to staff perceptions, a finding of the study was that patients spent a relatively small proportion of time in therapy departments and a much greater amount of time in disengaged behaviour in the ward. Following the introduction of a goal planning system (Kennedy et al., 1991) the above behaviour patterns changed significantly. The overall pattern of interaction between patients and staff increased and patients spent a much greater proportion of their day in therapy areas, and when on the ward areas, spent a greater proportion of the time engaged in rehabilitation activities. Kennedy et al. (1991) conclude that goal planning is an effective way of reducing disengagement, increasing activity and increasing patient involvement in decision making.

McGrath and Adams (1999) found that goal planning was also an effective psychological intervention for reducing anxiety, which helped the individual cope with distress. They found that positive emotions and the development of a positive self-image occur through goal planning. The specific factors identified as facilitating this change were when the actual rate of approach to a goal was greater than the desired rate. These findings emphasize the need for the provision of accurate feedback about perform-ance and progress through the setting of specific goals with a realistic time frame for achievement.

There are many variations on the application of goal planning theory and this partly depends on the context of the service. However, the section below outlines the key aspects of the approach with practical examples.

Key strategies of goal planning

Client involvement

One of the key theoretical principles of goal setting theory is client involvement within the goal planning process because this enhances the individual's commitment, and therefore performance. There is a recognition that the provision of rehabilitation should be organized around the client's needs rather than being therapist-centred to enable the person to actively engage in their rehabilitation and for the goals to build upon the skills and routine of the individual so that these are generalized to the patient's natural environment (Houts and Scott, 1975). Research has found that goal setting provides a direction for the individual and helps to focus their attention on key objectives. Locke and Latham (2002) comment that goal setting energizes the person, with high goals leading to greater effort than low goals; facilitates persistence; and helps the individual develop knowledge and strategies to manage problems. As stated earlier, goal performance is strongest when people are committed to their goals; this commitment in turn is moderated by the importance of the outcomes and the individual's self-efficacy. Locke et al. (1997) consider the primary benefit of participation in decision making to be cognitive rather than motivational, that partici-pation stimulates information exchange. In their research, those who participated in formulating strategies performed the strategies better and had higher self-efficacy. Latham et al. (1988) found that in addition to this, a key aspect was to provide the individual with an explanation about the rationale and purpose for the goal because this enhances performance.

There is a substantial body of evidence that active involvement in goal planning facilitates goal attainment and patient satisfaction. LaFerriere and Calsyn (1978) report that adults with disabilities who are directly involved in goal setting are more likely to report greater motivation for change and Treischman (1974) comments that rehabilitation is more effective when the patient is involved with goal setting. Foley (1998) reviews the usefulness of goal planning within spinal cord injury rehabilitation and states that the involvement of a patient in setting goals and identifying priorities helps the individual to manage the consequences of their injury and facilitates adjustment by highlighting capabilities, giving the person a sense of control.

Orbell *et al.* (2001) found that self-efficacy and goal importance were related to achievement of activities of daily living skills following joint replacement surgery, and were more predictive of post-surgery outcome three months after surgery than medical variables and prior disability. They suggest their findings support the theoretical proposition that attractiveness of a goal and motivational arousal influence goal achievement. Webb and Glueckauf (1994) looked at involvement in goal planning and goal achievement within a traumatic brain-injured population. Participants in a high involvement condition demonstrated significant gains compared to the low involvement group over the time period of the intervention.

Duff *et al.* (1999) reported a survey of patients' views of goal planning. Patients reported that goal planning helped them to plan and be actively involved in their rehabilitation and provided them with information and clear goals. MacLeod and MacLeod (1996) completed a survey with spinal cord-injured patients a year after the introduction of a goal planning system. Patients reported goal planning to be informative and helpful and rated that they had a 'fair' to 'complete' amount of control over rehabilitation through the goal planning process. There was a significant relationship between provision of information and patient sense of control.

Multidisciplinary approach

In physical rehabilitation, clients present with a complex array of problems which are beyond the mechanics of an actual disease or injury and involve all aspects of an individual's life. A comprehensive multidisciplinary team is at the heart of the provision of effective rehabilitation services and no one professional group can meet all of the multi-faceted needs of these patients. Some common needs in physical disability concern activities of daily living, physical well-being and self-care, mobility, social issues, accommodation, employment, family support, sexuality and psychological well-being. If we take one aspect, such as learning to dress oneself, there are specific skills that a physiotherapist, occupational therapist (OT) and nurse bring to this area. For example, the patient may need to develop skills in balance or be able to lift their arms in order to put on a top; such skills will be worked on by the physiotherapist. The OT, in turn, may work on specific upper limb skills and practise dressing, perhaps identifying techniques or aides required by the individual. The nursing team then works with the patient on a daily basis to implement these skills and contextualize them, and together with the patient can provide a feedback loop about whether further skills are required. Each professional brings their specific expertise to a problem but needs to work in conjunction with the others to practically solve the difficulty. Where this does not take place, confusion exists with each group narrowly viewing the patient's needs from their own perspective, rather than working collaboratively on client-driven goals. So, in the above example, the OT may start dressing practice before the person has gained the requisite balance skills. This not only reduces the likelihood of the person successfully achieving the goal, which in turn impacts on their self-efficacy and motivation, but also the individual only develops skills to deal with prescribed areas (e.g. dressing on a hospital bed) rather than an overall problem-solving framework.

McGrath and Adams (1999) comment that goal planning, when properly applied, is effective in resolving conflict among team members because the focus is naturally on client-driven goals which forces collaborative inter-disciplinary work. In reviewing the essential elements of goal planning, McGrath and Davis (1992) identified goal incompatibility, either within or between professions, or between the clients' and professionals' views, as one of the main contributors to rehabilitation planning going wrong. This highlights the interrelationship between the two key strategies discussed so far: client involvement and multidisciplinary team working.

Needs assessment

The effectiveness of rehabilitation planning is related to the process through which needs are assessed and identified. Wade (1998a), in a review of assessment in rehabilitation, cites evidence that up to 75 per cent of disabilities in hospital inpatients are unrecognized by physicians, although a lower rate of failure was found in outpatients (Calkins *et al.*, 1991). Wade (1998a) suggests that uni-professional assessment leads to failure in identifying some of the problems experienced by the individual and that assessment that focuses specifically on disability will be more comprehensive in identifying an individual's problem (Cunningham *et al.*, 1996). Wade (1998b) concludes that assessment should be structured, multidisciplinary and conducted by specialized rehabilitation services to avoid failure in identifying the multi-faceted needs of an individual with a physical disability. Multidisciplinary assessment also enables the identification of common goals between members of a team, which is essential in achieving a consistent approach to behaviour change, as outlined above.

There are a substantial number of assessment tools used in rehabilitation. The remainder of this section highlights some of the important considera-tions for assessment and provides specific examples of tools used in goal planning settings that utilize this approach.

There is a need at the outset to consider whether to use a global assess-ment tool which has been designed for use with many populations or one that is specific to your client group. Glueckauf (1993) provides a comprehensive overview of assessment in rehabilitation and discusses the principles involved in selecting an assessment tool. Glueckauf suggests that assessment tools in rehabilitation need to have as a basic premise the concept of the 'expert consumer' with professional and consumer advocates being involved in the design and evaluation process. Assessment devices need to be sensitive to small increments of change as well as addressing the more global issue of the amount of assistance required to complete a task or the ability of the client to independently perform a task (Keith and Lipsey, 1993). This is particularly critical in rehabilitation because the skills worked on are often fine, such as someone who is currently receiving 75 per cent support with a transfer increasing their independence by 25 per cent. If the overall rating is one of either complete independence or dependence, then this person would clearly still fail even though their skills and ability have improved. An important consideration when designing an assessment tool is that the evaluation is 'theory driven', that the assessment questions should be guided by some explicit conceptualization of the causal process through which the intervention is expected to have effects (Keith and Lipsey, 1993).

McGrath and Davis (1992), in examining this area, make the distinction between interdisciplinary assessment (which they suggest is based on 'social participation', identifying the client's ability to assume valued roles and the impediments to this) and a multidisciplinary approach which focuses on 'activities' (such as problems with self-care or speech and language) (*International classification of impairments, disabilities and handicaps*: ICIDH-2; World Health Organization, 2001). The latter, they suggest, fits easily into professional categories and boundaries but does not encourage a client-focused approach (the former). They suggest that a multidisciplinary approach is supported by many assessment tools commonly used in rehabilitation, such as the Barthel Index (Mahoney and Barthel, 1965) and Functional Independence Measure (FIM; Hamilton and Granger, 1990), and although these provide a reliable and measurable outcome, they do not reflect client needs and address the principles of goal planning theory outlined above. Wade and de Jong (2000) comment that assessment also needs to assess participation, perceived needs and ability from the client's perspective rather than the outside perspective of the rater.

Comprehensive approaches

Comprehensive assessment in rehabilitation should emphasize the individual's strengths rather than weaknesses, and focus on their needs rather than disabilities. Building on the existing strengths of an individual helps compensate for loss of function. Being clear about somebody's strengths helps us to identify the resources of the individual and the reinforcers that are most meaningful and motivating for them. Individuals may have physical strengths, such as the ability to type or enjoy sport, or have skills in a craft; mental strengths, such as a facility with numbers; special interests which they enjoy and are knowledgeable about, like literature or cookery; and social strengths, such as having a wide circle of supportive friends.

Two approaches to assessment that have been developed by physical rehabilitation services are the life goals approach (developed by McGrath and Adams, 1999, working in brain injury) and the needs assessment approach (developed by Kennedy and colleagues (Kennedy and Hamilton, 1999; Berry and Kennedy, 2002) working in spinal cord injury). The life goals approach utilizes Carver and Scheier's (1990) control model of affect to explain the emotional impact of brain injury on life goals. McGrath *et al.* (1995) have developed a life goals questionnaire which is administered on admission, the findings of which structure the goal planning meeting. Sivaraman Nair (2003) reviews a number of scales which measure life goals and comments on the merits of this approach.

The Needs Assessment Checklist (NAC; Kennedy and Hamilton, 1999) was developed for a spinal cord injured population because existing measures were found to be too generalized in their measurement of incremental behaviour change, providing too many floor and ceiling effects. The NAC was developed through consultation with patients and the multidisciplinary team. Rehabilitation domains were generated within which specific areas of need and the behavioural indicators were then identified and agreed. For example, a domain area is activity of daily living, a need area is dressing, and a behavioural indicator is ability to dress the upper half of the body. Another critical factor which distinguishes the NAC from other measures is that independence is rated on both physical and verbal means, thus someone who will not recover sufficient physical function for a task (such as dressing their top half) can still achieve maximum independence by being knowledgeable about and able to instruct others in its completion. The NAC has been found to be both a reliable and valid measure of rehabilitation (Berry and Kennedy, 2002).

The setting of goals is directly derived from the assessment tool used and goals are set between the patient and the multidisciplinary team in a collaborative relationship. The following section outlines how to do this effectively.

Setting specific goals

A key component of goal planning is that goals need to be specific and set at the right level, not too easy and not unrealistically high, but challenging (Stetcher *et al.*, 1995; Bar-Eli *et al.*, 1997; Wade, 1999). Research has found that people achieve less when 'do your best' goals are set, compared to the setting of specific but difficult goals (Locke and Latham, 1990). This is because 'do your best' goals have no external frame of reference, so people cannot judge what to achieve or whether they have achieved it. Theodorakis *et al.* (1996) comment on the usefulness of goal setting with injured athletes. They state that specific, difficult and challenging goals lead to a higher level of task performance than general goals. They found that specific personal goal setting was the mediator between ability and performance and was related to self-efficacy expectations, confidence and self-satisfaction. Bower *et al.* (1996) found that setting specific measurable goals was more strongly associated with skill acquisition than conventional or intensive physiotherapy in children with cerebral palsy.

Levels of goal setting

There are many variants to the application of goal setting, but most systems use three levels. The first level is an aim or need and refers to the area in which the goal is to be set, for example activities of daily living. The second is an objective or goal and specifies behaviour, what is to be learned, e.g. the development of a specific skill, and how. Goals need to be generally achievable within weeks or a couple of months. The overriding principle is for a goal to be clear and specific. The third level is commonly referred to as targets. Targets are much more immediate and outline the specifics of who will be involved in meeting the target, the action, conditions and level of success. It is a supplementary level to the overall goal and each goal may have a number of targets before the goal itself is achieved. For example 'Jennifer must be able to cook' is not a specific enough goal because this could range from beans on toast to a cordon bleu meal. The setting of the goal will also depend upon the individual's previous skill in her area. Jennifer may have been a very established cook with a number of strengths in this area or beans on toast may be the limit of her ability and, importantly, interest. So a goal must specify who (Jennifer) will do what (cook spaghetti Bolognese), under what conditions (in occupational therapy, in a month's time) and to what degree of success (independently). Targets will therefore underpin the achievement of this goal and may include: 'Jennifer to be assessed for a knife splint and cut up vegetables in the first week'; 'The physiotherapist and Jennifer to improve arm strength so that Jennifer can lift a pan clear of the stove in the second week'; and 'Jennifer and the OT to go on a shopping trip to buy ingredients prior to cooking the meal'. If the client has a cognitive impairment the targets could include organization and planning skills in the execution of the shopping task or cooking the meal, or a much longer-term goal which includes rehearsal. This is where the flexibility of the approach lies, in that goals and targets can be as detailed as required.

In rehabilitation it is common for clients to have a number of long-term or complex goals which need to be broken down into a series of small steps or targets. Bar-Eli *et al.* (1994) comment on the need for both short- and long-term goals in order to produce lasting and self-regulated behaviour change and state that the proximity of the goal can also serve to increase performance. In particular they emphasize the role of immediate goals in providing direct incentives and feedback about progress. So, for example, a longer-term goal may be for a child to return to school after a protracted period of time in hospital. This can be made much more attainable by identifying the smaller goals within it.

Case vignette 12.1

Mark is a 10-year-old boy with cerebral palsy who is able to walk with the aid of calipers and a stick. He lives in Cambridge with his mother and two younger siblings, one aged four and the other nine months. His stepfather left three months ago and Mark has not seen him since, although he has visited his siblings while Mark was at school. He enjoys playing on the computer and goes to his local swimming club. Mark does not like reading and his teachers are beginning to wonder if he will cope with secondary school when he moves up in one year's time. He will be spending about a month in hospital and as a consequence the risk is that he will fall further behind his peers.

In the above example, a longer-term goal is for Mark's educational needs to be assessed by an educational psychologist and liaison established with the school special needs teacher, and a decision to be made about his secondary school provision. Mark's physical needs have also changed, so a medium-term goal is for his new requirements/needs to be established. Short-term targets with this would be for the local community OT to contact the school (and secondary school) and visit with the family to assess the environment for adaptations. A visit may in turn highlight further targets such as accessibility, and support or transport issues, before the overall goal of returning to school can be achieved. In the meantime three short-term/immediate targets could be set:

1   Mark to maintain contact with the school through attending the school fete and emailing/seeing friends.
2   The school to advise the hospital teacher and the family about work that Mark can complete while in hospital, including the setting of specific tasks or tests (e.g. spelling/maths) for Mark at regular intervals – some of which may be able to be achieved interactively with peers.

3   The physiotherapist to identify sports that Mark can become involved with at secondary school and practise these with him.

McGrath and Adams (1999) state that a strength of the goal planning process is that it is explicitly hierarchical. They conceptualize the three levels as: basic therapeutic activities (targets) which are linked to higher order objectives, which are in turn linked to a higher order aim. They consider that these should be personally meaningful and related to the individual's higher order reference values. So, learning to dress oneself is related to being able to go out with friends, which in turn is related to a resumption of independence. It is this higher order aim which is related to the individual's self-image and self-efficacy, the achievement of which facilitates adjustment. Wade (1999) considers the three-level process to be related to level of organizational involvement and makes links with the model of illness outlined in the ICIDH-2 (World Health Organization, 2001). Wade (1999) considers that an aim involves organizations in general society, often outside health, and that to impact at the 'participation' level (thus focusing on social roles, etc.), one needs to involve both the patient and their family. The objective or goal includes one organization and two or more professionals and considers 'activity' (behaviour), the context, environment and attitudes. Wade (1999) considers targets to involve one or more named people and can be at any level of the ICIDH-2 model.

Case vignette 12.2

Henry is a 60-year-old retired solicitor. He and his wife live in a detached farmhouse in Norfolk with toilet and bathing facilities on the first floor. Henry had a right-sided stroke two months ago and has neglect of his left side. He is also incontinent of urine. He has speech difficulties which frustrate him greatly and impact upon his ability to communicate with his family and friends. He has a supportive family, two of his children live abroad and one lives in London. Henry's interests prior to his stroke included sailing, golf, reading a daily newspaper and doing the crossword, and listening to classical music.

From the above example Henry has a number of needs, but perhaps the most initially pressing involve speech/cognition, activity and housing. An immediate goal could be for Henry to be assessed by the speech and language therapist, with the aim of improving his speech and also his ability to communicate his needs and wishes. A medium-term goal could be set of Henry reading the newspaper and completing a crossword. This would involve the speech and language therapist, OT and clinical psychologist doing joint work to increase Henry's cognitive functioning and setting incremental targets such as reading a short paragraph through to an article, or letter/word puzzles of increasing complexity leading to a crossword. Many potential activity goals (both short and long term) could be set. Immediate targets could include teaching Henry to dress himself and use strategies to accommodate his left-sided neglect in this task, with a longer-term goal of resuming some of his valued activities, for example, attending a classical music concert. Another long-term goal would be for him to return home. This would involve a number of short-term/immediate targets:

1   The hospital OT to contact Henry's wife within one day to outline the need and rationale for a visit and to see if it can be made, finding out suitable dates for her.
2   The hospital OT to make a referral to the community OT within one week and request that Henry's home is assessed.
3   A home visit to take place within four weeks and transport to be arranged.

Clinical context

In clinical settings, limited work has been done on staff ability to set specific goals and predict outcome, despite the fact that this is a cornerstone of rehabilitation practice. Squires *et al.* (1991) found that physiotherapists working with older adults were able to accurately predict and set goals and the timescale for change, in relation to the level of mobility required for discharge. Duff *et al.* (2004) conducted a retrospective audit of rehabilitation practice in spinal cord injury. They found a high achievement rate (72 per cent following the first goal planning meeting and 68 per cent thereafter), with only a small proportion of goals being overachieved (2 per cent) or partially achieved (4 per cent), which points to the ability of therapists to predict achievement and set realistic goals. Furthermore, the goal planning approach used was found to correlate with the assessment and discharge measure of rehabilitation outcome (the NAC), providing support for the use of a structured goal planning approach.

Rehabilitation planning in practice

Many injuries require a period of acute care which inevitably creates a degree of dependency. Although necessary at this early stage, such dependency hampers later rehabilitation when the emphasis must be on enabling the person to achieve as great a degree of independence as possible. Rehabilitation is a two-part process of enabling the individual to develop the skills they need, and in turn, empowering them to use these skills. It is a partnership of learning and self-responsibility rather than a prescriptive process which requires compliance. It involves the client identifying their needs and aims with the treating clinicians, and the clinicians utilizing their skills as directed by the client and their needs, rather than having a predetermined checklist of what needs to be achieved.

The role of a keyworker

The provision and organization of goal planning is often coordinated through using a keyworker system. A keyworker is most commonly a member of the multidisciplinary team working with the patient such as, for example, an OT or nurse who takes on the additional team role of facilitating the goal planning process. The keyworker role is a complex one and is crucial in the effectiveness and ethos of the overall goal planning system for the individual patient. The role includes facilitating the use of the key strategies outlined above, ensuring a patient-centred approach from the team through minimizing role conflict and ambiguity. It involves *coordinating* the rehabilitation team, *supporting* the team and patient through the setting of appropriate goals and level of difficulty, *facilitating* the individual's rehabilitation and acting as the patient's *advocate*. This latter role of *empowerment* is one of the most significant and will be discussed in greater detail later in this chapter. Keyworkers maintain an overview of the goal planning process for the individual and have practical roles of organizing and conducting the goal planning meetings, and perhaps the completion of the assessment tool. The keyworker is an 'expert resource' for the patient, with the ability to direct the patient about how to gain information within the organization, rather than being the holder of all the knowledge about the individual's needs. A keyworker's role often includes negotiation between individual team members, or the patient and the clinical team. This most commonly occurs when a patient has different goals from the team. The team has a responsibility to provide an explanation for their recommendation and the consequences of not pursuing a certain goal, for example contractures in the case of a patient refusing to wear splints. In such an example a crucial first step in engaging in the process may be to concentrate on the common goals and return to more difficult ones later. So advocacy involves helping the patient to discover their views and feelings, to think in a creative way about their resources, to provide information and explore options, and to support the person in thinking through the issues of their disability. It also involves conveying faith in the person and their skills and gently challenging negative beliefs. Being a keyworker can also involve talking through anxieties which may be an indicator that the individual does not feel they have the skills to cope with a new challenge. Successfully meeting fears provides powerful feedback and increases confidence; negotiating realistic goals and targets is an important way of achieving this. Successful patient–provider communication is fundamental to the effective provision of rehabilitation services, because unless we know about the person's condition from their perspective and the context of their life, we cannot know how best to support their rehabilitation (Inui and Carter, 1985).

Empowerment

The most significant role of the keyworker is one of empowerment. Empowerment is now recognized as one of the key factors in the provision of rehabilitation services for chronic conditions (Department of Health, 2001). A goal planning approach encompasses the principles of the self-management or Expert Patient programmes (as they have become known in the UK) because it is based upon patients developing the knowledge, confidence and motivation to manage their own skills in order to take effective control over their condition or disability.

The introduction outlined the core aspects of rehabilitation, which in physical disability often occurs after an acute episode in which the person's life and function change. Rehabilitation is about enabling the person to accommodate these changes in their life. Common experiences of patients with chronic conditions are: lack of involvement in decisions; no one to talk to about anxieties and concerns; lack of clear information about tests and/ or treatments; insufficient information for family and friends; insufficient information about recovery (Coulter, Picker Institute, 2001, cited in Department of Health, 2001). Effective rehabilitation planning is about enabling the person to develop the skills required for them to manage their needs for the rest of their life. These skills are knowing how to recognize and act upon symptoms; to be able to deal with acute problems or exacerbations of the condition; to effectively use medicines and treatments; to comprehend the implications of professional advice; to be able to access services, social services, leisure activities etc.; to manage work or employment; to develop strategies to deal with the psychological consequences of the condition or disability; to learn to cope with other people's responses to the condition or disability; and, where relevant, to establish a stable pattern of sleep and rest for dealing with fatigue (Department of Health, 2001). These need to be key features of the provision of rehabilitation planning, because the behaviours patients initially learn to manage their changed physical condition will be with them for the rest of their lives. If patients learn about partnership and develop an understanding about their condition from the earliest stages of their adjustment, these skills will be utilized throughout. Many physical disability services provide lifespan services to their clients; therefore teaching self-management skills helps to manage these resources effectively. There is evidence of reduced primary care contact following self-management programmes because of the development of patients' skills to manage their condition.

The research evidence is that the impact of self-management approaches reduces the likelihood of the more disabling aspects of chronic conditions such as symptoms, pain, reduced social activities and isolation, lack of employment and problems of psychological adjustment and life satisfaction. Also, there is evidence of improved adherence and healthful behaviours (exercise, cognitive symptom management, coping, and communications with physicians), improved health status (self-reported health, fatigue, disability, social/role activities and health distress) and decreased days in hospital (Department of Health, 2001). User-led self-management programmes have been developed by a number of groups such as the Multiple Sclerosis Society, Changing Faces, the British Heart Foundation and the Spinal Injuries Association. There are five core self-management skills: problem solving; decision making; resource utilization; formation of a patient–professional relationship; and taking action. However, the evidence is that important though these skills are, they are not the key to effective self-management. The key is empowerment, to change the individual's confidence and belief that they are able to take control over their life despite their condition or disability.

Von Korff et al. (1997), in their article on collaborative management of chronic illness, identify many of the principles of goal planning as being part of patient self-management. They consider four aspects of collaborative management: first, a collaborative definition of the problem, followed by goal setting and planning. The third element is teaching health skills. The provision of structured patient education and teaching about the condition is a necessary and complementary system to a goal planning approach. Von Korff et al. cite evidence from diabetes, oncology, arthritis, HIV, back pain, asthma, coronary care, amputation and Parkinson's disease about the effectiveness of health education. The fourth element is active, sustained follow-up from the health care provider, which, as commented upon above, is often a feature of physical disability services.

Goal planning and self-management initiatives also help improve adherence in chronic conditions. In diabetes, dietary management improved following self-management and goal setting (Glasgow et al., 1996) and in brain injury the gains made during goal planning were maintained on follow-up in a group that were taught self-monitoring techniques (Webb and Glueckauf, 1994). Oldridge et al. (1999) found improved adherence and outcome in patients post myocardial infarction that followed a goal setting programme compared to those who participated in usual care. Kennedy and Swalwell (1995) found that patients with a spinal cord injury who had participated in a goal planning programme had maintained their rehabilitation goals six months post discharge. Bar-Eli et al. (1994) found that adolescents with physical injury and behavioural problems were more likely to maintain the gains made during goal setting if they were involved in the process of setting goals and had a mixture of long- and short-term goals to achieve.

Implementing goal planning

A goal planning approach radically alters the orientation and provision of rehabilitation services. It steps away from traditional professional boundaries to put patients' needs at the heart of service provision. As highlighted earlier (Keith and Lipsey, 1993; Kennedy et al., 1988), implementing a goal planning system can alter all aspects of patient's and staff's therapeutic day and their achievements. Georgiades and Phillimore (1975) wrote a seminal paper about achieving successful organizational change. Any change needs to be identified and desired by those affected, so it is important to involve current patients, staff and user groups in reviewing the service and making change. Also, having a key group of people who are committed and behaviourally supportive to following through the change process is crucial (Locke and Latham, 2002). A plan for change should focus on the macro, organizational level as well as the individuals within it. Locke and Latham (2002) suggest that there is a need to make a public commitment to implementing the process as this enhances the likelihood of change taking place and thus enhances performance.

Kennedy and Pearce (1993) outline the strategies for change used to implement goal planning within a spinal cord injury rehabilitation service. First, they mapped out the needs of the individuals within the service which led to the development of a NAC containing behavioural indicators of performance. The needs were mapped out by a group of staff who were both operationally active and committed to the goal planning process and the checklist was developed and piloted in consultation with patients and staff. The NAC came to be used as both an assessment and outcome tool associated with the programme. A staff training package incorporating the key strategies of goal planning was also developed, which included specific teaching on the skills required to be a keyworker. A project monitoring team oversaw the whole process and met regularly throughout the implementation. The service has undergone a number of audits (Kennedy and Swalwell, 1995; Kennedy et al., 1996; Duff et al., 1999, 2004) and the system refined in the light of these.

Davis et al. (1992) outline the process of introducing goal planning within a brain injury rehabilitation setting. They comment on the importance of involving staff within the change process and the need to make gradual incremental change to staff working practice. Initial staff concerns were that the new approach increased the time demand for them to attend meetings. Their study found that time was required to be invested initially to implement the system, but that in the long term, time spent in planning meetings reduced the need for reactive 'crisis' meetings. They also found that the new interdisciplinary approach streamlined the admission and rehabilitation pathways, providing a consensus in terminology. A later audit of the same service (McGrath *et al.*, 1995) identified training needs for staff which included videos of well and poorly run goal planning meetings and quarterly question and answer training sessions to enhance staff adherence to the key strategies.

Conclusion

Goal planning theory is a well-established and frequently utilized system for facilitating patient involvement in rehabilitation and in the organization of rehabilitation provision as a whole. The practice of goal planning has developed into a robust behavioural approach which can be utilized with any clinical group. There is evidence that behavioural change is more likely to occur when goal planning is used (Wade, 1998b), and evidence that supports the provision of problem-orientated, well-organized and coordinated multidisciplinary rehabilitation services (Wade and de Jong, 2000). There is a need for more published clinical evidence of the effectiveness of the approach (Wade, 1998a). Research is particularly required in evaluating process issues of the approach, such as client involvement. For example, the amount of patient communication and speech within a meeting, satisfaction assessments following goal planning meetings (rather than a global assessment of the system as a whole), and adherence. Rehabilitation outcome data are also required in order to understand the effectiveness of particular aspects of the approach. Although further research is needed, a number of studies have demonstrated that effective goal-orientated rehabilitation planning enhances the lives of people with disabilities and can provide commissioners and practitioners with detailed information about rehabilitation and the actual needs of a client group, thus enabling strategic provision of services. Studies have also shown that systematic rehabilitation planning can empower and involve patients to address their needs, and that these are involved in the individual's achievement and service outcome.

References

Bandura, A. (1986). *Social foundations of thought and action: A social-cognitive theory*. Englewood Cliffs, NJ: Prentice-Hall.

Bar-Eli, M., Hartman, I. and Levy-Kolker, N. (1994). Using goal setting to improve physical performance of adolescents with behaviour disorders: The effect of goal proximity. *Adapted Physical Activity Quarterly*, 11, 86–97.

Bar-Eli, M., Tenenbaum, G., Pie, J. S., Btesh, Y. and Almog, A. (1997). Effect of goal difficulty, goal specificity and duration of practice time intervals on muscular endurance performance. *Journal of Sports Sciences*, 15, 125–135.

Berry, C. and Kennedy, P. (2002). A psychometric analysis of the Needs Assessment Checklist (NAC). *Spinal Cord*, 41, 490–501.

Bower, E., McLellan, D. L., Arney, J. and Campbell, M. J. (1996). A randomised controlled trial of different intensities of physiotherapy and different goal-setting procedures in 44 children with cerebral palsy. *Developmental Medicine and Child Neurology*, 38(3), 226–237.

Calkins, D. R., Rubenstein, L. V., Clearly, P. D., Davies, A. R., Jette, A. M. A., Fink, A., Kosecoff, J., Young, R. T. and Delbanco, T. L. (1991). Failure of physicians to recognize functional disability in ambulatory patients. *Annals of Internal Medicine*, 114, 451–454.

Carver, C. S. and Scheier, M. F. (1990). Origins and function of positive and negative affect: A control process review. *Psychology Review*, 97, 19–36.

Cunningham, C., Horgan, F., Keane, N., Connolly, P., Mannion, A. and O'Neil, D. (1996). Detection of disability by different members of an interdisciplinary team. *Clinical Rehabilitation*, 10, 247–254.

Davis, A., Davis, S., Moss, N., Marks, J., McGrath, J., Hovard, L., Axon J. and Wade, D. (1992). First steps towards an interdisciplinary approach to rehabilitation. *Clinical Rehabilitation*, 6, 237–244.

De Kock, U., Saxby, H., Felce, D., Thomas, M. and Jenkins, J. (1988). Individual planning for adults with severe or profound mental handicaps in a community-based service. *Mental Handicap*, 16, 152–158.

Department of Health (2001). *The Expert Patient: A new approach to chronic disease management for the 21st century*. London: Department of Health.

Duff, J., Evans, M. and Kennedy, P. (2004). Goal planning: A retrospective audit of rehabilitation process and outcome. *Clinical Rehabilitation*, 18, 275–286.

Duff, J., Kennedy, P. and Swalwell, E. (1999). Clinical audit of physical rehabilitation: patients' views of goal planning. *Clinical Psychology Forum*, 129, 34–38.

Foley, A. (1998). A review of goal planning in the rehabilitation of the spinal cord injured person. *Journal of Orthopaedic Nursing*, 2(3), 148–152.

Georgiades, N. J. and Phillimore, L. (1975). The myth of the hero-innovator and alternative strategies for organizational change. In C. C. Kiernan and F. P. Woodford (eds) *Behaviour modification with the severely retarded: Study group of the Institute for Research into Multiple Handicap* (pp. 313–319). New York: Associated Scientific Publishers.

Glasgow, R. E., Toobert, D. J. and Hampson, S. E. (1996). Effects of a brief office-based intervention to facilitate diabetes dietary self-management. *Diabetes Care*, 19(8), 835–842.

Glueckauf, R. L. (1993). Use and misuse of assessment in rehabilitation. In R. L. Glueckauf, L. B., Secrest, G. R. Bond and E. C. McDonel (eds) *Improving assessment in rehabilitation and health* (pp. 33–60). Newbury Park, CA: Sage.

Hamilton, B. B. and Granger, C. V. (1990). *Guide for the use of uniform data set for medical rehabilitation*. Buffalo, NY: Research Foundation of State University of New York.

Houts, P. and Scott, R. (1975). *Goal planning with developmentally disabled persons: Procedures for developing an individualized client plan*. Hershey, PA: Department of Behavioural Science, Pennsylvania State University College of Medicine.

Inui, T. S. and Carter, W. B. (1985). Problems and prospects for health services research on provider–patient communication. *Medical Care*, 23(5), 521–538.

Keith, R. A. and Lipsey, M. W. (1993). The role of theory in rehabilitation assessment, treatment and outcomes. In R. L. Gluekauf, L. B. Secrest, G. R. Bond and E. C. McDonel (eds) *Improving assessment in rehabilitation and health* (pp. 33–60). Newbury Park, CA: Sage.

Kennedy, P. and Hamilton, L. R. (1999). The needs assessment checklist: A clinical approach to measuring outcome. *Spinal Cord*, 37(2), 136–139.

Kennedy, P. and Pearce, N. (1993). Goal planning, needs assessment and advocacy. *Health Services Management*, 89, 17–19.

Kennedy, P. and Swalwell, E. (1995). Clinical audit of physical rehabilitation: Goal planning and needs assessment. *Auditorium*, 2, 25–28.

Kennedy, P., Fisher, K. and Pearson, E. (1988). Ecological evaluation of a rehabilitation environment for spinal cord injured people: Behavioural mapping and feedback. *British Journal of Clinical Psychology*, 27, 239–246.

Kennedy, P., Henderson, J. and Gallagher, S. (1996). Improving goal attainment with spinal cord injured patients. *Journal of the Association for Quality in Healthcare*, 3, 145–150.

Kennedy, P., Walker, L. and White, D. (1991). Ecological evaluation of goal planning and advocacy in a rehabilitative environment for spinal cord injured people. *Paraplegia*, 29, 197–192.

LaFerriere, L. and Calsyn, R. (1978). Goal attainment scaling: An effective treatment technique in short term therapy. *American Journal of Community Psychology*, 6, 271–282.

Latham, G. P., Erez, M. and Locke, E. (1988). Resolving scientific disputes by the joint design of crucial experiments by the antagonists: Application to the Erez–Latham dispute regarding participation in goal setting. *Journal of Applied Psychology*, 73, 753–772.

Locke, E. and Latham, G. (1990). *A theory of goal setting and task performance.* Englewood Cliffs, NJ: Prentice-Hall.

Locke, E. A. and Latham, G. P. (2002). Building a practically useful theory of goal setting and task motivation. *American Psychologist*, 57(9), 705–717.

Locke, E. A., Alavi, M. and Wagner, J. (1997). Participation in decision making: An information exchange perspective. In G. Ferris (ed.) *Research in personnel and human resources management* (Vol. 15, pp. 293–331). Greenwich, CT: JAI Press.

Locke, E., Frederick, E., Bobko, P. and Lee, C. (1984). Effect of self-efficacy, goals and task strategies on task performance. *Journal of Psychology*, 69, 241–251.

McGrath, J. R. and Adams, L. (1999). Patient-centred goal planning: A systematic psychological therapy? *Topics in Stroke Rehabilitation*, 6(2), 43–50.

McGrath, J. R. and Davis, A. M. (1992). Rehabilitation: Where are we going and how do we get there? *Clinical Rehabilitation*, 6, 225–235.

McGrath, J. R., Marks, J. A. and Davis, A. M. (1995). Towards interdisciplinary rehabilitation: Further developments at Rivermead Rehabilitation Centre. *Clinical Rehabilitation*, 9, 320–326.

MacLeod, G. M. and MacLeod, L. (1996). Evaluation of client and staff satisfaction with a goal-planning project implemented with people with spinal cord injuries. *Spinal Cord*, 34, 525–530.

Mahoney, F. I. and Barthel, D. W. (1965). Functional evaluation: The Barthel Index. *Maryland State Medical Journal*, 14, 61–65.

Norris-Baker, C., Stephens, M. A., Rintala, D. H. and Willems, E. P. (1981). Patient behavior as a predictor of outcomes in spinal cord injury. *Archives of Physical Medicine & Rehabilitation*, 62(12), 602–608.

Oldridge, N., Guyatt, G., Crowe, J., Feeny, D. and Jones, N. (1999). Goal attainment in a randomized controlled trial of rehabilitation after myocardial infarction. *Journal of Cardiopulmonary Rehabilitation*, 19, 29–34.

Orbell, S., Johnston, M., Rowley, D., Davey, P. and Espley, A. (2001). Self-efficacy and goal importance in the prediction of physical disability in people following hospitalisation: A prospective study. *British Journal of Health Psychology*, 6(1), 25–40.

Ryan, T. A. (1970). *Intentional behaviour*. New York: Ronald Press.

Sivaraman Nair, K. P. (2003). Life goals: The concept and its relevance to rehabilitation. *Clinical Rehabilitation*, 17, 192–202.

Squires, A., Rumgay, B. and Perombelon, M. (1991). Audit of contract goal setting by physiotherapists working with elderly patients. *Physiotherapy*, 77(12), 790–795.

Stetcher, V. J., Seijts, G. H., Kok, G. J., Latham, G. P., Glasgow, R., DeVellis, B., Meertens, R. M. and Bulger, D. W. (1995). Goal setting as a strategy for health behaviour change. *Health Education Quarterly*, 22(2), 190–200.

Theodorakis, Y., Malliou, P., Papaioannou, A., Beneca, A. and Filactakidou, A. (1996). The effect of personal goals, self efficacy, and self satisfaction on injury rehabilitation. *Journal of Sport Rehabilitation*, 5, 214–223.

Treischman, R. B. (1974). Coping with a disability: A sliding scale of goals. *Archives of Physical Medicine and Rehabilitation*, 55, 556–560.

Von Korff, M., Gruman, J., Schaefer, J., Curry, S. J. and Wagner, E. H. (1997). Collaborative management of chronic illness. *American College of Physicians*, 127(12), 1097–1102.

Wade, D. T. (1998a). Editorial: Evidence relating to assessment in rehabilitation. *Clinical Rehabilitation*, 12, 183–186.

Wade, D. T. (1998b). Editorial: Evidence relating to goal planning in rehabilitation. *Clinical Rehabilitation*, 12, 273–275.

Wade, D. T. (1999). Goal planning in stroke rehabilitation: What? *Topics in Stroke Rehabilitation*, 6(2), 8–15.

Wade, D. T. and de Jong, B. A. (2000). Recent advances in rehabilitation. *British Medical Journal*, 320, 1385–1388.

Webb, P. M. and Glueckauf, R. L. (1994). The effects of direct involvement in goal setting on rehabilitation outcome for persons with traumatic brain injuries. *Rehabilitation Psychology*, 39(3), 179–188.

World Health Organization (2001). *International classification of impairments, disabilities and handicaps (ICIDH-2)*. Geneva: World Health Organization.

Chapter 13

Innovations in technology and their application to rehabilitation

Mary D. Slavin

Introduction

Innovations in technology: the context

The remarkable innovations in science and technology that have occurred over the last fifty years have tremendous potential to improve rehabilitation by enhancing approaches to therapeutic interventions and improving service delivery. Concomitant with innovations in technology, a major shift in conceptual frameworks for science and medicine has occurred. Conceptual frameworks are habitual ways of thinking that provide the lens through which problems are viewed; they influence solutions that are considered and stimulate us to ask some questions while ignoring other questions or issues. Innovations in technology are adapted and used in rehabilitation within a context. Therefore, it is important to examine scientific conceptual frameworks and consider the effect they have on the use of technology in rehabilitation.

Traditional scientific conceptual frameworks are rooted in a Cartesian-Newtonian model that emphasizes reductionism, determinism, and dualism. Through the lens of this traditional conceptual framework, technology is integrated into therapeutic interventions and directed at 'fixing' malfunctioning parts. Over the last century, scientific advances in many arenas have challenged the traditional Cartesian-Newtonian model and a new conceptual framework has emerged (Prigogine and Stengers, 1984). This new conceptual framework reflects the influence of systems theory, articulated by Ludwig von Bertalanffy in the 1940s as an alternative to the Cartesian-Newtonian model (von Bertalanffy, 1968). Table 13.1 compares the basic principles of Cartesian-Newtonian and systems theory approaches.

Systems theory has been applied in many fields including physics, economics, and management. The following elements of system theory are relevant to a conceptual framework for rehabilitation: (1) characteristics of a system as a whole are not exhibited by the parts alone; (2) a system's behavior may be chaotic and achieve equilibrium through a trial and error

Table 13.1 Evolution in conceptual framework for science and medicine

Cartesian/Newtonian		General systems 'theory'
Atomistic: reductionism, fragmentation	$\Longrightarrow$	*Holism/emergence*: the system exhibits properties that are not contained in the parts alone.
Deterministic: cause and effect – the output is proportional to the input	$\Longrightarrow$	*Chaotic*: small changes in input can lead to large changes in output and/or there may be many possible outputs for a given input.
Dualistic: laws governing a system's behavior may be deduced from observations	$\Longrightarrow$	*Subjective*: some aspects of the system may not be describable by objective means.

process often described as self-adapting or self-organizing; (3) a system is actively organized in terms of a goal and changes in the system reflect goal-directed behavior; and (4) the system uses feedback to match the goal with behavior. Through the lens of a conceptual framework influenced by systems theory, technological innovations adapted and used in rehabilitation would focus on emergent behavior within the context of a goal-directed activity. Technology would be used to promote behavioral change by providing effective feedback on performance.

Developments in neuroscience, consistent with a systems theory approach, have also had an impact on conceptual frameworks for rehabilitation. Traditional views of a fixed, static nervous system have been challenged by studies demonstrating a dynamic capacity for self-organization in the central nervous system. Research demonstrates that cortical sensory maps, once considered fixed representations in the adult brain, are dynamically maintained and altered by injury and use (Nudo, 2003; Nudo and Milliken, 1996; Nudo *et al.*, 1996). New theories of brain function suggest that practice and repetition alter central nervous system structure and function, a capacity not heretofore considered feasible. Thus new developments in neuroscience provide a rationale for therapeutic interventions in rehabilitation that emphasize practice and repetition to affect the neural substrate and produce behavioral change. Consistent with this component of a conceptual framework for rehabilitation, innovations in technology would be adapted to provide patients with opportunities to engage in practice and repetition.

Innovations in technology: need

There is an urgent need to develop and implement the most effective and efficient treatment approaches in rehabilitation. Financial constraints and efforts to control costs (Ottenbacher *et al.*, 2004) have created a sense of urgency and, consequently, there is great interest in using technology to enhance rehabilitation efforts. In addition to its use as an adjunct to therapeutic interventions, technology can also improve service delivery. Appropriate use of innovations in technology can increase the effectiveness and efficiency of rehabilitative care so that all persons served have every opportunity to reach their maximum potential. Since the need is great, it is likely that technological innovations that are shown to enhance the efficacy and efficiency of rehabilitative care will be widely adopted.

This chapter explores innovations in technology that may be used in rehabilitation to: (1) augment therapeutic interventions through the use of computer technology, the Internet, and robotic devices; and (2) enhance the efficacy and efficiency of service delivery.

Technology to augment therapeutic interventions

Computers, cybertherapy and virtual reality

Computers are incorporated into most aspects of modern life and have great potential to serve as a powerful adjunct to therapeutic approaches used in rehabilitation. The most basic application of computer technology in rehabilitation involves specially designed computer programs that are used to assist in training. Computer-assisted training is currently used to treat clients with visual and hearing problems, motor impairments, mental retardation, and dyslexia (Sik Lanyi et al., 2004). Patients with brain injury who used a computerized memory training program showed significant improvements in memory and self-efficacy (Tam and Man, 2004). Children with attention deficit hyperactivity disorder (ADHD) who used a computer program to train working memory had a significant treatment effect post-intervention and at follow-up. Use of the program also improved response inhibition and reasoning and reduced parent-rated inattentive ADHD symptoms (Klingberg et al., 2005).

Cybertherapy is a more sophisticated application that combines computer technology with communication and information technologies to improve healthcare processes (Riva et al., 2004). Virtual reality (VR) is a central component of cybertherapy. VR uses computer-generated sensory cues to provide a powerful experience while tracking and recording subject behavior (Riva et al., 2004). A review of the literature since the early 1990s documents the growth of VR applications in medicine. A MEDLINE/PubMed search using the terms 'virtual reality' and 'rehabilitation' identified 156 citations from 1995–2005, but only three citations from 1990–1994 (accessed September 2005). Retrieved literature demonstrates a shift in the use of VR. While VR was primarily used as an aid to surgical training and planning in the early 1990s (Satava, 1994), it is currently used primarily in neurorehabilitation (Rizzo et al., 2004).

Figure 13.1 Virtual reality (VR) system (photo courtesy of Clarkson University)

VR system features

VR systems employ computer hardware and software to create two- or three-dimensional artificial or virtual environments. Virtual environments mimic, to varying degrees, aspects of a real environment. A person interacts with the virtual environment by using special devices that provide sensory input from the computer to the user. These sensory inputs include visual, auditory, and/or haptic inputs that simulate what the user would experience in a real environment. VR systems incorporate sensors to monitor the user's actions so that the system can produce computer-generated environments that match the user's activity. Sensors track user activity and provide feedback about performance.

VR systems primarily focus on visual input. The most basic system uses a conventional computer monitor to provide a two-dimensional display of a virtual environment and the user's action within the environment. More sophisticated VR systems completely immerse the user inside the virtual environment by using goggles, a helmet, or a face mask for visual input (Figure 13.1). Auditory information is delivered via headphones. Some systems also provide haptic information via gloves, pens, joysticks, or exo-skeletons to give the user a sense of touch and allow the user to feel a variety of textures as well as changes in texture.

Table 13.2 Advantages of virtual reality (VR)

- Capacity to systematically deliver and control dynamic, interactive 3D stimuli within an immersive environment difficult to present using other means.
- Capacity to create more ecologically valid assessment and rehabilitation scenarios.
- Delivery of immediate performance feedbacks in a variety of forms and sensory modalities.
- Provision of 'cueing' stimuli or visualization tactics designed to help guide successful performance to support an error-free learning approach.
- Capacity for complete performance capture and the availability of a more naturalistic/intuitive performance record for review and analysis.
- Capacity to pause assessment, treatment, and training for discussion and/or integration of other methods.
- Design of safe testing and training environments that minimize the risks due to errors.
- Capacity to improve availability of assessment and rehabilitation by persons with sensorimotor impairments via the use of adapted interface devices and tailored sensory modality presentations built into virtual environment scenario design.
- Introduction of 'gaming' features into VR rehabilitation scenarios as a means to enhance motivation.
- Integration of virtual human representations (avatars) for systematic applications addressing social interaction.
- Potential availability of low-cost libraries of virtual environments that could be easily accessed by professionals.
- Option for self-guided independent testing and training by clients when appropriate.

Source: Rizzo *et al.* (2004b).

There is growing interest in using VR as a tool to extend and augment therapeutic interventions. The following features of VR make it well suited to a conceptual framework based on a systems theory approach: it (1) focuses on emerging behaviors; (2) emphasizes complex interactions of multiple systems; (3) provides appropriately challenging, task-specific activities in ecologically valid, yet safe and controlled environments; and (4) provides feedback to patient and clinician. During therapy, an individual patient's specific training needs are met by customizing virtual environments to allow patients to engage gradually and progressively in more challenging tasks and practice tasks over long periods of time. VR also motivates and keeps patients engaged in therapy by providing stimulating activities. Patient motivation is also enhanced because VR systems provide feedback to patients and allow clinicians to set goals and assess patient performance.

One might ask the question: Why create a virtual environment when patients can perform in the real world? VR allows the clinician to control stimuli the patient receives and provides an opportunity to measure physiological and/or kinematic responses that occur within natural complex environments (Keshner, 2004). The advantages of using VR as an adjunct to therapeutic interventions are outlined in Table 13.2.

VR applications: psychological

VR is an important cybertherapy tool (Riva *et al.*, 2004) and studies have examined the efficacy of VR training as an intervention for phobias and anxiety disorders including: acrophobia, agrophobia, fear of flying, fear of spiders, and erectile dysfunction (Krijn *et al.*, 2004; North *et al.*, 1998). VR was first used as an adjunct to systematic desensitization, a behavioral technique used to treat patients with phobias. Systematic desensitization encourages patients to visualize images of anxiety-producing stimuli that are progressively more disturbing. Since patients often have difficulty with mental imagery, VR is a powerful adjunct to the systematic desensitization approach. Using VR, patients interact with virtual environments that present carefully controlled anxiety-producing stimuli (North *et al.*, 1998). Clients with acrophobia who were treated with VR exposure therapy had a reduction in anxiety and avoidance behaviors (Rothbaum *et al.*, 2002a). In fact, treatment with VR was as effective as live exposure to anxiety-provoking stimuli (Emmelkamp *et al.*, 2001). Moreover, results were maintained at six-month follow-up (Emmelkamp *et al.*, 2004). VR therapy used in conjunction with cognitive and behavioral techniques to treat patients with agoraphobia resulted in a reduction of depression and anxiety and fewer panic attacks. These results were achieved with 33 per cent fewer sessions than use of cognitive and behavioral techniques alone (Vincelli *et al.*, 2003). VR therapy is also an effective treatment for fear of flying (Maltby *et al.*, 2002; Rothbaum *et al.*, 2002a, 2002b). VR is more effective than conventional therapy for treating body image disturbances in individuals who are obese and have binge-eating disorders (Riva *et al.*, 2002) and results are maintained at six-month follow-up (Riva *et al.*, 2003).

VR creates a special and protected virtual environment that can be safely explored in a clinical setting and provides a bridge between the clinical setting and the real environment. Scenarios that the patient may encounter in the real world can be simulated with VR and practiced safely, under the supervision of trained professionals (Botella *et al.*, 2004a, 2004b). Virtual environments used to treat patients with acrophobia include a virtual balcony and a 10-story building with an external glass elevator. Virtual environments with a closed elevator and room with moving walls were developed to treat claustrophobia (Sik Lanyi *et al.*, 2004). In addition to monitoring behavioral changes, the efficacy of VR therapy can be examined by monitoring physiological responses, such as skin resistance (Wiederhold *et al.*, 2002).

VR applications: cognitive

Using virtual environments for cognitive testing in neuropsychological assessments is a promising application of VR technology. Neuropsychological assessments using VR can help rehabilitation efforts to address specific impairments (Schultheis and Mourant, 2001; Schultheis *et al.*, 2002). Neuropsychological assessments augmented by VR include assessment of prospective memory in patients post-stroke (Brooks *et al.*, 2004) and cognitive function (Zhang *et al.*, 2003) and spatial memory (Skelton *et al.*, 2000) in patients with traumatic brain injury. VR is an effective method for diagnostic testing for the following reasons: (1) real-life situations are simulated in a controlled laboratory setting; (2) test stimuli are reliably produced in a consistent manner; (3) complex test stimuli are more challenging and, therefore, testing provides a more realistic simulation of experiences the patient will encounter.

The Wisconsin Card Sorting Test (WCST) is commonly used by neuropsychologists to assess executive function. However, there is great concern that the WCST does not adequately challenge patients and, consequently, the WCST may not provide a valid assessment of the challenges patients face in the real world. Realistic, interactive, three-dimensional virtual environments can provide a challenging test of executive functioning and studies support the usefulness of neuropsychological testing with VR (Elkind *et al.*, 2001; McGeorge *et al.*, 2001). A study comparing a VR test of executive function called the 'Look for a Match' with the WCST found that performance on the VR test was lower, indicating that the VR test is more challenging (Elkind *et al.*, 2001). Findings from VR testing of patients with deficits in executive functioning reveal that patients find VR testing more enjoyable (Elkind *et al.*, 2001) and VR test findings significantly correlate with behavior in the real world (McGeorge *et al.*, 2001). VR has also been successfully used to assess spatial learning and memory in patients with traumatic brain injury (Skelton *et al.*, 2000).

VR has great potential as a method to assess and practice activities of daily living. With VR training patients can perform and practice activities of daily living in safe, progressively challenging environments that are reliably reproduced. Successful applications of VR in activities of daily living include a virtual supermarket to assess and train cognitive ability (Lee *et al.*, 2003) and an immersive kitchen (Christiansen *et al.*, 1998). The immersive kitchen requires multiple steps in meal preparation; it provides a reliable way to assess performance in patients with traumatic brain injury (Christiansen *et al.*, 1998) and is a good predictor of actual performance in the kitchen (Zhang *et al.*, 2003). VR is also used in cognitive rehabilitation of patients with dysexecutive symptoms. A VR application, called the V-STORE, requires patients to solve tasks that are progressively more challenging and requires patients to use the following abilities: programming, abstraction, short-term memory, and attention (Lo Priore *et al.*, 2003).

The ability to practice in a safe environment is critically important when assessing driving skills. VR is used to safely assess driving ability with scenarios that are realistic, interactive, and standardized (Schultheis and

Mourant, 2001). VR assessments of driving ability in patients with Alzheimer's disease demonstrate that visuospatial impairment, reduced useful field of view, and reduced perception of three-dimensional structure-from-motion strongly predict crashes (Rizzo et al., 2001). VR driving assessments demonstrate that patients with traumatic brain injury do not have difficulty with driving speed but make errors on secondary tasks performed while driving (Lengenfelder et al., 2002). These findings provide evidence of the impact of cognitive deficits on driving and are useful in making decisions about a patient's readiness to resume driving. Test results also identify areas to address in therapy to improve driving ability.

VR applications: motor

VR training for patients with motor impairments simulates real motor tasks and provides augmented feedback regarding performance. With VR motor training clinicians can control the many aspects of the motor task more effectively than they could in real-world activities. VR also provides an opportunity to measure physiological and/or kinematic responses by having patients engage in reproducible environments with varying degrees of complexity (Keshner, 2004). VR training promotes motor skill acquisition because it allows patients to engage in sustained activity. As an adjunct to conventional therapy, VR has great potential because it increases the frequency, duration, and intensity of practiced tasks (Sisto et al., 2002).

A group from the Massachusetts Institute of Technology (Cambridge, Massachusetts, USA) uses VR to improve upper extremity motor function in patients who have had stroke (Holden et al., 1999). The VR system they developed is based on the principle of learning by imitation and uses pre-recorded movements of a virtual 'teacher' to demonstrate optimal movement patterns for different tasks (Holden et al., 2002). The system uses an electromagnetic tracking device to record and display patient movements while simultaneously displaying the optimal, desired movement path provided by the 'teacher'. During training, patients attempt to match the desired movement while the clinician controls the frequency of visual feedback, speed of motion and other components to maximize training effects. Studies using this system demonstrate that VR training improves motor performance and that patients are able to transfer new motor skills to real-world tasks and untrained spatial locations (Holden and Dyar, 2002; Holden et al., 1999, 2000). There are efforts to develop VR systems to train other movements. Another VR system uses a cyberglove in a virtual environment where the patient tries to 'catch' a butterfly to improve hand function. Patients recovering from stroke who used this system showed improvements in hand movement (Boian et al., 2002).

VR provides stimulating environments that motivate patients. Results from a study using VR to treat children with cerebral palsy indicate that

VR play is a motivating activity. Features of environments that produced higher levels of volition included challenge, variability, and competition (Harris and Reid, 2005). VR also provides stimulating environments for balance training. One balance training system inserts a video image of the user into a virtual environment. In the environment the user can engage in a variety of challenging activities which include: (1) a juggling task that requires the user to reach sideways while juggling virtual balls; (2) a conveyer belt task that has the user turn sideways to pick up a virtual box from a virtual conveyer belt, turn and place the box on a second virtual conveyer belt; and (3) a snowboard task where the user learns to avoid trees, rocks, and other virtual objects (Sveistrup, 2004). During balance training, task difficulty is modified by increasing the number of virtual objects or increasing the speed at which the objects or environment move (Sveistrup, 2004). Balance training VR systems have been used to treat older patients and patients with traumatic brain injury. While studies indicate no significant differences between the VR balance training and training with traditional approaches, participants in VR programs are more enthusiastic about the program and have more confidence in their balance ability (Sveistrup, 2004).

The future of computer-based and VR therapies

There has been considerable progress incorporating computer-based and VR approaches into rehabilitation, but the potential has not been fully realized. This is likely to change soon – a panel of psychotherapy experts listed VR and computerized therapies among the top five therapeutic approaches of the future (Norcross et al., 2002). VR systems can be developed for psychological, cognitive, and motor applications and used to assist in assessment and training activities. It is likely that advances in VR technology will lead to the development of more useful VR systems at a lower cost (Rizzo et al., 2004b).

There is a great need for randomized clinical trials to assess the efficacy of VR training compared to standard therapy (Krijn et al., 2004). However, since the outcomes with VR treatment may be similar to outcomes with conventional treatment, studies should also examine patient satisfaction, motivation, and the economic impact of VR. Positive outcomes in these measures may support the use of VR as a therapeutic intervention even if the treatment effect is similar to traditional approaches. More research is needed to determine whether VR can be used to treat a broader scope of disorders, including depression, schizophrenia, drug addiction, and autism (Wiederhold and Wiederhold, 2004). While initial results indicate that persons with dementia have no significant detrimental psychological or physical effects from VR treatment, the impact of cognitive and psychological impairments on VR use warrants further investigation.

VR can be used as a supplement or alternative to conventional therapy and is easily adapted for use in inpatient, outpatient and home-based care settings. The development and incorporation of VR systems in rehabilitation will likely increase because VR provides patients with extended opportunities for interaction without necessarily increasing demands on staff (Deutsch *et al.*, 2004). One promising area for VR is home-based rehabilitation. When combined with telemedicine applications, VR provides stimulating interventions that allow clients to continue therapy at home (Sveistrup *et al.*, 2003) and documents patient performance.

Tele-rehabilitation

Recent advances in communication such as the Internet, e-mail and videoconferencing have had, and will continue to have, an enormous impact on health care. Tele-medicine and tele-rehabilitation evolved from the early use of technology to exchange patient information to the use of advanced patient monitoring systems. Advances in methods to remotely monitor patient responses and provide treatment interventions open up new possibilities for home care. In the future, tele-rehabilitation applications will use cutting-edge communication technologies to treat and monitor patients in their homes.

Linking VR and the Internet provides a mechanism for VR to be widely used and presents interesting possibilities for home-based therapy. This application in rehabilitation has the potential to increase client involvement and improve patient outcomes while keeping costs down. Libraries of VR scenarios that are appropriate for treating a variety of patient conditions are available via the Internet. The European Union VEPSY Updated – Telemedicine and Portable Virtual Environments for Clinical Psychology – research project (http://www.cybertherapy.info) supports a website with a library of virtual environments. The environments are designed for clinical assessment and treatment of social phobia, panic disorders, male sexual disorders, and obesity and eating disorders.

VR combined with videoconferencing has been used to develop a home-based program for upper extremity rehabilitation post-stroke. This system is an economical approach that provides patients with extended opportunities for practice and repetition in the home (Piron *et al.*, 2002). A feasibility study using tele-rehabilitation VR to deliver occupational therapy at home demonstrated the potential of this approach (Rydmark *et al.*, 2002). Home-based VR rehabilitation provides an effective treatment medium for patients who live in remote areas or those who have difficulty leaving the home, as is the case for individuals with agrophobia (Wiederhold and Wiederhold, 2005).

Videoteleconferencing provides an alternative for speech-language pathology assessments (Brennan *et al.*, 2004), voice therapy (Mashima *et al.*, 2003) and neuropsychological evaluations (Hildebrand *et al.*, 2004); study results demonstrate that videoteleconferencing assessments are not substantially different from in-person assessments. Additionally, if patients can become comfortable using the technology for assessment (Hildebrand *et al.*, 2004) they are more likely to be able to continue with these methods in treatment (Mashima *et al.*, 2003). Using videoteleconferencing for home assessments prior to discharge is a cost-effective method for identifying potential accessibility problems in home environments and for prescribing appropriate modifications (Sanford *et al.*, 2004).

There is some evidence that tele-rehabilitation is effective for motor training. A systematic review of studies investigating the effects of distance motor training with VR and robotic devices shows that these interventions are promising; however, the strength of evidence for these relatively new approaches is poor (van Dijk and Hermens, 2004). More large-scale, well-designed studies are needed to determine if tele-rehabilitation is effective and practical. Tele-rehabilitation efficacy studies should include additional outcome measures, such as patient satisfaction and cost, since these factors may favor use of tele-rehabilitation, even if treatment effects are similar to conventional approaches.

Ambient intelligence

There is a growing awareness that the environment has a significant effect on disability. According to the World Health Organization's *International classification of functioning, disability and health*, disability is a function of the relationships between disabled persons and their environment (World Health Organization, 2001). Technology can mitigate the effects of disabling conditions by providing support to overcome environmental restrictions, thereby promoting independent function. Ambient intelligence (AI) is an interesting approach to increasing independence by using technology to overcome environmental restrictions. AI uses human/computer interfaces to compensate for or to extend an individual's ability to perform activities. The Information Society Technologies Advisory Group (ISTAG) of the European Community is the driving force behind the AI movement. The ISTAG vision for the future is one where humans are surrounded by intelligent interfaces that are widely distributed and imbedded in everyday objects such as furniture, clothes, and vehicles.

Tele-rehabilitation and AI require active devices with low-energy requirements that operate wirelessly. Sensors used in AI and tele-rehabilitation can be placed in the home to allow measurement of patient activity and behavior (Dittmar *et al.*, 2004) or worn by the patient. Wrist devices are effective for combining sensors, circuits, supply, display, and wireless transmission. The development of unobtrusive sensors that can be integrated into wearable systems is critical to continuing advances in AI and tele-rehabilitation (Bonato, 2005). Clothing also offers many possibilities for locating sensors. Fabric-based interfaces are in the early stage of testing for tele-rehabilitation with patients post stroke (De Rossi et al., 2004).

AI is the 'effective and transparent support to the activity of the subject/s through the use of information and communication technologies' (Riva, 2004: 20). The use of technology in AI is substantially different from VR. VR puts an individual inside a computer-generated world while AI puts the computer inside the world to assist with everyday activities. AI moves computers into the background of the environment and intelligent inter-faces forward. AI guides the activity of the user and matches the computer interface to user characteristics. AI also provides feedback and tracks and records activity (Morganti and Riva, 2005). AI allows for the continuation of rehabilitation in the natural environment and AI support can be modified to meet individual needs as patients' functional status changes. Aspects of AI have been used to design an intelligent environment to assist older adults with dementia with activities of daily living by using sensing agents (Mihailidis et al., 2004).

Robotics

Initial efforts to use robotics in rehabilitation focused on developing robotic devices to replace the function of missing body parts: an application that is consistent with a traditional Cartesian-Newtonian conceptual framework. In the early 1990s, the first 'therapeutic' robotic devices were developed. Therapeutic robotic devices provide opportunities for patients to engage in task-oriented, repetitive activities while providing feedback on perfor-mance. This shift in the use of robotic devices reflects the influence of systems theory and advances in neuroscience that focus on repetition and practice (Burgar et al., 2000). Investigations are currently underway to examine the use of therapeutic robotic devices to assist, evaluate, and document motor rehabilitation (Riener et al., 2005). Therapeutic robotic devices are of particular interest because they provide a cost-effective adjunct to clinical practice and allow continued practice beyond the time that patients spend working directly with therapists (Lum et al., 2002).

Using robotic devices to assist in upper extremity rehabilitation of patients following stroke is a promising area of research; several groups are currently conducting clinical trials of interventions using different robotic designs. One therapeutic robotic design, the mirror-image motion enabler (MIME), operates in unilateral and bimanual modes. In the unilateral mode, the MIME robot moves the subject's arm passively or provides the necessary assistance to movement using selected preprogrammed upper extremity movement trajectories. In the bilateral mode, the subject practices bimanual, coordinated movements that are controlled by the unaffected upper extremity. Training in the bilateral mode seeks to promote plasticity

Figure 13.2 Patient using the MIT-Manus robotic training system (photo courtesy of the Massachusetts Institute of Technology)

of undamaged ipsilateral pathways that may contribute to motor recovery of the involved extremity (Burgar *et al.*, 2000).

The MIT-Manus robot is another therapeutic robotic design used for post-stroke upper extremity rehabilitation. Patients sit at a table with their lower arm and wrist in a brace that is attached to the arm of the MIT-Manus robot (Figure 13.2). A video screen prompts the person to begin an exercise that involves a specific arm movement. If the person does not begin to move, the robot initiates arm movement. If the person begins to actively move during robot-assisted movement, the robot adjusts to provide the guidance and assistance as needed.

The efficacy of robotics for post-stroke upper extremity rehabilitation has been documented in several studies. A search of literature on the efficacy of robotics for post-stroke upper extremity rehabilitation (MEDLINE/ PubMed [1966 – September 2005] and the Science Citation Index [1973 – September 2005] databases) using the terms 'robotics', 'rehabilitation', and 'stroke' identified 62 studies. Of those studies, 13 studies focused on upper extremity rehabilitation, used standard clinical outcome measures, and were published in English (Fasoli *et al.*, 2005). Table 13.3 summarizes findings from five studies that compared the efficacy of robotic therapy to a control group.

For the most part, robotic training improves the movements that were trained (Fasoli *et al.*, 2003; Lum *et al.*, 2002). Robotic training also

Table 13.3 Summary: efficacy of robotic therapy in post-stroke upper extremity rehabilitation

Study	Sample	Treatment	Outcome measures	Reported outcomes
Aisen et al. (1997)	N = 20 Exp: 10 Control: 10	Exp: planar robot-aided Rx with MIT-Manus Control: 'sham Rx' weekly to biweekly contact with robot Dosage: Exp: 5× week/4–5 weeks; Control: 1× per week robot exposure	FM (66 max) MSS S/E MSS W/H Motor power FIM	p = 0.21 p = 0.002 NS hand p = 0.36 P = 0.10 NS
Volpe et al. (2000)	N = 56 Exp: 30 Control: 26	Exp: planar robot-aided Rx with MIT-Manus Control: 'sham Rx' weekly to biweekly contact with robot Dosage: Exp: 5× week/4–5 weeks; Control: 1× per week robot exposure	FM S/E (42 max) MSS S/E MSS W/H Motor power FIM motor	NS p < 0.01 NS p < 0.001 p < 0.01
Burgar et al. (2000)	N = 21 Exp: 11 Control: 10	Exp: MIME robot-assisted reaching movements Control: conventional Rx using NDT approach Dosage: 24 sessions over 8 weeks	FM UE total score FM S/E FM W/H Barthel	NS p < 0.05 (robot > control) NS between groups NS
Volpe et al. (2001)	N = 96 Exp: 56 Control: 40	Exp: planar robot-aided Rx with MIT-Manus Control: 'sham Rx' weekly to biweekly contact with robot Dosage: Exp: 5× week/4 weeks; Control: 1× per week robot exposure	FM S/E (42 max) MSS S/E Motor power FIM	NS p < 0.001 p < 0.005 NS
Lum et al. (2002)	N = 27 Exp: 13 Control: 14	Exp: Targeted reaching movements with MIME robot Control: conventional Rx based on NDT Dosage: 24 1-hr sessions over 2 months	FM (one group) FM (between groups) Barthel FIM	p < 0.001 p < 0.05 (robot > control) NS at 1 and 2 months NS at 1 and 2 months

Exp = experimental; FIM = Functional Independence Measure ®; FM = Fugl-Meyer Assessment; MSS = Motor Status Scale; S/E = shoulder/elbow; sham Rx = sham treatment; UE = upper extremity; W/H = wrist/hand.
Source: Adapted from Fasoli et al. (2005).

improves reaching ability (Lum *et al.*, 2002) and increases strength (Lum *et al.*, 2002) and power (Fasoli *et al.*, 2003). In one study training effects were sustained at four-month follow-up (Fasoli *et al.*, 2004) and another study demonstrated that the improved outcome was sustained after three years (Volpe *et al.*, 1999).

Researchers are beginning to investigate the efficacy of robotic therapeutic devices for gait-training activities. Robotic devices may assist therapists by providing task-specific practice activity of stepping during body-weight-supported treadmill training, which can be difficult to manage in patients with limited mobility (Hornby *et al.*, 2005). One robotic device, the Lokomat, consists of a treadmill and a powered exoskeleton. Since it is well established that repeated practice trains for specific activation patterns, robotic applications for gait training must be careful to match characteristics of the gait pattern that is produced with robotic devices to the desired gait pattern (Hidler and Wall, 2005). Further research using control groups and carefully designed protocols is necessary to determine whether robotic devices can be used effectively for gait training.

The use of robotic devices in rehabilitation provides opportunities for extended practice and the intensity of robotic training would be difficult to replicate in routine clinical practice. One research group reported that one-hour robotic training sessions, three times per week for six weeks, provided patients with the opportunity to make over 10,000 movements of the shoulder and elbow to reach targets (Volpe, 2004). Positive results from clinical trials of upper extremity use of robotic devices demonstrate the importance of activity-based therapies. One limitation of current robotic therapy is that only a few movements are practiced. Future developments in robotic applications will allow for training in a greater variety of movement, greater ability to interact with devices, and will incorporate virtual environments into robotic training (Hesse *et al.*, 2003). One barrier to the use of robotic devices is the fear among therapists that they will be replaced (Hesse *et al.*, 2003). This fear may subside if research demonstrates results that could not be achieved with conventional approaches to therapy.

Technology to enhance the efficacy and efficiency of service provision

Information management

The explosion of medical research information published in biomedical journals and widely disseminated via the Internet has not been matched by effective methods to process and use this information. Consequently, current research is not readily integrated into rehabilitation practice. The volume of available research information is daunting – even the most diligent clinician cannot keep up. As the US Institute of Medicine (IOM) report *Crossing the quality chasm* noted, 'Between the healthcare we have and the care we could have lies not just a gap, but a chasm' (Institute of Medicine, 2001: 1). This chasm is due, in large part, to a failure to translate and promote appropriate application of research findings. Indeed, the failure to translate new knowledge into clinical practice and healthcare decision making is one of two major barriers preventing human benefit from advances in biomedical sciences (Sung *et al.*, 2003). Acknowledgement of the 'chasm' between research and practice has led to dissatisfaction with old models of dissemination that relied on publications in scientific journals and continuing education to introduce research evidence into clinical practice.

An emerging paradigm for bridging the 'chasm' between research knowledge and clinical practice focuses on knowledge translation (KT). KT is 'the exchange, synthesis, and ethically-sound application of knowledge within a complex set of interactions among researchers and users' (http://www.cihr-irsc.gc.ca/e/29418.html). Translational blocks can be removed only through the collaborative efforts of multiple stakeholders (Sung *et al.*, 2003). The Canadian Institutes of Health Research (CIHR) recommend that knowledge translation efforts create 'environments conducive to two-way exchange of knowledge and that capitalize on inter- and trans-disciplinary integration of expertise' (http://www.cihr-irsc.gc.ca/e/29418.html). Other CIHR recommendations to promote KT include 'an obvious pipeline of knowledge flow; creativity; and the proper alignment of resources to influence change and ensure sustainability' (http://www.cihr-irsc.gc.ca/e/29418.html).

There is great potential to use technology to mitigate some of the barriers to knowledge translation. Sophisticated information management systems can screen research studies to identify the most relevant studies for professionals working with specific patient populations, summarize important findings, and disseminate findings. Armed with wireless, hand-held computers, clinicians would have ready access to this targeted information in clinical settings. In this manner, technology can help clinicians integrate research evidence into day-to-day practice and clinical decision making.

Patient assessment and outcomes management

Rehabilitation begins and ends with patient assessment. Patient assessments are part of the outcomes used to gauge the efficacy of interventions for individual patients and for quality improvement efforts within the healthcare system. Therefore, it is critical to have valid, precise, and efficient methods for measuring patient health or functional status outcomes. Traditional outcome measures are comprised of test items that are limited in their ability to accurately describe patients with a wide range of ability (Hambleton, 2000) and, consequently, they lack precision and breadth or are too cumbersome to be feasible.

Computer adaptive testing (CAT) is a technological advance that provides a precise measure of health status or function with relatively few test items. CAT uses artificial intelligence to customize individual patient assessments by selecting specific test items that are best suited for individual patients from a large test item pool. Item pools are constructed using item response theory (IRT) to calibrate test items along a continuum of item difficulty. The computer program uses patient responses to select test items with a level of difficulty that is best suited for an individual patient's ability level. In this manner, only those test items that are most appropriate for each respondent are administered. CAT assessments significantly reduce respondent burden (Ware *et al.*, 2005) and can be used across a broad range of patient abilities and in multiple settings (Andres *et al.*, 2004). Because test items are matched to the patient's ability level, CAT eliminates the ceiling and floor effects that are often a problem with traditional patient assessments (Revicki and Cella, 1997). CAT applications that are currently available for use in rehabilitation include assessment of functional ability in adults (Andres *et al.*, 2004) and children (Haley *et al.*, 2005), headache-related disability (Bayliss *et al.*, 2003) and impact (Ware *et al.*, 2003), shoulder evaluation (Cook *et al.*, 2005) and depression (Gardner *et al.*, 2004).

CAT methods have great potential for providing valid, effective, and efficient patient assessments in a number of domains relevant to rehabilitation. According to the US National Institutes of Health (NIH) Roadmap for Accelerating Medical Discovery to Improve Health, 'Technologies, such as a computerized adaptive health assessment, could revolutionize how symptoms and treatment outcomes are assessed. Equipped with these tools, scientists will be better equipped to understand how patients perceive changes in their health status resulting from new treatments, thereby directing research to therapies that would be most highly valued by patients' (National Institutes of Health, 2005).

Conclusion

Historically, the rehabilitation field has been slow to adopt innovations. However, the availability of advances in technology combined with a more sophisticated conceptual framework for rehabilitation and increased pressure to get better results creates an environment conducive to innovation. Innovations in computer technology, cybertherapy, and robotics are well suited for a conceptual framework for rehabilitation that focuses on emergent behavior, adaptation, feedback, and practice. Clinical studies demonstrate that therapeutic interventions characterized by high-intensity treatments and sustained practice (Kwakkel *et al.*, 1999, 2004) and early, repetitive, and targeted stimulation (Feys *et al.*, 2004) result in increased functional ability and long-term improvements. Evidence from basic neuroscience and clinical sciences confirms the importance of repetition and suggests that activity-dependent plasticity is a mechanism that underlies functional recovery (Volpe, 2004) and behavioral change. Finally, external pressures to improve the efficacy and efficiency of rehabilitation efforts will facilitate change and promote the adoption of technological innovations that enhance therapeutic interventions and service delivery methods.

References

Aisen, M., Krebs, H., Hogan, N., McDowell, F. and Volpe, B. (1997). The effect of robot-assisted therapy and rehabilitative training on motor recovery following stroke. *Archives of Neurology*, 54(4), 443–446.

Andres, P., Black-Schaffer, R., Ni, P. and Haley, S. (2004). Computer adaptive testing: A strategy for monitoring stroke rehabilitation across settings. *Topics in Stroke Rehabilitation*, 11(2), 33–39.

Bayliss, M., Dewey, J., Dunlap, I., Batenhorst, A., Cady, R. and Diamond, M. (2003). A study of the feasibility of internet administration of a computerized health survey: The headache impact test (HIT). *Quality of Life Research*, 12, 953–961.

Boian, R., Sharma, A., Han, C., Merians, A., Burdea, G., Adamovich, S., Recce, M., Tremaine, M. and Poizner, H. (2002). Virtual reality-based post-stroke hand rehabilitation. *Studies in Health Technology and Informatics*, 85, 64–70.

Bonato, P. (2005). Advances in wearable technology and applications in physical medicine and rehabilitation. *Journal of Neuroengineering Rehabilitation*, 2(1), 2.

Botella, C., Villa, H., Garcia-Palacios, A., Banos, R. M., Perpina, C. and Alcaniz, M. (2004a). Clinically significant virtual environments for the treatment of panic disorder and agoraphobia. *Cyberpsychology and Behaviour*, 7(5), 527–535.

Botella, C., Villa, H., Garcia Palacios, A., Quero, S., Banos, R. and Alcaniz, M. (2004b). The use of VR in the treatment of panic disorders and agoraphobia. *Studies in Health Technology and Informatics*, 99, 73–90.

Brennan, D., Georgeadis, A., Baron, C. and Barker, L. (2004). The effect of video-conference-based telerehabilitation on story retelling performance by brain-injured subjects and its implications for remote speech-language therapy. *Telemedicine Journal and e-health*, 10(2), 147–154.

Brooks, B., Rose, F., Potter, J., Jayawardena, S. and Morling, A. (2004). Assessing stroke patients' prospective memory using virtual reality. *Brain Injury*, 18(4), 391–401.

Burgar, C., Lum, P., Shor, P. and Van der Loos, M. (2000). Development of robots for rehabilitation therapy: The Palo Alto VA/Stanford experience. *Journal of Rehabilitation Research and Development*, 37(6), 663–673.

Christiansen, C., Abreu, B., Ottenbacher, K., Huffman, K., Masel, B. and Culpepper, R. (1998). Task performance in virtual environments used for cognitive rehabilitation after traumatic brain injury. *Archives of Physical Medicine and Rehabilitation*, 79(8), 888–892.

Cook, K., Roddey, T., O'Malley, K. and Gartsman, G. (2005). Development of a flexilevel scale for use with computer-adaptive testing for assessing shoulder function. *Journal of Shoulder and Elbow Surgery*, 14(1 Suppl S), 90S–94S.

De Rossi, D., Lorussi, F., Scilingo, E., Carpi, F., Tognetti, A. and Tesconi, M.

(2004). Artificial kinesthetic systems for telerehabilitation. *Studies in Health Technology and Informatics*, 108, 209–213.

Deutsch, J., Merians, A., Adamovich, S., Poizner, H. and Burdea, G. (2004). Development and application of virtual reality technology to improve hand use and gait of individuals post-stroke. *Restorative Neurology and Neuroscience*, 22(3–5), 371–386.

Dittmar, A., Axisa, F., Delhomme, G. and Gehin, C. (2004). New concepts and technologies in home care and ambulatory monitoring. *Studies in Health Technology and Informatics*, 108, 9–35.

Elkind, J., Rubin, E., Rosenthal, S., Skoff, B. and Prather, P. (2001). A simulated reality scenario compared with the computerized Wisconsin Card Sorting Test: An analysis of preliminary results. *Cyberpsychology and Behaviour*, 4(4), 489–496.

Emmelkamp, P., Bruynzeel, M., Drost, L. and van der Mast, C. (2001). Virtual reality treatment in acrophobia: A comparison with exposure in vivo. *Cyberpsychology and Behaviour*, 4(3), 335–339.

Emmelkamp, P., Krijn, M., Hulsbosch, A., de Vries, S., Schuemie, M. and van der Mast, C. (2004). Virtual reality treatment versus exposure in vivo: A comparative evaluation in acrophobia. *Behaviour Research and Therapy*, 40(5), 509–516.

Fasoli, S., Krebs, H. and Hogan, N. (2005). Rehabilitation robotics for the paretic arm after stroke: An efficacy review. Presented to the American Congress of Rehabilitation Medicine, Chicago, IL, USA, September.

Fasoli, S., Krebs, H., Stein, J., Frontera, W., Hughes, R. and Hogan, N. (2003). Effects of robotic therapy on motor impairment and recovery in chronic stroke. *Archives of Physical Medicine and Rehabilitation*, 84(4), 477–482.

Fasoli, S., Krebs, H., Stein, J., Frontera, W., Hughes, R. and Hogan, N. (2004). Robotic therapy for chronic motor impairments after stroke: Follow-up result. *Archives of Physical Medicine and Rehabilitation*, 85(7), 1106–1107.

Feys, H., De Weerdt, W., Verbeke, G., Steck, G., Capiau, C., Kiekens, C., Dajaegar, E., van Hoydonck, G., Vermeersch, G. and Cras, P. (2004). Early and repetitive stimulation of the arm can substantially improve the long-term outcome after stroke: A 5-year follow-up study of a randomized trial. *Stroke*, 35(4), 924–929.

Gardner, W., Shear, K., Kelleher, K., Pajer, K., Mammen, O., Buysse, D. and Frank, E. (2004). Computerized adaptive measurement of depression: A simulation study. *BMC Psychiatry*, 6(4), 13.

Haley, S., Ni, P., Fragala-Pinkham, M., Skrinar, A. and Corzo, D. (2005). A computer adaptive testing approach for assessing physical functioning in children and adolescents. *Developmental Medicine and Child Neurology*, 47(2), 113–120.

Hambleton, R. (2000). Emergence of item response modeling in instrument development and data analysis. *Medical Care*, 38(9 Suppl), II60–65.

Harris, K. and Reid, D. (2005). The influence of virtual reality play on children's motivation. *Canadian Journal of Occupational Therapy*, 72(1), 21–29.

Hesse, S., Schmidt, H., Werner, C. and Bardeleben, A. (2003). Upper and lower extremity robotic devices for rehabilitation and for studying motor control. *Current Opinion in Neurology*, 16(6), 705–710.

Hidler, J. and Wall, A. (2005). Alterations in muscle activation patterns during robotic-assisted walking. *Clinical Biomechanics*, 20(2), 184–193.

Hildebrand, R., Chow, H., Williams, C., Nelson, M. and Wass, P. (2004).

Feasibility of neuropsychological testing of older adults via videoconference: Implications for assessing the capacity for independent living. *Journal of Telemedicine and Telecare*, 10(3), 130–134.

Holden, M. and Dyar, T. (2002). Virtual environment training: A new tool for rehabilitation. *Neurology Report*, 26, 62–71.

Holden, M., Todorov, E., Callahan, J. and Bizzi, E. (1999). Virtual environment training improves motor performance in two stroke patients. *Neurology Report*, 23, 57–67.

Holden, M., Dyar, T., Callahan, J., Schwamm, L. and Bizzi, E. (2000). Motor learning and generalization following virtual environment training in a patient with stroke. *Neurology Report*, 24, 170–171.

Holden, M., Dyar, T., Callahan, J., Schwamm, L. and Bizzi, E. (2002). Quantitative assessment of motor generalization in the real world following training in a virtual environment in patients with stroke. *Neurology Report*, 25, 129–130.

Hornby, T., Zemon, D. and Campbell, D. (2005). Robotic-assisted, body-weight-supported treadmill training in individuals following motor incomplete spinal cord injury. *Physical Therapy*, 85(1), 52–66.

Institute of Medicine (2001). *Crossing the quality chasm: A new health system for the 21st century*. Washington, DC: National Academies Press.

Keshner, E. (2004). Virtual reality and physical rehabilitation: A new toy or a new research and rehabilitation tool? *Journal of Neuroengineering Rehabilitation*, 1(1), 8.

Klingberg, T., Fernell, E., Olesen, P., Johnson, M., Gustafsson, P., Dahlstrom, K., Gillberg, C. G., Forssberg, H. and Westerberg, H. (2005). Computerized training of working memory in children with ADHD – a randomized, controlled trial. *Journal of the American Academy of Child and Adolescent Psychiatry*, 44(2), 177–186.

Krijn, M., Emmelkamp, P., Olafsson, R. and Biemond, R. (2004). Virtual reality exposure therapy of anxiety disorders: A review. *Clinical Psychology Review*, 24(3), 259–281.

Kwakkel, G., Wagenaar, R. C., Twisk, J. W., Lankhorst, G. J. and Koetsier, J. C. (1999). Intensity of leg and arm training after primary middle-cerebral-artery stroke: A randomised trial. *Lancet*, 354(9174), 191–196.

Kwakkel, G., van Peppen, R., Wagenaar, R., Wood Dauphinee, S., Richards, C., Ashburn, A., Miller, K., Lincoln, N., Partridge, C., Wellwood, I. and Langhorne, P. (2004). Effects of augmented exercise therapy time after stroke: A meta-analysis. *Stroke*, 35(11), 2529–2539.

Lee, J., Ku, J., Cho, W., Hahn, W., Kim, I. Y., Lee, S., Kang, Y., Kim, D. Y., Yu, T., Wiederhold, B. K., Wiederhold, M. D. and Kim, S. (2003). A virtual reality system for the assessment and rehabilitation of the activities of daily living. *Cyberpsychology and Behaviour*, 6(4), 383–388.

Lengenfelder, J., Schultheis, M., Al-Shihabi, T., Mourant, R. and DeLuca, J. (2002). Divided attention and driving: A pilot study using virtual reality technology. *Journal of Head Trauma Rehabilitation*, 17(1), 26–37.

Lo Priore, C., Castelnuovo, G., Liccione, D. and Liccione, D. (2003). Experience with V-STORE: Considerations on presence in virtual environments for effective neuropsychological rehabilitation of executive functions. *Cyberpsychology and Behaviour*, 6(3), 281–287.

Lum, L., Burgar, C., Shor, P., Majmundar, M. and Van der Loos, M. (2002). Robot-assisted movement training compared with conventional therapy techniques for the rehabilitation of upper-limb motor function after stroke. *Archives of Physical Medicine and Rehabilitation*, 83(7), 952–959.

McGeorge, P., Phillips, L., Crawford, J., Garden, S., Della Sala, S., Milne, A., Hamilton, S. and Callender, J. S. (2001). Using virtual environments in the assessment of executive dysfunction. *Presence: Teleoperators & Virtual Enviroments*, 10(4), 375–383.

Maltby, N., Kirsch, I., Mayers, M. and Allen, G. (2002). Virtual reality exposure therapy for the treatment of fear of flying: A controlled investigation. *Journal of Consulting and Clinical Psychology*, 70(5), 1112–1118.

Mashima, P., Birkmire-Peters, D., Syms, M., Holtel, M., Burgess, L. and Peters, L. (2003). Telehealth: Voice therapy using telecommunications technology. *American Journal of Speech and Language Pathology*, 12(4), 432–439.

Mihailidis, A., Carmichael, B. and Boger, J. (2004). The use of computer vision in an intelligent environment to support aging-in-place, safety, and independence in the home. *IEEE Transactions on Information Technology in Biomedicine*, 8(3), 238–247.

Morganti, F. and Riva, G. (2005). Ambient intelligence for rehabilitation. In G. Riva, F. Vatalaro, F. Davide and A. M. Davide (eds) *Ambient intelligence*. Amsterdam: IOS Press.

National Institutes of Health (2005). Re-engineering the clinical research enterprise: Dynamic assessment of patient-reported chronic disease outcomes. Retrieved 18 July 2006 from http://nihroadmap.nih.gov

Norcross, J., Hedges, M. and Prochaska, J. (2002). The face of 2010: A Delphi poll on the future of psychotherapy. *Professional Psychology: Research and Practice*, 33(3), 316–322.

North, M., North, S. and Coble, J. (1998). Virtual reality therapy: An effective treatment for phobias. *Studies in Health Technology and Informatics*, 58, 112–119.

Nudo, R. (2003). Adaptive plasticity in motor cortex: Implications for rehabilitation after brain injury. *Journal of Rehabilitation Medicine*, 41 Suppl, 7–10.

Nudo, R. and Milliken, G. (1996). Reorganization of movement representations in primary motor cortex following focal ischemic infarcts in adult squirrel monkeys. *Journal of Neurophysiology*, 75(5), 2144–2149.

Nudo, R., Wise, B., SiFuentes, F. and Milliken, G. (1996). Neural substrates for the effects of rehabilitative training on motor recovery after ischemic infarct. *Science*, 272, 1791–1794.

Ottenbacher, K., Smith, P., Illig, S., Linn, R., Ostir, G. and Granger, C. (2004). Trends in length of stay, living setting, functional outcome, and mortality following medical rehabilitation. *Journal of the American Medical Association*, 292(14), 1687–1695.

Piron, L., Tonin, P., Atzori, A., Zanotti, E., Massaro, C., Trivello, E. and Dam, M. (2002). Virtual environment system for motor tele-rehabilitation. *Studies in Health Technology and Informatics*, 85, 355–361.

Prigogine, I. and Stengers, I. (1984). *Order out of chaos: Man's new dialogue with nature*. New York: Bantam Books.

Revicki, D. and Cella, D. (1997). Health status assessment for the twenty-first century: Item response theory, item banking and computer adaptive testing. *Quality of Life Research*, 6(6), 595–600.

Riener, R., Nef, T. and Colombo, G. (2005). Robot-aided neurorehabilitation of the upper extremities. *Medical & Biological Engineering & Computing*, 43(1), 2–10.

Riva, G. (2004). The psychology of ambient intelligence: Activity, situation and presence. In G. Riva, F. Davide, F. Vatalaro and M. Alcaniz (eds) *Ambient intelligence: The evolution of technology, communication and cognition towards the future of human–computer interaction* (pp. 19–34). Amsterdam: IOS Press.

Riva, G., Bacchetta, M., Baruffi, M. and Molinari, E. (2002). Virtual-reality-based multidimensional therapy for the treatment of body image disturbances in binge eating disorders: A preliminary controlled study. *IEEE Transactions on Information Technology in Biomedicine*, 6(3), 224–234.

Riva, G., Bacchetta, M., Cesa, G., Conti, S. and Molinari, E. (2003). Six-month follow-up of in-patient experiential cognitive therapy for binge eating disorders. *Cyberpsychology and Behavior*, 6(3), 251–258.

Riva, G., Botella, C., Castelnuovo, G., Gaggioli, A., Mantovani, F. and Molinari, E. (2004). Cybertherapy in practice: The VESPY updated project. *Studies in Health Technology and Informatics*, 99, 3–14.

Rizzo, A., Strickland, D. and Bouchard, S. (2004b). The challenge of using virtual reality in telerehabilitation. *Telemedicine Journal and e-health*, 10(2), 184–195.

Rizzo, M., McGehee, D., Dawson, J. and Anderson, S. (2001). Simulated car crashes at intersections in drivers with Alzheimer disease. *Alzheimer Disease and Associated Disorders*, 15(1), 10–20.

Rizzo, A., Schultheis, M., Kerns, K. and Mateer, C. (2004a). Analysis of assets for virtual reality applications in neuropsychology. *Neuropsychological Rehabilitation*, 14, 207–239.

Rothbaum, B., Hodges, L., Smith, S., Lee, L. and Price, L. (2002a). A controlled study of virtual reality exposure for fear of flying. *Journal of Consulting and Clinical Psychology*, 6, 1020–1026.

Rothbaum, B., Hodges, L., Anderson, P., Price, L. and Smith, S. (2002b). Twelve-month follow-up of virtual reality and standard exposure therapy for the fear of flying. *Journal of Consulting and Clinical Psychology*, 70(2), 428–432.

Rydmark, M., Broeren, J. and Pascher, R. (2002). Stroke rehabilitation at home using virtual reality, haptics and telemedicine. *Studies in Health Technology and Informatics*, 85, 434–437.

Sanford, J., Jones, M., Daviou, P., Grogg, K. and Butterfield, T. (2004). Using telerehabilitation to identify home modification needs. *Assistive Technology*, 16(1), 43–53.

Satava, R. (1994). Emerging medical applications of virtual reality: A surgeon's perspective. *Artificial Intelligence in Medicine*, 6(4), 281–288.

Schultheis, M. and Mourant, R. (2001). Virtual reality and driving: The road to better assessment for cognitively impaired populations. *Presence: Teleoperators & Virtual Environments*, 4(1), 431–439.

Schultheis, M., Himelstein, J. and Rizzo, A. (2002). Virtual reality and neuro-psychology: Upgrading the current tools. *Journal of Head Trauma Rehabilitation*, 17(5), 378–394.

Sik Lanyi, C., Laky, V., Tilinger, A., Pataky, I., Simon, L., Kiss, B., Simon, V., Szabo, J. and Pall, A. (2004). Developing multimedia software and virtual reality worlds and their use in rehabilitation and psychology. *Studies in Health Technology and Informatics*, 105, 273–284.

Sisto, S., Forrest, G. and Glendinning, D. (2002). Virtual reality applications for motor rehabilitation after stroke. *Topics in Stroke Rehabilitation*, 8(4), 11–23.

Skelton, R., Bukach, C., Laurance, H., Thomas, K. and Jacobs, J. (2000). Humans with traumatic brain injuries show place-learning deficits in computer-generated virtual space. *Journal of Clinical and Experimental Neuropsychology*, 22(2), 157–175.

Sung, N., Crowley, W. J., Genel, M., Salber, P., Sandy, L., Sherwood, L., Johnson, S. B., Catanese, V., Tilson, H., Getz, K., Larson, E. L., Scheinberg, D., Recce, E. A., Slavkin, H., Dobs, A., Grebb, J., Martinez, R. A., Korn, A. and Romoin, D. (2003). Central challenges facing the national clinical research enterprise. *Journal of the American Medical Association*, 289(10), 1305–1306.

Sveistrup, H. (2004). Motor rehabilitation using virtual reality. *Journal of NeuroEngineering and Rehabilitation*, 1(10), 1–8.

Sveistrup, H., McComas, J., Thornton, M., Marshall, S., Finestone, H., McCormick, A., Babulic, K. and Mayhew, A. (2003). Experimental studies of virtual reality-delivered compared to conventional exercise programs for rehabilitation. *Cyberpsychology and Behaviour*, 6(3), 245–249.

Tam, S. and Man, W. (2004). Evaluating computer-assisted memory retraining programmes for people with post-head injury amnesia. *Brain Injury*, 18(5), 461–470.

van Dijk, H. and Hermens, H. (2004). Distance training for the restoration of motor function. *Journal of Telemedicine and Telecare*, 10, 63–71.

Vincelli, F., Anolli, L., Bouchard, S., Wiederhold, B., Zurloni, V. and Riva, G. (2003). Experiential cognitive training in the treatment of panic disorders with agoraphobia: A controlled study. *Cyberpsychology and Behaviour*, 6(3), 321–328.

Volpe, B. (2004). 'Stroke, stroke': A coxswain's call for more work and more innovation. *Journal of Rehabilitation Research and Development*, 41(3A), vii–x.

Volpe, B., Krebs, H., Hogan, N., Edelsteinn, L., Diels, C. and Aisen, M. (1999). Robot training enhanced motor outcome in patients with stroke maintained over 3 years. *Neurology*, 53(8), 1874–1876.

Volpe, B., Krebs, H., Hogan, N., Edelsteinn, L., Diels, C. and Aisen, M. (2000). A novel approach to stroke rehabilitation: Robot-aided sensorimotor rehabilitation. *Neurology*, 54(10), 1938–1944.

Volpe, B. T., Krebs, H. I. and Hogan, N. (2001). Is robotic training for post-stroke rehabilitation realistic? *Current Opinion in Neurology*, 14(6), 745–752.

von Bertalanffy, L. (1968). *General system theory*. New York: Braziller.

Ware, J. J., Gandek, B., Sinclair, S. and Bjorner, J. (2005). Item response theory and computerized adaptive testing: Implications for outcomes measurement in rehabilitation. *Rehabilitation Psychology*, 50(1), 71–78.

Ware, J. J., Kosinski, M., Bjorner, J., Bayliss, M., Batenhorst, A., Dahlof, C., Tepper, S. and Dowson, A. (2003). Application of computerized adaptive testing (CAT) to the assessment of headache impact. *Quality of Life Research*, 12(8), 935–938.

Wiederhold, B. and Wiederhold, M. (2004). The future of cybertherapy: Improved options with advanced technologies. *Studies in Health Technology and Informatics*, 99, 263–270.

Wiederhold, B. and Wiederhold, M. (2005). The future of cybertherapy: Improved options with advanced technology. In G. Riva, C. Botella, P. Legeron and G. Optale (eds) *Cybertherapy: Internet and virtual reality as assessment and rehabilitation tools for clinical psychology and neuroscience*. Amsterdam: IOS Press.

Wiederhold, B., Jang, D., Kim, S. and Wiederhold, M. (2002). Physiological monitoring as an objective tool in virtual reality therapy. *Cyberpsychology and Behaviour*, 5(1), 77–82.

World Health Organization (2001). *International classification of functioning, disability and health*. Geneva: World Health Organization.

Zhang, L., Abreu, B., Seale, G., Masel, B., Christiansen, C. and Ottenbacher, K. (2003). A virtual reality environment for evaluation of a daily living skill in brain injury rehabilitation: Reliability and validity. *Archives of Physical Medicine and Rehabilitation*, 84(8), 1118–1124.

Index